MICROSOFT WORD

Version 5.0   Advanced Functions   IBM®

USING MICROSOFT® WORD

Version 5.0   Advanced Functions   IBM®

Janet R. Wilson
Seattle University

Patricia A. Shepard
Bellevue Community College

WCB Wm. C. Brown Publishers

Book Team
Editor *Kathy Shields*
Software Hotline and Developmental Support Technician *Lisa Schonhoff*
Production Coordinator *Peggy Selle*

WCB **Wm. C. Brown Publishers**
President *G. Franklin Lewis*
Vice President, Publisher *George Wm. Bergquist*
Vice President, Publisher *Thomas E. Doran*
Vice President, Operations and Production *Beverly Kolz*
National Sales Manager *Virginia S. Moffat*
Advertising Manager *Ann M. Knepper*
Marketing Manager *Craig S. Marty*
Production Editorial Manager *Colleen A. Yonda*
Production Editorial Manager *Julie A. Kennedy*
Publishing Services Manager *Karen J. Slaght*
Manager of Visuals and Design *Faye M. Shilling*

Microsoft ® Word is a registered trademark of Microsoft Corporation.

IBM ® is a registered trademark of International Business Machines Corporation.

Hewlett-Packard ® and LaserJet + ® are registered trademarks of Hewlett-Packard Company.

Cover design by Dale Rosenbach

Copyright © 1991 by Wm. C. Brown Publishers. All rights reserved

Library of Congress Catalog Card Number: 89-82514

ISBN: 0-697-11708-1

No part of this publication may be reproduced, stored in a retrieval system, or transmitted, in any form or by any means, electronic, mechanical, photocopying, recording or otherwise, without the prior written permission of the publisher.

Printed in the United States of America by Wm. C. Brown Publishers,
2460 Kerper Boulevard, Dubuque, IA 52001

USING MICROSOFT WORD VERSION 5.0 ADVANCED FUNCTIONS

TABLE OF CONTENTS

PREFACE	IX
PART 1	**1**
CHAPTER 1 INTRODUCTION	2
Objectives	3
How to Use the Text	3
PART 2	**5**
CHAPTER 2 CREATING NEWSPAPER STYLE COLUMNS	6
Formatting Multiple Columns	6
Controlling Column Breaks	9
Using Print PreView to View Both Pages	9
CHAPTER 3 USING SIDE-BY-SIDE PARAGRAPH FORMATTING	11
Creating a Document with Side-by-side Paragraphs in Two Columns	11
Creating a Document with Side-by-side Paragraphs in Three Columns	15
CHAPTER 4 EDITING A TABLE	19
Changing the Tab Set Position for a Column	20
Moving a Column	21
Adding Tab Marks for a New Column	22
Deleting a Column	22
Clearing all Tabs	22
Setting New Tabs	23
Copying a Column	24
REINFORCEMENT EXERCISES	25
PART 3	**33**
CHAPTER 5 USING LINE DRAW FEATURES	34
Using the Format Border Menu	34
Using Tabs to Draw Horizontal Lines	39
Using Vertical Tabs to Insert Lines in a Table	40
Using the Arrow Keys to Draw Lines	41

CHAPTER 6 GRAPHICS LAYOUT — 44

Using the Format Position Menu to Create a Newsletter — 44
Using Show Layout to Display the Text on the Screen in Two Columns — 52
Positioning Paragraphs Outside the Margins — 54
Using the Capture.COM Program — 59
Using the Library, Link, Graphics Menu — 63

CHAPTER 7 FORMS — 66

Creating a Form — 68
Filling in the Form — 71
Creating and Using a Guide for Filling in a Preprinted Form — 72

REINFORCEMENT EXERCISES — 76

PART 4 — 83

CHAPTER 8 USING MERGE — 84

Merging a Form Letter with a Data Document — 84
Using Set and Ask Variables in a Form Letter — 87
Using Merge to Produce Labels in a Single Column — 90
Using Merge to Produce Labels in Multiple Columns — 91
Merging Addresses with Different Numbers of Lines — 94
Using IF/ENDIF Instructions — 96
Using the INCLUDE Instruction — 97
Using Merge to Fill in a Form — 99

CHAPTER 9 SORTING TEXT — 102

Sorting Paragraphs — 102
Sorting the Lines of a Table — 105
Sorting Columns in a Table — 105
Sorting Records in a Data Document — 106

REINFORCEMENT EXERCISES — 107

PART 5 — 113

CHAPTER 10 USING MATH — 114

Add — 114
Subtract — 115
Multiply — 115
Divide — 116
Totaling a Column in a Table — 116
Percentages — 118
Creating a Table and Performing Multiple Calculations — 119

REINFORCEMENT EXERCISES — 123

PART 6 — 129

CHAPTER 11 USING MACROS — 130

Using the Supplied Macros — 130
Creating a Macro — 131
Running a Macro using Control Codes — 133
Editing a Macro — 134
Deleting a Macro — 135
Writing a Macro Containing a SET Instruction — 135
Writing a Macro Containing Several Macro Instructions — 139

REINFORCEMENT EXERCISES — 145

PART 7 — 151

CHAPTER 12 USING THE FOOTNOTE MENU — 152

Entering a Footnote — 152
Revising Footnote Text — 153
Deleting a Footnote — 154
Moving a Footnote — 154
Formatting the Footnote Numbers — 155
Printing Footnotes at the End of the Document — 155

CHAPTER 13 USING ANNOTATIONS — 156

Entering an Annotation — 156
Printing Annotations at the Bottom of the Page — 157

CHAPTER 14 USING BOOKMARKS — 158

Designating Text as a Bookmark — 158
Using a Bookmark for Cross Referencing — 159
Removing a Bookmark Designation — 160

REINFORCEMENT EXERCISES — 161

PART 8 — 165

CHAPTER 15 USING STYLE SHEETS — 166

Changing the NORMAL.STY Style Sheet — 167
Creating a Style Sheet — 168
Using a Style Sheet — 172
Creating a Style Sheet to use with an Outline — 174
Printing the Style Sheet — 176
Attaching the Style Sheet — 176
Revising the Formatting of a Style — 178
Creating a Style by Example — 178

REINFORCEMENT EXERCISES — 180

PART 9		185
CHAPTER 16 OUTLINING		186
	Typing Text in Outline View	187
	Numbering an Outline	189
	Adding Text to an Outline	189
	Collapsing and Expanding Outline Subheadings and Text	191
	Using Organize Outline	192
	Printing an Outline without the Text	193
	Attaching a Style Sheet	193
CHAPTER 17 CREATING AN INDEX		194
	Designating Text for the Index	194
	Compiling an Index	197
	Editing the Index	197
	Using the Supplied Macro "Index_entry.mac" to Designate Text for an Index Entry	198
CHAPTER 18 CREATING A TABLE OF CONTENTS		200
	Designating Text for the Table of Contents	200
	Compiling the Table of Contents	203
	Adding Page Numbering to the Document	204
REINFORCEMENT EXERCISES		205
APPENDIX I	QUICK REFERENCE GUIDE TO MICROSOFT WORD BASIC FUNCTIONS	213
APPENDIX II	QUICK REFERENCE GUIDE TO MICROSOFT WORD ADVANCED FUNCTIONS	249
APPENDIX III	PROMPT SHEET FOR USING MICROSOFT WORD	287
APPENDIX IV	GLOSSARY OF TERMS	289
INDEX		293

PREFACE

AUDIENCE This book is intended to be used at the college level by students who have some familiarity with computers, but who need to learn specific application programs in computer laboratory environments. It is expected that those using this text would be comfortable with the basic functions of Microsoft Word: creating, saving, and printing a document; formatting text with tabs, character, paragraph, and division formatting; using special features including the spelling program, Thesaurus, glossary entries, splitting windows, and the Library Document retrieval menu for file management.

The text is designed to enable a student to work through the lessons on his/her own, or it may be used in a more traditional classroom setting. The text was written to be used in software application classes at the four-year, community college level, or in adult education classes. It might also be effective at the high school level in advanced courses. This, however, was not the intended audience and so would be up to the individual instructor.

APPROACH A step-by-step approach guides the students through the various procedures used to produce realistic word processing documents. This means that students will be "learning by doing," which includes making some mistakes. The text anticipates these "errors" and includes responses and solutions to possible problems that may occur during the word processing work.

A section of reinforcement exercises is included at the end of each part. These exercises include recall questions and answers, plus several practice documents giving students the opportunity to apply the features learned in each part to production work.

FEATURES Each part includes chapters covering related procedures.

Part 1 :
   Chapter 1 Introduction
Part 1 includes the objectives of the advanced text and lists the various features to be covered. In addition, instructions are presented for using the text.

Part 2 :
    Chapter 2 Creating Newspaper Style Columns
    Chapter 3 Using Side-by-side Paragraph Formatting
    Chapter 4 Editing a Table
    Reinforcement Exercises

Part 2 presents the various functions used for producing documents containing columns. Word 5 allows the user to format text in multiple newspaper type columns or to enter text in side-by-side columns. This section also gives instructions for editing tables and includes moving, deleting, or copying tabular columns.

Part 3 :
    Chapter 5 Using Line Draw Features
    Chapter 6 Graphics Layout
    Chapter 7 Forms
    Reinforcement Exercises

Part 3 consists of learning to use the Format Border menu to draw boxes and lines around text, to use tabs to draw horizontal and vertical lines, and to use the direction (arrow) keys to draw lines. The chapter on graphics includes using the Format pOsition menu to set paragraphs in specific positions and to format them in different sizes. It also provides instruction in using the Capture.COM program to save screen images and using the Library Link Graphic program to import the image into a Word document. The final chapter in this part shows students how to create and fill in forms.

Part 4 :
    Chapter 8 Using Merge
    Chapter 9 Sort Text
    Reinforcement Exercises

The various merge features are covered in chapter 8. The students will merge a main document with a data document in order to produce personalized letters. They will also learn to write various merge instructions in a main document in order to tailor the merge to various specifications, and they will use merge to produce labels. Chapter 9 gives instructions in using the Library Sort menu to sort text both alphabetically and numerically.

Part 5 :
    Chapter 10 Using Math
    Reinforcement Exercises

Students will learn how to use the various math operators with numbers in order to add, subtract, multiply, divide or work with percents. In addition to simple math problems, the text contains instructions for setting up forms, filling in columns with numbers, and performing various calculations to produce percentages and totals.

Part 6:
    Chapter 11 Using Macros
    Reinforcement Exercises

Knowing how to create and use macros is essential for efficient word processing functions. In this chapter, students will learn to use the supplied macros, as well as create their own, both by recording keystrokes, and by writing macros. In addition, they will learn to edit their macros and maintain the glossary, which is the storage file for macros as well as for glossary entries.

Part 7:
    Chapter 12 Using the Footnote Menu
    Chapter 13 Using Annotations
    Chapter 14 Using bookmarks
    Reinforcement Exercises

Formatting references is the focus of part 7. The footnote and the annotation features are very similar. The main difference is that footnotes are formatted with numbers as the reference and annotations may be formatted with any character, plus the date and time, as part of the reference. Annotations are new in Word 5, as are bookmarks. Chapter 14 covers formatting blocks of text as bookmarks and using the bookmark name to insert a cross-reference to a page number.

Part 8:
    Chapter 15 Using Style Sheets
    Reinforcement Exercises

The use of style sheets for automatic formatting is one of the most popular and efficient functions of Microsoft Word. Chapter 15 shows students how to create and use their own style sheets, as well as how to change the NORMAL.STY, the default style sheet.

Part 9:
    Chapter 16 Outlining
    Chapter 17 Creating an Index
    Chapter 18 Creating a Table of Contents
    Reinforcement Exercises

The outline feature in Microsoft Word is somewhat different from other word processing programs. Not only does it allow the user to write outlines in traditional outline format, but it also provides for entering text in the outline and for using the "ORGANIZE" mode to edit large documents. Chapters 17 and 18 show students how to designate text in document for indexes and for table of contents. The Library Table and Library Index menus are then used to compile these references, with accompanying page numbers, at the end of the document .

Preview   Each chapter begins with a preview of the functions to be learned including a description of the functions, possible uses of the functions, and other general comments pertinent to each particular feature.

Step-by-step instructions	Following the preview are exercises leading the student through the steps necessary to produce a document using the specific features in that chapter. The text the student is to type and the keystrokes used for commands or features are printed in bold type. The text of the practice exercises is displayed in a box. Sideheadings are printed in 12 point, bold, all caps, and indicate a specific feature to be covered. Sub-sideheadings are printed in 12 point, bold, first letter capitalized, and indicate step-by-step instructions for using that feature. *"Notes:"* are additional comments, information, or explanations of possible problem areas and are shown in italic.
Reinforcement exercises	Reinforcement exercises are included at the end of each part. These exercises consist of recall questions which are intended to assist the student in understanding the features learned in the preceding exercises. By answering the questions, the student is able to summarize and recall the steps used for each feature. Following the recall questions are practice exercises applying the functions learned to actual document production.
Quick Reference Guides	This text contains two Quick Reference Guides. Appendix I consists of a guide to the basic functions and may be used as a review of the various basic features such as character, paragraph, and division formatting, setting tabs, using the Spelling program and the Thesaurus, plus other basic features. Appendix II is a guide to the advanced features learned in this text. These guides summarizes the keystrokes used for the various functions and list them in alphabetical order. Students are encouraged to use these guides in working through the practice exercises and in producing their own documents.
Prompt sheet	Appendix III provides the student with a two-page prompt sheet listing the function keys and the features assigned to each, plus the speed keys used to apply various types of character or paragraph formatting. In addition, other keystrokes used to move the highlight and perform functions such as entering new paragraphs, new lines, new pages, or new division marks are included. This is different from the Quick Reference Guide, which gives instructions for use, as well as the keystrokes.
Glossary of Terms	Appendix IV consists of a glossary of computer terms as well as terms common to Microsoft Word.

INSTRUCTOR'S MANUAL An Instructor's Manual is included in the package along with the text book and consists of the following:

* A description of the organization of the text.

* A description of the organization of the instructor's manual.

* An outline of each Part consisting of:
  Learning objectives
  Teaching techniques
  Chapter outline
  Lecture outline for each chapter
  The solutions to the recall questions
  The solutions to the practice exercises

* A test bank including:
  A test for each part: 2 through 9.
  A comprehensive test covering parts 2, 3, 4, and 5.
  A comprehensive test covering parts 6, 7, 8, and 9.
  A final test covering all parts: 2 through 9.

* Solutions to the test bank

* A Hands-on test consisting of four parts:

  1. Creating and using a macro
  2. Using graphics to create and print a flier
  3. Using graphics to create a form
  4. Filling in the form and using math for calculating totals.

* Solutions to the hands-on test

* A set of twenty-four transparency masters of the various menus and screens, plus examples of documents displaying some of the features learned in this text.

ACKNOWLEDGMENTS

We wish to thank the many users and teachers who worked through the earliest versions of this text and made valuable suggestions which have been incorporated in the final product. Those who helped are the staff of the Business and Office Division at Bellevue Community College, and Bellevue Community College computer instructors, Anna Wanaski and Sheila Fix, who were among the first to use the original work. We also appreciated the support and encouragement offered by computer authors, Carole Boggs Matthews and Martin Matthews, whose experience and insights were invaluable. Family and closest friends are to be thanked for their endurance, patience, understanding, and encouragement. Without that, this project would not have been completed. To Kathy Shields and the excellent staff at Wm. C. Brown publishers, we are grateful for their guidance and support. And finally, a warm thank you to the reviewers who provided many helpful comments and suggestions.

Janet Wilson, Seattle University

Patricia Shepard, Bellevue Community College

PART 1

CHAPTER 1   INTRODUCTION   2

    Objectives   3
    How to Use the Text   3

CHAPTER 1
INTRODUCTION

This text is intended to be used upon completion of <u>Using Microsoft Word Basic Functions</u>. In order to get the most out of this text, you should be comfortable with the basic features of Microsoft Word: creating and saving a document; editing text; selecting blocks of text; formatting including character, paragraph, and division formatting; setting tabs; using special features such as the Spelling program and the Thesaurus; using the Search and the Replace menus; creating and using glossary entries; and creating and using summary sheets.

The advanced features covered in this text include: formatting text in newspaper columns and side-by-side paragraphs; using the line draw features which include formatting text in boxes or with lines, using the tab key to draw horizontal lines, and using the Ctrl F5 key for line drawing; using the Format pOsition menu and the Library Link menu to produce documents containing graphics. You will also learn how to use the merge functions to produce mass mailings and address labels; use the sort feature to alphabetize and list items numerically; use the math function to add, subtract, multiply, and divide; create and use macros; insert and number footnotes and annotations automatically; and format and use bookmarks for cross-referencing. Finally, you will learn to use the powerful style sheet function to format text automatically; use the outline feature to organize and write documents; and use the index and table of contents to compile references for your document.

The advanced functions are presented with step-by-step instructions for producing documents incorporating the specific functions in each chapter. At the end of each part, a reinforcement chapter is incorporated containing recall questions and answers plus several practice exercises which enable students to apply the functions to document production.

OBJECTIVES

The objectives of this text are to:

1. Provide a tool for classroom learning.

2. Present the material in a logical, orderly manner.

3. Use practice exercises throughout to aid in a clearer understanding of the features of Microsoft Word 5.0.

4. Use recall exercises and reinforcement documents at the end of each chapter for maximum recall and retention of the material presented.

5. Provide a quick reference guide to both basic and to advanced features. The quick reference guide summarizes the keystrokes used for each function and lists them in alphabetical order.

6. Provide a prompt sheet listing the functions in alphabetical order and shows the speed key for each function.

7. Provide a glossary of computer terms.

8. Provide an index for quick location of information.

HOW TO USE THE TEXT

Each chapter in this text is organized in several parts.

*   A preview discusses the functions to be covered, briefly explaining what they are, and how they may be used. Also included is other pertinent information affecting how you use the function.

*   Step-by-step instructions guide you through the procedure for using Word to produce the document in the practice exercises.

*   Text shown in a box is a practice exercise.

*   Text printed in bold is text which is to be typed, or indicates the keystrokes used to perform various functions.

*   Notes are printed in italic and provide additional information about the function. The information in the notes sometimes gives you alternative ways of using the function or tips and suggestions for its application.

*   Sections containing recall questions, reinforcement documents, and answers to the recall questions, are included in parts 2 through 9. These reinforcement exercises enable you to immediately apply the functions to other documents, thereby helping you retain what has been learned.

*   Appendices I and II are Quick Reference Guides included at the end of the text--appendix I consists of the basic functions not included in this text, and appendix II consists of the advanced functions. The functions are listed in alphabetical order so they are easy to locate. Use the Quick Reference Guides when you prepare the reinforcement documents. It will be easier to use than to work through the exercises a second time.

*   Appendix III is the prompt sheet listing the functions and the keystrokes used for each, plus speed keys for formatting and other keyboard actions.

*   Appendix IV consists of a glossary of computer terms and other terms specifically associated with Microsoft Word features.

PART 2

CHAPTER 2   CREATING NEWSPAPER STYLE COLUMNS   6

    Formatting Multiple Columns   6
    Controlling Column Breaks   9
    Using Print PreView to View Both Pages   9

CHAPTER 3   USING SIDE-BY-SIDE PARAGRAPH FORMATTING   11

    Creating a Document with Side-by-side Paragraphs in Two Columns   11
    Creating a Document with Side-by-side Paragraphs in Three Columns   15

CHAPTER 4   EDITING A TABLE   19

    Changing the Tab Set Position for a Column   20
    Moving a Column   21
    Adding Tab Marks for a New Column   22
    Deleting a Column   22
    Clearing all Tabs   22
    Setting New Tabs   23
    Copying a Column   24

REINFORCEMENT EXERCISES   25

CHAPTER 2

CREATING NEWSPAPER STYLE COLUMNS

PREVIEW

Multiple column layout allows you to type text in two or more columns similar to newspaper columns. As the text is typed, it automatically wraps from one column to the next. The Format Division Layout menu is used to specify the number of columns, the space between columns, and also to indicate if the division break is continuous.

In all versions of Microsoft Word prior to version 5.0, a heading, title, or banner to be printed over two or three columns on a page had to be formatted as a running-head. In Version 5.0, all you have to do is set "division break" in the Format Division Layout menu at "Continuous." This allows several different types of column formatting to be displayed on one page.

Show layout mode is also new in Version 5.0, and is used to display your text on the screen in the columns as they will be printed. This feature, in addition to Print preView, enables you to see how your text will look and to make any changes to the columns before you print.

When typing text in multiple columns, you may either format it in columns before typing, or you may type the text in one column, then apply the column formatting. In the following document, you will be changing the formatting as you type the text.

FORMATTING MULTIPLE COLUMNS

You will be typing the text shown in the box below.

```
                    THE OFFICE OF TODAY

     One of the more dramatic changes observed in the
office of today is the conspicuous absence of the
typewriter, the standard office tool for over a century.
     Rapidly replacing the typewriter as a means of
recording data and conveying facts essential to the world
of business is the computer and related computer
terminals.  Many businesses have begun to use the computer
terminal as the primary means of storing and communicating
information.
     With the ability of computer systems to communicate
with one another, it has also been noted that many offices
are utilizing these devices for electronic mail,
conferences between executives, and other communications
needs.
     Without a doubt, the computer is an integral part of
the modern business environment, and an understanding of
the applications and use of computer systems is an
important part of the job skills for office employees.
```

To type the title:

1. Press: **Alt C** to center.
2. Press: **Caps Lock.**

Using Microsoft Word Advanced Functions, Part 2

3. Type: **THE OFFICE OF TODAY** and press **Enter** twice.
4. Press: **Alt P** to return to normal paragraph formatting, and press **Caps Lock** to restore lowercase mode.

To set division break at continuous:

1. Press: **Esc.**
2. Choose: **Format, Division, Layout.**
3. Press: the **down arrow** to move to "division break" field.
4. Press: **C** or the **space bar** to choose "Continuous."
5. Press: **Enter** to return to the document screen.

Note: *A division formatting mark is displayed, and the text above the mark is formatted for one column with the "division break" field set at "Continuous." This means that additional text formatted in multiple columns can be added below this division mark, and all text will be printed on the same page. If "division break" field is not set at "Continuous," then each new division will begin printing on a new page.*

To specify the number of columns for remaining text and to set division break at continuous:

1. Move: the **highlight** to the line below the division mark.
2. Press: **Esc.**
3. Choose: **Format, Division, Layout.**
4. Move: the **highlight** to the "number of columns" field.
5. Type: **2** to specify the number of columns.
6. Leave the "space between" field at 0.5".
7. Move: the **highlight** to the "division break" field.
8. Press: **C** or the **space bar** to set at "Continuous."
9. Press: **Enter** to return to the document screen and press **Enter** again to insert a blank line.
10. Move: the **highlight** to the blank line. This is where you will begin typing the text to be formatted in multiple columns.

Your screen should look like the example shown below. Notice the bracket, which is now at position 2.7 in the Ruler line, indicating the right margin for the column.

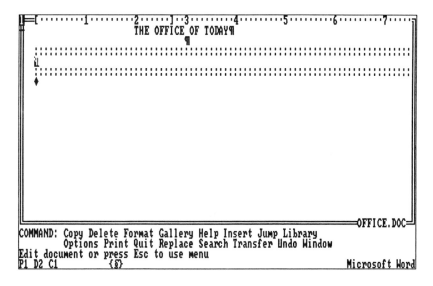

11.	Press:	**Alt 2** to double-space.
12.	Type:	the text in the box on page 6.

Note: *The text will be displayed on the screen in one long column.*

<u>To change the default drive with a hard disk system to save on a floppy disk in Drive A:</u>

Note: *If you are using a dual disk system, Drive B is the default drive and you will not need to make a change.*

13.	Press:	**Esc.**
14.	Choose:	**Transfer, Options.**
15.	Type:	**A:.**
16.	Move:	the **highlight** to the "save between sessions" field and select "Yes."
17.	Press:	**Enter** to return to the document.

18. Press **Ctrl F10** to save the document. Name it **office.**

To use "Show layout on/off" to display both columns as they will be printed:

1.	Press:	**Alt F4.**
	or	
2.	Press:	**Esc.**
3.	Choose:	**Options.**
4.	Set:	"show layout" field at "Yes."

Note: *An* **LY** *will be displayed in the status line to indicate the mode.*

An example of how your text will look is shown below. Your line endings may not be identical to those in the example, depending upon the font size you are using.

```
╔═[·······1·······2·······3·······4·······5·······]══╗
║              THE OFFICE OF TODAY¶                  ║
║                       ¶                            ║
║::::::::::::::::::::::::::::::::::::::::::::::::::::║
║    One of the more         conferences between     ║
║  dramatic changes observed  executives, and other   ║
║  in the office of today is  communications needs.¶  ║
║  the conspicuous absence of    Without a doubt, the ║
║  the typewriter, the        computer is an integral ║
║  standard office tool for   part of the modern business ║
║  over a century.¶           environment, and an     ║
║     Rapidly replacing the   understanding of the    ║
╚═════════════════════════════════════════════OFFICE.DOC═╝
COMMAND: Copy Delete Format Gallery Help Insert Jump Library
         Options Print Quit Replace Search Transfer Undo Window
Edit document or press Esc to use menu
P1 D1 C21          {§}                    LY        Microsoft Word
```

5.	Press:	**Alt F4** to leave show layout mode.

Note: *It is easier to edit text when you are not in show layout mode as this mode slows down the way Word works.*

CONTROLLING COLUMN BREAKS

After entering text in columns, you may discover one column is considerably longer than the other, and you wish to make them appear more even. Text may be moved from the end of one column to the beginning of the next column by positioning the **highlight** where you wish to end the first column and pressing **Ctrl Alt Enter** to insert a "new column" mark--which appears as a row of dots. All of the column text below that mark will be moved to beginning of the next column.

To move text from column one to column two:

1. Move: the **highlight** to the left margin, even with the paragraph beginning "**With the ability. . .**"

Note: *You want the highlight to be positioned at the left margin in order to include the tab mark with the rest of the text.*

2. Press: **Ctrl Alt Enter** to insert the new column mark. A row of dots will appear at the end of the first column, and the text below the mark will now be printed in the second column.

To move text from page 1 to page 2:

Also insert a new column mark at the beginning of the fourth line from the end of the text to move text to the second page--just for purposes of practice at this time.

1. Move: the **highlight** to the fourth line up from the end of column two.
2. Press: **Ctrl Alt Enter** to insert a column break.

Note: *If the status line does not display the page number, go to the Options menu, move the highlight to "paginate" field, press "A" to select "Auto," and press Enter to return to the document. A page number will now be displayed in the status line.*

USING PRINT PREVIEW TO VIEW BOTH PAGES

1. Press: **Ctrl F9.**
   or
2. Press: **Esc.**
3. Choose: **Print, preView.**

In the Print preView menu:
4. Choose: **Options.**

In the Options menu:
5. Press: **2** or **space bar** to choose "2-page."
6. Press: **Enter** to display the two pages of column text.

An example of how your text should look is shown below. Line endings shown below may not be identical to your line endings.

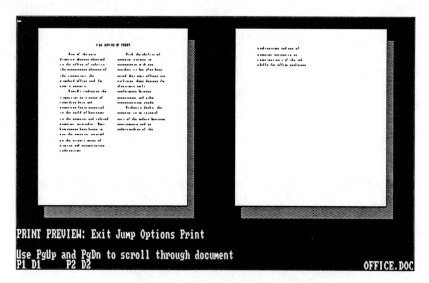

7. Press: E to choose **Exit** to return to the document.
8. Press **Ctrl F10** to save the changes.
9. Check your printer for paper, and press **Ctrl F8** to print.
10. Press **Esc** and choose **Transfer, Clear, All** to clear the screen.

CHAPTER 3

USING SIDE-BY-SIDE PARAGRAPH FORMATTING

PREVIEW

Side-by-side paragraphs allow the user to align blocks of text horizontally as well as vertically. It is useful for typing schedules, scripts, question and answer type text where the question is displayed in one column and the corresponding answer will be typed in the adjacent column, or for comparing items with a description of one in the left paragraph and a corresponding description in the right paragraph.

When using side-by-side formatting, type the paragraph that will appear at the left in the first row, followed by remaining paragraphs as they appear from left to right across the page. Directly following the first row of paragraphs, type the next row in order from left to right, and repeat for the remaining rows of paragraphs. See the text in the box on page 12. After the text is typed for all paragraphs, use the Format, Paragraph menu to set left and right indents (the indents control the line length of each "column"), and set the "side-by-side" field at "Yes."

An example of side-by-side paragraph formatting is shown below.

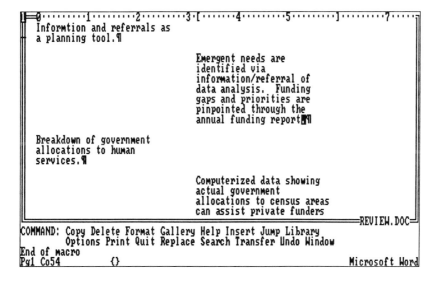

CREATING A DOCUMENT WITH SIDE-BY-SIDE PARAGRAPHS IN TWO COLUMNS

The text in the box on page 12 will be used in this exercise. After formatting for side-by-side paragraphs it will look like the screen print shown above.

To enter text for the side-by-side paragraphs:

1. Type: the title, shown on the following page, centered and in all caps.
2. Press: **Enter** three times, press **Alt P** to return to normal paragraph formatting, and press **Caps Lock** to return to lowercase.
3. Type: the text for the first paragraph--**Information and referral as a planning tool.**
4. Press: **Enter.**

5. Type: the text for the paragraph to the right--**"Emergent needs are identified via. . .",** and continue to the end of the paragraph.
6. Press: **Enter.**
7. Repeat for the remaining two paragraphs. Do not leave a space between paragraphs.

```
                      REVIEW OF ACTIVITIES

Information and referrals as a planning tool.(press Enter)
Emergent needs are identified via information/referral of
data analysis.  Funding gaps and priorities are pinpointed
through the annual funding report.(press Enter)
Breakdown of government allocations to human
services.(press Enter)
Computerized data showing actual government allocations to
census areas can assist private funders as well as human
service planners in prioritizing needs.(press Enter)
```

To prepare for formatting:

When you are using side-by-side paragraphs, you must calculate where you wish to set the right indent for the paragraphs in the left column, and where you wish to set a left indent for the paragraphs in the second column. These indents determine the length of the line for the paragraph and act as the <u>right margin</u> for the paragraphs in column 1, and as the <u>left margin</u> for the paragraphs in column 2. In the text above, the first paragraph will be printed at the left, the second paragraph will be printed starting on the same line as the first, but will be printed at the right side of the page.

To calculate the width and position of side-by-side paragraphs:

<u>Determine the width of typing area:</u>
    Two 1.25" margins equal 2.5" minus 8.5" in paper = 6" for the typing area.
        (These are the defaults.)

<u>Calculate width of each paragraph:</u>
    You have 6" of typing area:
        if column 1 = 2.75 and
        if column 2 = 2.75,
        then the total typing area = 5.5" which would leave .5" between columns.

<u>Calculate the indents for each paragraph.</u>
    Right Indent (the position where lines in column 1 will end) = the width of typing area in column 2 (2.75) + the space between (.5) = 3.25

    Left Indent (the position where the lines in column 2 will begin) = the width of the typing area of column 1 (2.75) + space between (.5) = 3.25

To format the paragraphs so they will print side-by-side:

The procedure is to format all paragraphs in the first vertical column, then format all paragraphs in the next vertical column and so on until all formatting is completed. When you learn to use style sheets, you may create a style by recording the formatting for each paragraph and apply the formatting to remaining paragraphs with the style key code.

To format paragraph 1:
1. Move: the **highlight** to the first paragraph.
2. Press: **Esc.**
3. Choose: **Format, Paragraph.**

In the Format Paragraph menu:
4. Move: the **highlight** to the "right indent" field and type **3.25**.
5. Move: the **highlight** to the "space before" field and type **1** (to enter a blank line between each paragraph).
6. Move: the **highlight** to the "side-by-side" field and select "Yes."
7. Press: **Enter** to return to text.

Note: The text automatically readjusts to fit the new paragraph formatting command.

To format paragraph 3:

Format paragraph 3 before formatting paragraph 2 in order to use **F4** to repeat the formatting for paragraphs in the same vertical column. This speeds up the formatting tasks considerably.

8. Move: the **highlight** to any position in paragraph 3 "Breakdown of government . . . "
9. Press: **F4** to repeat the formatting.

To format paragraph 2:
10. Move: the **highlight** to the second paragraph (which is to be to the right of the first paragraph).
11. Press: **Esc.**
12. Choose: **Format, Paragraph.**
13. Set: "left indent" field at 3.25.
14. Set: "space before" field at 1.
15. Set: "side-by-side" field at "Yes."
16. Press: **Enter.**

To format paragraph 4:
17. Move: the **highlight** to paragraph 4.
18. Press: **F4** to repeat the formatting.

Your screen will look like the example shown below.

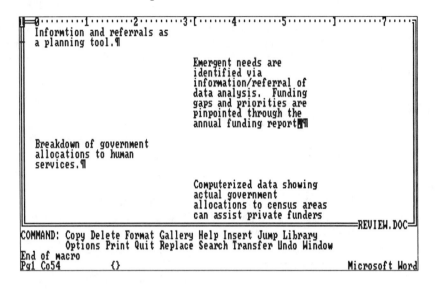

To show paragraphs side-by-side:

1. Press: **Alt F4** to go to show layout mode-- an **LY** will be displayed in the status line.

Your text should resemble the example shown below.

```
                        REVIEW OF ACTIVITIES
Information and referrals      Emergent needs are identified
as a planning tool.            via information/referral of
                               data analysis.  Funding gaps
                               and priorities are pinpointed
                               through the annual funding
                               report.

Breakdown of government        Computerized data showing
allocations to human           actual government alloca-
services.                      tions to census areas can
                               assist private funders as
                               well as human service
                               planners in prioritizing
                               needs.
```

2. Press: **Alt F4** to leave the show layout mode.

Note: *Leave the show layout mode when you wish to edit the text. You don't necessarily have to do this, but show layout mode slows down editing and moving the highlight.*

To use Print preView to view the entire document:

1. Press: **Ctrl F9** to go to Print preView to see the placement on the page.
2. Press: **E** to choose Exit to return to the document screen.

3. Press **Ctrl F10** to save the document, name it **review**. If a summary sheet menu appears when you save, press **Enter** to bypass it.
4. Press **Ctrl F8** to print. Be sure the printer is on line and the paper is adjusted.
5. Press **Esc** and choose **Transfer, Clear, All** to clear the screen.

CREATING A DOCUMENT WITH SIDE-BY-SIDE PARAGRAPHS IN THREE COLUMNS

The concepts for creating a document with side-by-side paragraphs in three columns are the same as those used in the previous document. However, in this exercise the center paragraphs will have to be formatted with both left and right indents in order to create the margins. An example of your final document is shown below.

In this exercise you will be using the **F4** key again to "Repeat last edit."

```
                    OFFICE AUTOMATION SEMINAR

                         April 16, 1990

8:30-9:00         Continental Breakfast              Room 103

9:00-10:30        "Office Trends in Today's          Room 104
                  Business Environment"
                  Dr. Allison Edwards,
                  author of best-seller:
                  High Tech Trends

10:30-11:00       Coffee Break                       Room 103

11:00-3:00        Employee Development               Room 201
                  Courses:   In-house
                  and college courses
```

To enter text for the side-by-side paragraphs.

1. Center and type the title in all caps; center and type the date.
2. Press **Enter** three times.
3. Press **Alt P** after the date to return to normal paragraph.
4. Type the paragraphs as you did in the preceding exercise. Remember to type the paragraph in the left column first, followed by the paragraph in the middle column, and finally the paragraph in the third column. Repeat for each of the remaining rows of paragraphs. Be sure there are no blank lines between paragraphs. Your text should look like the example in the box on the following page.

Note: *When entering the name "Dr. Allison Edwards," insert spaces by pressing Ctrl space bar, instead of just the space bar, to insert nonbreaking spaces to keep the name and title on one line.*

```
          OFFICE AUTOMATION SEMINAR

             April 16, 1990

8:30-9:00
Continental Breakfast
Room 103
9:00-10:30
"Office Trends in Today's Business Environment" (do not
press Enter) Dr. Allison Edwards, author of best-seller:
High Tech Trends
Room 104
10:30-11:00
Coffee Break
Room 103
11:00-3:00
Employee Development Courses:   In-house and college
courses
Room 201
```

To format the paragraphs in column 1:

1.	Move:	the **highlight** into the first paragraph "**8:30-9:00**."
2.	Press:	**Esc.**
3.	Choose:	**Format, Paragraph.**
4.	Set:	"right indent" at 4.5.
5.	Set:	"space before" at 1.
6.	Set:	"side-by-side" at "Yes."
7.	Press:	**Enter.**

To use the "Repeat last edit" (F4 key) command to format the remaining paragraphs which will be in the first column:

1.	Move:	the **highlight** into the 4th paragraph "**9:00-10:30**" which will be the second paragraph in column 1.
2.	Press:	**F4** to repeat the formatting.
3.	Repeat:	steps 1 and 2 for the remaining two paragraphs (showing the hours) that will appear in the first vertical column.

To format the paragraphs in column 2:

1.	Move:	the **highlight** into the second paragraph "**Continental Breakfast.**"
2.	Press:	**Esc.**
3.	Choose:	**Format, Paragraph.**
4.	Set:	"left indent" field at 1.7.
5.	Set:	"right indent" field at 1.7.
6.	Set:	"space before" at 1.
7.	Set:	"side-by-side" at "Yes."
8.	Press:	**Enter.**
9.	Move:	the **highlight** to the fifth paragraph "**Office Trends . . .**"

Using Microsoft Word Advanced Functions, Part 2

10. Press: **F4** to repeat the edit.
11. Repeat steps 1 through 10 for the remaining two paragraphs (containing the name of the event) to be formatted for the middle column.

To format the paragraphs in column 3:

1. Move: the **highlight** to the third paragraph "**Room 103.**"
2. Repeat the procedures given for the paragraphs for the first two columns using the settings given below.

   Set "left indent" field at 4.5.
   Set "space before" field at 1.
   Set "side-by-side" at "Yes."

3. Move: the **highlight** to the sixth paragraph "**Room 104.**"
4. Press: **F4** to repeat edits and repeat for the remaining paragraphs (room numbers) in column 3.

An example of your text is shown below.

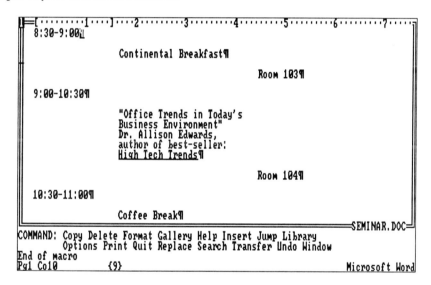

5. Press: **Alt F4** to go to show layout mode.
   or
6. Press: **Ctrl F9** to go to Print preView to see how the paragraphs will look when they are printed.

Your text should resemble the document shown below.

```
                    OFFICE AUTOMATION SEMINAR

                        April 16, 1990

8:30-9:00           Continental Breakfast              Room 103

9:00-10:30          "Office Trends in Today's          Room 104
                    Business Environment"
                    Dr. Allison Edwards,
                    author of best-seller:
                    High Tech Trends

10:30-11:00         Coffee Break                       Room 103

11:00-3:00          Employee Development               Room 201
                    Courses:   In-house
                    and college courses
```

7. Save the document, name it **seminar,** and print.

Note: *Microsoft Word includes in its program five preset styles to help in setting up side-by-side paragraphs. These styles are located on the Utilities Disk. If these files were not copied to the Word directory when the program was installed, refer to the Microsoft Word manual for instructions for copying those files. If you are using a diskette system, the Utilities disk must be in a disk drive in order to use the files. The section on Style Sheets in this text will give instructions for using supplied styles.*

8. Clear the screen.

CHAPTER 4

EDITING A TABLE

PREVIEW

In the text <u>Using Microsoft Word Basic Functions</u> you learned how to set tabs and type a table. A quick review of those steps are as follows:

1. Press **Alt F1** to go to the Tab Set menu.

2. Either type the position number and letter corresponding to the type of tab to be set, or move the **highlight** to the position where you want to set a tab, and type the letter indicating the type of tab. If a leader character is to be set, type the leader character or type "b" to select "Blank."

3. Repeat for additional tab settings. Reminder: If the tab or one of the arrow keys is pressed, the **highlight** will be moved from the ruler line to the menu. Press **F1** to return the **highlight** to the ruler line.

4. Press **Enter** to return to the document screen.

5. When typing the lines in the table, press **Shift Enter** at the ends of each line, rather than the **Enter** key so the text is formatted as one paragraph. If you press **Enter** at the end of each line, then when you edit the table you must "select" the entire table.

Once the new tabs have been set and the text for each column is typed, the columns may be easily moved, deleted, copied, or tab sets may be deleted and new ones entered. You will use **Shift F6** (column selection on/off) to "select" or highlight a column before moving, deleting, or copying it.

To create the table

(See the example on the following page.)
Tabs will be set at:
- 0.5 = left flush tab
- 2.8 = center tab
- 4.5 = decimal tab
- 5.5 = right flush tab

To set tabs:
1. Move: the **highlight** to the position where the table will begin.
2. Press: **Alt F1**.
   or
3. Press: **Esc**.
4. Choose: **Format, Tab, Set** to display the Format Tab Set menu.

In the Format Tab Set menu:
5. Type: **0.5** to specify the position--1/2 inch from left margin--for the first Left Flush Tab.

Note: *You must type the 0 in front of the decimal. If a period is typed first, a dot will be set as the leader character for that tab set.*

6. Type: **L** to specify the type of tab to be set.

7.	Type:	**2.8** to specify the position for the second column.
8.	Type:	**C** to set a Center Tab.
9.	Type:	**4.5** to specify the position for the third column.
10.	Type:	**D** to set a Decimal Tab.
11.	Type:	**5.5** to specify the position for the last column.
12.	Type:	**R** to set a Right Flush Tab.
13.	Press:	**Enter** to return to typing area.

To enter the text:

<u>To display all tab marks, new line marks (down arrows), and dots representing spaces:</u>
1.	Press:	**Esc.**
2.	Choose:	**Options.**
3.	Move:	the **highlight** to the "show non-printing symbols" field and choose "All."

<u>To display the ruler line if it is not displayed:</u>
4.	Move:	the **highlight** to the "show ruler" field and choose "Yes."
5.	Press:	**Enter** to return to the document screen.

<u>To enter the text:</u>
6.	Press:	**Tab** (an arrow representing the tab mark is displayed) and type **Thermometer**.
7.	Press:	**Tab** and type **XT4804**.
8.	Press:	**Tab** and type **$** (press **space bar** four times) **7.50**. The dots between the $ sign and the seven represent spaces.
9.	Press:	**Tab** and type **250**.
10.	Press:	**Shift Enter** to format the table as one paragraph. A down arrow will be displayed at the right margin.

11. Repeat for the remaining lines of the table in the box below, pressing **Shift Enter** at the end of each line; however, press **Enter** instead of **Shift Enter** at the end of the last line.

```
Thermometer          XT4804         $     7.50      250
Oscilloscope         XQ55             2,999.99       62
Electrocardiograph   XQ58             3,255.95       21
Hemostat             T57423              12.50       15
One liter beaker     X7                   4.95      175
Balance              XT48               950.00       73
```

Note: *Be sure you have a down arrow at the end of each line except the last.*

12. Press **Ctrl F10** to save the document. Name it **table**.

CHANGING THE TAB SET POSITION FOR A COLUMN

To move the second column 1/4 inch to the right--to position 3:

1.	Move:	the **highlight** to any position in the paragraph (table).
2.	Press:	**Alt F1** to display the Format Tab Set menu.
3.	Press:	the **right arrow** to move the **highlight** to the **C** (tab position for column 2).
4.	Press:	**Delete** to delete the tab.

Using Microsoft Word Advanced Functions, Part 2

Note: The text will change, but don't worry about it. As long as you entered the appropriate number of tab marks, the columns will line up properly when you set the new tab position.

5. Move: the **highlight** to the 3.
6. Type: **C** to set a Center Tab at the new position.
7. Press: **Enter** to return to the document.

Note The second column automatically readjusts to the new tab stop.

Note: When working in the Tab Set menu, if the Tab key is pressed to move the highlight into the "alignment" or "leader character" field, return the highlight to the "Tab set" field and press **F1** key to <u>return the highlight to the ruler line</u>. You will then be able to use the arrow keys to move the highlight to various positions. Sometimes this is a more effective way of setting tabs, than to type a position number.

MOVING A COLUMN

To move the second column in front of the first column:

1. Move: the **highlight** to the **X** in the first line of column 2.
2. Press: **Shift F6** to turn Column Select on--a CS will be displayed in the Status Line.
3. Press: the **right arrow** to move the **highlight** to one space beyond the last character in the first line--this will include the tab mark following the column entry.
4. Press: **down** arrow to highlight the entire column.

Your table should resemble the example shown below.

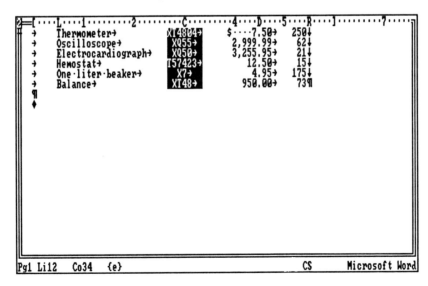

5. Press: **Delete** key to move the column into scrap.
6. Move: the **highlight** to the first character of first column (**T** in **Thermometer**)
7. Press: **Insert** to insert the column text from scrap.

Note: The column has been moved. Now the tabs have to be changed to correspond to the column text.

To change the tab sets:

To change the tab in column 1 to a Center tab:
1. Press: **Alt F1**.
2. Move: the **highlight** to L at position 0.5 and delete it with the **Delete** key.
3. Type: **0.7**.
4. Type: C to set a Center Tab which automatically realigns the column.

To change the tab in column 2 to a Left flush tab.
5. Type: **1.5** in the "position" field.
6. Type: L to set a Left Flush Tab--column 2 moves to 1.5.

To delete the Center tab:
7. Move: the **highlight** to C and press **Delete**. The remaining columns will automatically adjust to the appropriate tab sets.
8. Press: **Enter** to return to the document.

ADDING TAB MARKS FOR A NEW COLUMN

Tab marks need to be added for the new column at the right margin. The text for this column will be entered in the math instructions in chapter 10.

1. Press: the **End** key to move the **highlight** to end of first line.
2. Press: the **Tab** key to insert a tab mark.
3. Press: the **down arrow** to move to next line.
4. Press: the **Tab** key.
5. Repeat steps 3 and 4 for the remaining lines.

DELETING A COLUMN

To delete column 1:

1. Use **Shift F6** to "select" the column--be sure to include the trailing tab marks, but no not include the tab marks at the left margin.

2. Press: **Delete**.

Note: *Ignore the alignment and the ruler line. New tabs will be set for the entire table in the next step.*

CLEARING ALL TABS

1. Press: **Esc.**
2. Choose: **Format Tab Reset-all**.

(Don't panic--the columns will appear scrambled.)

Using Microsoft Word Advanced Functions, Part 2   23

SETTING NEW TABS

To set new tabs including a tab stop for the additional column to be entered later:

1. Press: **Alt F1.**
2. Set: a Left flush tab at 0.5.
3. Set: a Decimal tab 3.5.
4. Set: a Right flush tab at 4.5.
5. Set: a Decimal tab at 5.5.

Your screen should resemble the example shown below.

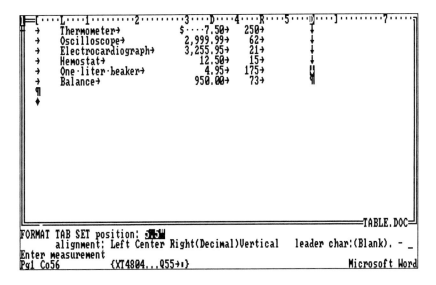

6. Press: **Enter** to return to the typing area. The columns will automatically adjust to the new tab sets.

7. Press **Ctrl F10** to save the edits. This document will be used in the Math Section.

8. Press **Esc** and choose **Transfer, Clear, All** to clear the screen.

<u>To change the screen so that only paragraph marks are displayed:</u>
1. Press: **Esc.**
2. Choose: **Options.**
3. Move: the **highlight** to the "show non-printing symbols" field.
4. Press: **P** or the **space bar** to set the response at "Partial."

COPYING A COLUMN

Note: *An exercise for this procedure has not been included; however, if you want to experiment with this in another document, follow the instructions below. The document "table" does not have enough space to copy a column and maintain the correct formatting of the columns.*

The procedures for copying a column to another position are similar to the other procedures for editing columns.

1. "Select" the column.
2. Press **Alt F3** to copy the column to scrap.
3. Move the **highlight** to the new position where the column is to be copied.
4. Press **Insert** to copy.

REINFORCEMENT EXERCISES

FUNCTIONS REVIEWED

Chapter 2:
> Formatting multiple columns
> Formatting titles over columns
> Controlling column breaks

Chapter 3:
> Formatting side-by-side paragraphs in two columns
> Formatting side-by-side paragraphs in three columns

Chapter 4:
> Creating a table
> Changing a column position
> Moving a column
> Deleting a column
> Clearing all tabs
> Setting new tabs

RECALL QUESTIONS

Answers to recall questions are on page 31.

1. Which menu is used to indicate the number of columns for a multi-columned document?

2. If you wish to type a headline or banner over several columns, what response must you choose in the "division break" field?

3. In which menu is the "division break" field located?

4. What combination of keystrokes is used to manually begin a new column?

5. How do you move the highlight from the left column to the next column to the right?

6. Which menu is used to format paragraphs as side-by-side paragraphs?

7. What is the advantage of using side-by-side formatting, rather than tabs to type paragraphs in corresponding columns?

8. How do you set the "margins" for side-by-side paragraphs?

9. What keys are pressed to go to column selection mode?

10. What keys are press to go to show layout mode?

11. Describe show layout mode?

12. How do you format a table as one paragraph?

13. What speed key is used to go to Print preView?

14. Define Print preView.

15. How do you reset the original tab settings?

DOCUMENT 1: NEWSPAPER STYLE COLUMNS

1. Create the document on the following page. Type it as a single-column document, and then change it to a two-column document.

2. Center the heading and the date/volume line over both columns.

3. Add bold to the heading and increase the font size to 14 point for the title. Use 12 point for the date/volume line and underline that line.

4. Enter a column break just before the heading **New Travel Policies:**.

5. Proof the document carefully, and run a spell check.

6. Go to Print preView to see how the document will look when it is printed.

7. Print a copy of the document.

8. Save it as **quartly.**

KTECH CORPORATION QUARTERLY

June 1990   Volume 2

ATTENDING CONFERENCES

This month's issue is devoted to attending conferences. Several important conferences are coming up this summer and fall that many of you will be attending.

During the past the standard procedure for attending and reporting on these conferences has been very casual. This was a good way to operate for many reasons: it cut down on the paperwork, increased the attendance to the conferences, and thus brought back to the company much valuable information.

Changing Times:

As all of you are aware, KTech Corporation has increased in size from 75 employees in 1985 to today's over 800 employees. This is a substantial increase, and it has not been easy to deal with the increased functions that accompany such a jump in the number of personnel.

Those of you who have been with the company since 1985 or earlier are to be commended for your cooperation and assistance in guiding KTech through a relatively easy transition from a very small company to one that is now competitive in the industry.

For these reasons, the management feels that better procedures are needed for those attending conferences so that the information may be shared by all.

New Travel Policies:

Beginning with the summer conference to be held in San Francisco, each employee will need to fill out an extended expense report and a summary of his/her participation in seminars at the conference.

The new forms will be in the office mail on Monday. Instructions are included with the form. Read over them carefully. If you have any questions regarding this extended expense form, please call personnel.

The Summary Report:

In addition, a summary report will now be required from each attendee. In the past a summary report was not required and each individual spoke briefly about his/her experience in a departmental meeting. As a small company, it was easy to share information in this manner. As a larger company, it is necessary to share information through written reports that can be shared by all employees.

The report should explain the following:

a. details of each seminar attended
b. the highlights of the conference as a whole
c. a summary of the most beneficial aspects of the conference
The report should be submitted to your department manager no later than two weeks after the return from the conference.

DOCUMENT 2: SIDE-BY-SIDE PARAGRAPHS

1. Create the document shown on the following page.

2. Use side-by-side paragraph formatting and type a centered heading set in a font size slightly larger than the rest of the text.

3. Set up the document approximately as shown.

4. Save the document as **seminar**.

5. Go to show layout mode to see the paragraphs as they will be printed.

6. Print a copy of the document.

COMPUTER TRAINING CONFERENCE
SUMMER 1990
San Francisco

Day 1

7:00-9:00	Coffee Introductions Keynote speaker	The General Conference Room
9:20-11:20	Sessions: Spreadsheet Presentations Word Processing in A New Age Database Management System	 The Orange Room The Blue Room The Green Room

12:00-1:30	Lunch
	
	Keynote speaker:
	  Jane Fenmore
	  SeaData, Inc., "Trends in Data Communications Technology"
		
		The General Conference Room

2:00-4:00	Sessions: MIS Designs for Small Organizations Why the Mainframe? Networking Graphics with the PC	 The Tropical Room The Arctic Room The North Room The South Room
6:00	Dinner/Social hour	The Grand Dining Room

ANSWERS TO RECALL QUESTIONS

1. Format Division Layout

2. Set "division break" at "Continuous."

3. Format Division Layout menu

4. Ctrl Alt Enter

5. Ctrl 5 (keypad 5) right arrow.

6. Format Paragraph

7. Using side-by-side formatting will always keep corresponding columns in the same line horizontally regardless of any editing.

8. The left and right indent fields in the Format Paragraph menu are set for each paragraph.

9. Shift F6

10. Alt F4

11. Show layout mode displays the text as it will be printed. For example, when you are typing text in columns, the text is not displayed in two or three columns next to each other unless you are in show layout mode.

12. Press Shift Enter at the end of each line in the table. This enables you to easily change the tabs. If you don't do this, you must "select" the entire table when you want to change the tab settings.

13. Ctrl F9

14. Print preView displays the full page as it will be printed. It shows the columns as they will be printed plus page numbers and headers and footers, if there are any. It also will show facing pages, or two consecutive pages.

15. Press Esc and choose Format Tab Reset-all.

PART 3

CHAPTER 5   USING LINE DRAW FEATURES   34

     Using the Format Border Menu   34
     Using Tabs to Draw Horizontal Lines   39
     Using Vertical Tabs to Insert Lines in a Table   40
     Using the Arrow Keys to Draw Lines   41

CHAPTER 6   GRAPHICS LAYOUT   44

     Using the Format Position Menu to Create a Newsletter   44
     Using Show Layout to Display the Text on the Screen in Two Columns   52
     Positioning Paragraphs Outside the Margins   54
     Using the Capture.COM Program   59
     Using the Library, Link, Graphics Menu   63

CHAPTER 7   FORMS   66

     Creating a Form   68
     Filling in the Form   71
     Creating and Using a Guide for Filling in a Preprinted Form   72

REINFORCEMENT EXERCISES   76

CHAPTER 5

USING LINE DRAW FEATURES

PREVIEW

The line draw feature is a flexible, easy-to-use way to enhance your text by adding lines or boxes for emphasis. In this section, you will learn how to add borders of various types and how to use the line draw mode. There are limits to the line draw features depending upon the type of printer you are using. Some of the following instructions may not work for you if your printer does not support the feature.

Microsoft Word 5.0 provides three different ways to draw lines.

1. Use the **Format Border** menu to format paragraphs in boxes, or to format paragraphs with vertical or horizontal lines at the top, bottom, left, or right sides. The Format Border menu also allows you to specify the type of lines--double or bold, for example--and to add shading in a box.

   Using the Format Border menu is a type of paragraph formatting; therefore, if **Alt P** is pressed to return to normal paragraph formatting when the **highlight** is in the paragraph, you will lose your borders.

2. Use the **Tab Set** menu to set Vertical Tabs in order to insert vertical lines in a table. The Tab Set menu is also used to draw horizontal lines with the underscore character set as a leader character for a tab.

3. Use **Line Draw mode--Ctrl F5--**to draw lines by pressing the arrow keys to move in various directions.

USING THE FORMAT BORDER MENU

This feature may be used to enhance banners, headings, or titles which are printed over column text.

In this exercise, you will be creating the heading shown below. The font for the text is Times Roman 14 bold. If this font is not available to you, choose the font which resembles it most closely in your "font name" and "font size" fields. Instruction is also included in this section to add gray shading; however, if your printer does not support that option, just ignore those instructions.

THE KTECH CORPORATION NEWSLETTER

To choose the Font Name and Size:
1. Press: **Alt F8** to go directly to the "Font Name" field in the Format Character menu.
2. Press: **F1** to display the list of available fonts.
3. Move: the **highlight** to the Times Roman font name.
4. Press: **F1** again to return to the menu.
5. Move: the **highlight** to the "Font Size" field.
6. Press: **F1** to display the list of font sizes.
7. Move: the **highlight** to select **14**, if that is displayed.

Using Microsoft Word Advanced Functions, Part 3

8.   Press: **Enter** to return to the document.

To use the Format Border menu to add bold lines above and below text:

To add the lines:
1.   Press: **Enter** and move the highlight above the page end mark.
2.   Press: **Esc.**
3.   Choose: **Format, Border.**

An example of the Format Border menu is shown below.

```
FORMAT BORDER type: None Box Lines      line style: Normal   color: Black
  left: Yes(No)       right: Yes(No)    above: Yes(No)       below: Yes(No)
  background shading: 0                 shading color: Black
Select option
Pg1 Co1           {}                                         Microsoft Word
```

4.   Press: **L** or press the **space bar** twice to choose "Lines."
5.   Move: the **highlight** to "above" field and set at "Yes."
6.   Move: the **highlight** to "below" field and set at "Yes."
7.   Move: the **highlight** to "line style" field.
8.   Press: **F1** to display the list of available options.
9.   Choose: **bold** if it is displayed in the list.
10.   Press: **Enter** to return to the document.

To add gray shading:
11.   Press: **Esc.**
12.   Choose: **Format, Border** to return to the menu.
13.   Move: the **highlight** to "background shading" field.
14.   Press: **F1** to display the list of available options.
15.   Choose: a number for the shading. The higher the number, the darker the shading.

Note: *If your printer does not support shading, a message to that effect will be displayed in this menu.*

16.   Press: **Enter** to return to the document screen and to display the bold lines above and below the paragraph code.

To format and type the text for the heading:

To choose bold formatting, font name, and font size:
1.   Press: **Esc.**
2.   Choose: **Format, Character** to display the menu.
3.   Press: **Y** to set "bold" field at "Yes."
4.   Move: the **highlight** to "font size" field.
5.   Type: **14** to set the font size.
6.   Move: the **highlight** to "font name" field.
7.   Press: **F1** to display the list of available fonts.
8.   Move: the **highlight** to "Times Roman" or the font name which most closely resemble Times Roman.
9.   Press: **Enter** to return to the document

To type the text:
10. Press: **Alt C** to center, and **Caps Lock** to go to uppercase mode.
11. Type: **THE KTECH CORPORATION NEWSLETTER**.
12. Press: **Enter**. (The formatting for the lines is repeated.)
13. Press: **Alt P** to return to normal paragraph formatting (be sure the **highlight** is in the paragraph below the heading).
14. Press: **Caps Lock** to return to lowercase, and press **Alt space bar** to return to normal character formatting (end "bold" and return to default font size).
15. Press: **Enter** twice to insert blank lines.

16. Press **Ctrl F9** or press **Esc** and choose **Print preView** menu to view the heading as it will be printed. If the lines appear to be touching the text, follow the instructions below to enter "new lines" above and below the text.
17. Choose **Exit** or press **Ctrl F9** to return to the document.

To insert new lines above and below the heading to increase the amount of white space between the border and the heading:
18. Move: the **highlight** to the beginning of the heading.
19. Press: **Shift Enter**. This allows the text to remain formatted as one paragraph.
20. Move: the **highlight** to the end of the heading.
21. Press: **Shift Enter** to insert a blank line below the text.

To view the heading:
22. Press **Ctrl F9** to use Print preView menu again to view the results of inserting extra lines.

23. Choose **Exit** or press **Ctrl F9** to exit Print preView menu, and move the **highlight** below the heading to proceed with the next exercise.

To use the Format Border menu to place a box around paragraph text:

You will be creating the document shown below. Your line endings may not be identical to those displayed depending upon the printer you are using.

```
     When typing text in a box, the borders
expand to fit around the text.  If you wish to
type two paragraphs in one box, press Shift
Enter twice at the end of the first paragraph,
rather than Enter.

     If you do not want a blank line between
paragraphs, press Shift Enter once at the end of
the first paragraph.
```

To create the box:
1. Press: **Esc.**
2. Choose: **Format, Border** to display the Border menu.
3. Press: **B** or the **space bar** to choose "Box."
4. Press: **Enter** to return to the document screen. A paragraph code in a box will be displayed.

Using Microsoft Word Advanced Functions, Part 3

<u>To type the text:</u>
5. Type: the text in the box. Press **Shift Enter** twice at the end of the first paragraph. If you don't, you will have two boxes, since the formatting is repeated each time you press **Enter** (the same as in other paragraph formatting).
6. Press: **Enter** to go to the line below the box.

Another box will be displayed.
7. Press: **Alt P** to return to normal paragraph formatting.
8. Press: **Enter** again to insert another blank line.

To use the Format Border menu to place a box around a list:

An example of the text is shown below. To demonstrate how the appearance of the box may be changed, this paragraph will be formatted with a two-inch left indent and a two-inch right indent, and the border will be in double lines. (The printer used to create this text does not support double lines, so the example shows a single line.)

```
        Beavers
        Bruins
        Cougars
        Huskies
```

1. Press: **Esc.**
2. Choose: **Format, Border, Box.**
3. Move: the **highlight** to "line style" field, and either type **double** or press **F1** to display the list of available line styles--if "double" is displayed, choose it.
4. Press: **Enter** to return to the document screen.
5. Type: the list in the box above inserting a tab in front of each item. Press **Shift Enter** at the end of each line except the last. Press **Enter** at the end of the paragraph. A new paragraph mark formatted in a box will appear. Press **Alt P** to return to normal paragraph formatting.

<u>To format the box with left and right indents:</u>
6. Move: the **highlight** up into the box (paragraph).
7. Press: **Esc.**
8. Choose: **Format, Paragraph.**
9. Move: the **highlight** to the "left indent" field.
10. Type: **2** to set a two-inch indent.
11. Move: the **highlight** to the "right indent" field.
12. Type: **2** to set a two-inch indent.
13. Press: **Enter** to return to the document screen. The paragraph displays the new indents.
14. Press: **Enter** after "Huskies".
15. Press: **Alt P** to return to normal paragraph formatting.
16. Press: **Ctrl F9** to go to Print preView.
17. Choose: **Exit** to return to the document.
18. Press: **Ctrl F10** to save the document. Name it **graphics**.
19. Press: **Ctrl F8** to print the document.
20. Clear the screen.

To use the Format Border menu to insert vertical lines in newspaper style columns:

In this exercise, you will add vertical lines to the newspaper style columns you created in the document **office** in Chapter 4. The Format Division Layout menu must be changed to indicate "0" spaces between columns. If you leave the "space between" field set at .5", two vertical lines will be displayed between the columns. After making this change, you will "select" the text in the columns and use the Format Border menu to add lines to the left and to the right of all of the paragraphs.

1. Load the document **office**.
2. To make the two columns even on one page, remove the column break at the end of column 2. To do this, move the **highlight** to the column break mark (row of dots) and press **Delete.**

To change "space between" to 0:
3. Move: the **highlight** to any position in Division 2 (the section of text formatted for two columns). Look at the status line to confirm your position.

Note: *A division is any section of text containing specific division formatting commands, such as margin settings, page length changes, multiple columns, or page numbers.*

4. Press: **Esc.**
5. Choose: **Format, Division, Layout.**
6. Move: the **highlight** to the "space between" field.
7. Type: **0** and press **Enter** to return to the document.

To "select" the text in the columns:
8. Move: the **highlight** to the first character in the first line of column one.
9. Press: **F6** to turn on "Extend."
10. Press: **Ctrl Page Down** to move the **highlight** to the end of the document to highlight the text.

To add vertical lines:
11. Press: **Esc.**
12. Choose: **Format, Border, Lines.**
13. Move: the **highlight** to the "left" field and set at "Yes."
14. Move: the **highlight** to the "right" field and set at "Yes."
15. Press: **Enter** to return to the document screen. Vertical lines will be displayed on both sides of the columns.

16. Press: **Alt F4** to go to "show layout" to display both columns on the screen.

Note: *If the column endings need to be adjusted, move the* **highlight** *to the position where you wish to insert a column break, and press* **Ctrl Alt Enter.** *This is easier to do in "show layout" mode; however, the process is slower in this mode.*

Using Microsoft Word Advanced Functions, Part 3

17. Press **Ctrl F9** to use the Print preView menu to display the page as it will be printed.

Your screen should resemble the text shown in the example below.

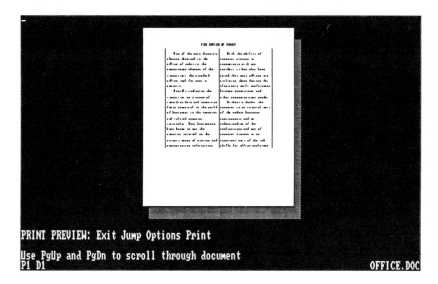

18.	Choose:	**Exit** or press **Ctrl F9** again to leave Print preView.
19.	Press:	**Alt F4** to leave "show layout" mode.
20.	Press:	**Ctrl F8** to print the document.

To save and clear the screen:

21.	Press:	**Esc** and choose **Transfer, Clear, All**.
22.	Press:	**Y** to save the edits and clear the screen.

USING TABS TO DRAW HORIZONTAL LINES

You may use a tab set with the underscore as a leader character to create a heading at the top of a page similar to the following example. To draw the line, set a right flush tab at position 5.5 with an underscore character as a leader. (You will not add the box. That is for display purposes only in this text.)

```
LESSON 1_____LINE DRAW
```

To set a tab with an underscore as a leader character:

1.	Press:	**Alt F1** to display the Format Tab Set menu.
2.	Type:	**5.5** in the "position" field.
3.	Type:	**R** to set the right flush tab.
4.	Type:	**Shift hyphen (_)** to set the underscore as the leader character.
5.	Press:	**Enter** to return to the document screen.
6.	Press:	**Caps Lock**.
7.	Type:	**LESSON 1** (at the left margin).
8.	Press:	**Tab** key to go to the Right Flush tab and draw the horizontal line.
9.	Type:	**LINE DRAW**.
10.	Press:	**Enter** to go to the next line.

11.	Press:	**Alt P** to return to normal paragraph (to restore the default tabs), and **Caps Lock** to return to lowercase.
12.	Press:	**Enter** three times to insert blank lines.

USING VERTICAL TABS TO INSERT LINES IN A TABLE

The Vertical Tab may be set at the positions where you wish to insert a line between columns in a table. In this section you will be creating the table shown below.

```
Item            Description         Amount

Corvette        Silver              6
300ZX           White               8
Ferrari         Red                 1
```

To set the tabs:

Tabs will be set at:

Left flush at 0.5 for the text in column 1.
Vertical Tab at 1.5.
Left flush at 2 for the text in column 2.
Vertical Tab at 4.
Left flush at 4.5 for the text in column 3.

1.	Press:	**Alt F1** to go to the Format Tab Set menu.
2.	Type:	**0.5** in the "Position" field.
3.	Type:	**L** to choose "left" alignment.
4.	Type:	**b** to return the "leader character" field to (Blank).

Note: *The "leader character" field was set for the "underscore" character; therefore, the "b" must be typed to restore the default (Blank).*

5.	Type:	**1.5** and a **V** to set a vertical tab. A vertical line appears in the ruler line.
6.	Type:	**2** and an **L** to set a left flush tab for column 2.
7.	Type:	**4** and a **V** to set a vertical tab.
8.	Type:	**4.5** and an **L** to set a left flush tab for column 3.
9.	Press:	**Enter** to return to the document.

Note: *The vertical lines are displayed on the screen in the first line, and they will be repeated each time Enter or Shift Enter is pressed to begin a new line.*

To create the table with vertical lines:

1.	Press:	the **Tab** key to go to position 0.5.
2.	Type:	**Item**.
3.	Press:	the **Tab** key to go to position 2.
4.	Type:	**Description**.
5.	Press:	the **Tab** key to go to position 4.5.
6.	Type:	**Amount**.

7. Press: **Enter** or **Shift Enter** twice to insert a blank line.
8. Repeat the steps above for typing the remainder of the table shown on the previous page.

After the last entry:
9. Press: **Enter** and **Alt P** to return to normal paragraph formatting.

10. Press: **Enter** again to insert another blank line.

If you want to add a box around the entire table:
11. "Select" all lines in the table if you pressed **Enter** at the end of each line. If you pressed **Shift Enter**, just move the **highlight** to any position in the table.

12. Press: **Esc.**
13. Choose: **Format, Border, Box.**
14. Press: **Enter** to return to the document.

Note: *A box will be displayed around all of the items; however, if you pressed **Enter** at the end of each line, a box would be displayed around each line. If the later happened, you will then have to press Shift Enter to insert a "new line" mark (a down arrow) at the end of each line, and delete the paragraph marks.*

*If you leave paragraph marks at the ends of each line, you can move the **highlight** into each paragraph and use the Format Border Lines menu to add lines on the right and the left sides of the paragraphs. The first paragraph in the table would also be formatted with a "line above" and the last paragraph would be formatted with a "line below." This would format the entire table in one box.*

15. Press **Ctrl F10** to save the document. Name it **lines.**
16. Clear the screen.

USING THE ARROW KEYS TO DRAW LINES

An easy way to create charts and graphs is to use the arrow keys to draw lines. Not only can you use a single line, but Word 5.0 provides several other characters which may be chosen to use in the line draw mode. The selection available to you depends upon your printer's capabilities. Also, not all printers support line draw, so it is advisable to do a simple line draw exercise, and then print it to see what your printer will do for you. The **Ctrl F5** key is used to go to line draw.

There are several rules you should follow when creating documents containing line draw.

1. Always use a fixed-pitch font (every character is the same width). Do not use a proportionally-spaced font. Since not all characters in a proportionally-spaced font are equal, this causes the text to change the alignment of the lines.

2. Use "overtype" mode in order to avoid moving the lines when typing text in a box or chart created in line draw. If you are in "insert" mode, the lines will be moved along with your text as you type.

3. Do not use formatting such as centering, tabs, or "space above" or "space below." Use the right or left arrow keys to move to the right or left, or use the space bar instead of centering or using tabs to move to the right. Use the up or down arrow keys to move to a new line position to enter text.

4. Avoid drawing lines around existing text. Draw the lines first, then enter the text. Formatting such as centering or tabs, can cause problems with your lines if you try to draw lines around text which has this formatting.

You will create the chart shown below.

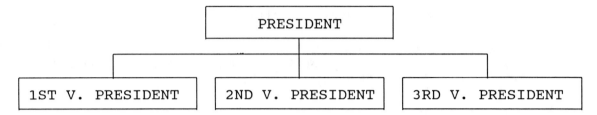

To use line draw to create a box:

1.	Press:	the **space bar** to move the **highlight** even with the 2 on the ruler line to begin the line draw about two inches from the left margin.
2.	Press:	**Ctrl F5** to go to "line draw" mode--an **LD** will be displayed in the status line.
3.	Press:	the **right arrow key** to draw a line to the 4 on the ruler line. This will make the box two inches wide.
4.	Press:	the **down arrow** twice to make the box two lines high.
5.	Press:	the **left arrow** to return the line even with 2 on the ruler line.
6.	Press:	the **up arrow** to draw a line up to the top line and complete the box.

Note: See the following instructions for moving from one position to another in order to draw other lines and boxes. You can move the arrow keys back over lines you have just drawn in order to go to a new position; however, if you move the arrow keys into a space without a line draw character in it, you will draw a line in that position. You would have to leave the Line Draw mode in order to delete any lines you do not want. See the instructions below for erasing lines.

To move from one position to another:

1. Press: **Ctrl F5** to exit Line Draw mode.
2. Move: the **highlight** to the center of the bottom line of the box on the screen.
3. Press: **Ctrl F5** to go to Line draw mode and press **down arrow** three times to draw a vertical line at the new position.

Continue drawing the lines and boxes for the remaining titles, using the arrow keys as described above. Make the boxes on the bottom row 1.7 in width.

To erase lines:

This is a quick way to edit line draw.

If you are in Line Draw mode:
1. Press: **Ctrl F5** to exit from Line draw mode.
2. "Select" the lines to be erased.
3. Press: **Delete** or **Backspace** to delete.

Note: When Delete is pressed, the lines to the right, if there are any, may be moved to the left. You would then have to press the space bar to move them back to the right. Sometimes gaps appear in the lines, and you would have to go back to line draw mode to correct this.

Using Microsoft Word Advanced Functions, Part 3   43

To type text in a box:

1. Press: **Ctrl F5** to exit Line Draw mode.
2. Move: the **highlight** to the position where text is to be typed.
3. Press: **F5** to go to Overtype mode. An **OT** will be displayed in the status line.
4 Type: the text in the example.

Note: *If the text does not fit in the box, you may have to abbreviate President.*

To change the line draw character:

Repeat steps above to create the same chart with a different line draw character, or to create your own design. Do this below the current document.

1. Press: **Esc.**
2. Choose: **Options** to go to the Options menu.
3. Move: the **highlight** to the "linedraw character" field.
4. Press: **F1** to display the available characters.
5. Move: the **highlight** to any character, and press **Enter** to return to the document.
6. Press: **Ctrl F5** to draw with the new character.

7. Before clearing the screen, repeat steps 1 through 5 to return the line draw character to the original single line character.

8. Press **Ctrl F10** to save the document **lines.**
9. Press **Ctrl F8** to print.
10. Clear the screen.

Note: *This text was created using a Hewlett-Packard LaserJet+ printer which does not support line draw; therefore the line draw exercise was created by using the Format Border Box option for the boxes, a Format Border Line for the horizontal line, and a vertical tab for the vertical lines. The second row of boxes were formatted as side-by-side paragraphs.*

CHAPTER 6

GRAPHICS LAYOUT

PREVIEW

The instructions in this chapter will show you how to use the **Format pOsition** menu to control the layout of pages by positioning paragraphs in text. This chapter will also include instructions for using the **Library Link Graphics** menu to import into a Word Document, graphics files saved by the **Capture.COM** program.

Format pOsition Menu

The **Format pOsition** menu allows you to format a paragraph by specifying the position on a page where the paragraph is to be printed. You may position the paragraph at the top of the page expanding over two columns; at the left or right margin corresponding to some additional text which "flows" around it; at the bottom of a column; or outside of the margins on facing pages. "Positioned" paragraphs are formatted in the same way all paragraphs are formatted. For example, they may be double-spaced, justified, formatted with a different font name and size, or formatted with bold or underlining.

Word uses the term "paragraph frame" when working with the **Format pOsition** menu. The paragraph frame refers to the rectangular space created by a paragraph and may or may not have an actual border around it. As you work with this feature, visualize the paragraph space as a frame. The frame is positioned on the page, and text or graphics may be manipulated within that frame.

Capture.COM

Instructions for using the **Capture.COM** program are included in this chapter. The Capture program saves a screen image as a graphics file and may then be imported into a Word document.

Library Link Graphics menu

The **Library Link Graphics** menu is used to import a graphic into a Word document. It is also used to align the graphic in a frame or change the width and height of the graphic. Use this menu to import a graphic saved with the Capture program, or use it to import graphics from other programs. The README.DOC stored on the Word Utilities disk 1 lists those programs: Lotus PIC files, PC Paintbrush PCX or PCC files, HPGL plotter files, PostScript files, Windows Clipboard, or Microsoft Pageview picture files.

USING THE FORMAT POSITION MENU TO CREATE A NEWSLETTER

In this exercise, you will be producing the first page of a newsletter. A copy of the final output is shown on the following page. The document includes the following types of positioned paragraphs:

*   The banner, which includes the name of the newsletter and the date line, is formatted to be positioned over a double column.

*   The box containing the telephone number is positioned at the left margin of the first column and will stay with the adjacent text.

*   The box in the center is at a fixed position in the center of the page.

*   The "promotions" paragraph is at a fixed position at the bottom of the right column. It does not have a box around it; however, think of it as being in a "frame."

```
          THE KTECH CORPORATION QUARTERLY

MARCH 1990                                    VOLUME 1
```

NEW COURSE OFFERINGS

```
KTech
Training
Dept.

456-7890
```

With so much to know about the fast changing world of business automation, the least of your worries should be learning how to take command of your personal computer. At KTech corporation, we want to help you take charge.

We have classes that help the new user get started. If you are just beginning, we will steer you in the right direction with "Word Processing for Beginners" which is a new class offered this month. All of our courses are offered on a regular basis.

```
INSIDE:

What's
Happening at
KTech This
Month.

Looking Back--
Where are They
Now?
```

Call the KTech Training Department for further information on course offerings and to register for classes scheduled this month.

Register early to get into the class of your choice.

All courses are hands-on, one person to a computer, unless otherwise specified.

DID YOU KNOW?

In 1960 IBM began installing its first commercial electronic computer system: the 1401 processor with 1.2K to 16K RAM. The standard was 8K RAM at the time. Few customers needed 16K.

This early system was quite different from computer systems in use today. There was no magnetic storage or operating system. Programs and data were stored on punch cards.

Once a week, service technicians powered down the system for about two hours to do preventive maintenance.

PROMOTIONS FOR APRIL

Joan Smith, Vice President, Sales

Benjamin MacDonald, Vice President, Accounting

Jeffrey Baldwin, Secretary, Corporate Investments

Molly Adams, Administrative Counsel

To set division formatting for two columns:

1. Press: **Esc.**
2. Choose: **Format, Division, Layout.**
3. Set: number of columns at 2 and leave the remaining fields at the default settings.
4. Press: **Enter** to return to the document screen.

To create and position the banner:

```
┌─────────────────────────────────────────────────────────────────────┐
│                   THE KTECH CORPORATION QUARTERLY                   │
│                                                                     │
│  MARCH 1990                                                VOLUME 1 │
└─────────────────────────────────────────────────────────────────────┘
```

1. Press: **Enter** and move the **highlight** to the line above the division mark.

To create a box for the heading:
2. Press: **Esc.**
3. Choose: **Format, Border, Box.**
4. Press: **Enter** to return to the document screen.

To use the Format pOsition menu to position the box over double columns:
5. Press: **Esc.**
6. Choose: **Format, pOsition** to display the menu.

An example of the menu is shown below.

```
FORMAT POSITION
     horizontal frame position: Left      relative to:(Column)Margins Page
     vertical frame position: In line     relative to:(Margins)Page
     frame width: Single Column           distance from text: 0.167"
Enter measurement or press F1 to select from list
Pg1 Col         {}                                        Microsoft Word
```

The responses to each of fields displayed in the menu above are the defaults for all paragraphs.

horizontal frame position: Left
All paragraphs are positioned at the left margin. The options available in this field are: left, centered, right, outside, inside, or a numeric value may be entered.

relative to: Column
A single column is the default for the text between the left and right margins. If Format Division Layout is set at two or three columns, then this response refers to the column in which the paragraph is positioned. "Margins" refers to the area between the left and right margins. "Page" refers to the position on the page, and may be outside the margins.

vertical frame position: In line
This means that the vertical position of a paragraph will be where the highlight is positioned when the text is typed. The paragraph will not be at a fixed position, but will move up or down the page as additional text is added or deleted above it. The other options in the field are: top, centered, bottom, or a numeric value may be entered. If any of these options is chosen, then the paragraph will be set at a fixed, vertical position.

relative to: Margins
: This response means the vertical position will be relevant to the margins which have been set. If the other option, "Page," is selected, then the vertical position will be relative to the page. For example, if "top" in the "vertical frame position" were selected and "Page" in the "relative to" field were selected, the paragraph would be positioned at the top <u>edge</u> of the paper.

frame width: single column
: The paragraph will extend from the left margin to the right margin of the column, whatever that measurement might be. If a different measurement is entered, that would change the width of the frame. If "double column" is selected, the paragraph would be positioned over two columns. The choices displayed when **F1** is pressed in this field depend upon the column layout chosen for the document.

distance from text: 0.167
: This is the amount of white space between the positioned paragraph frame and the text that flows around it. You may change this white space, by typing in a new measurement.

Be sure the **highlight** is positioned in the "horizontal frame position" field.

7.	Press:	**F1** to display the list of possible choices.
8.	Move:	the **highlight** to "Centered."
9.	Press:	**F1** to return the **highlight** to the menu.
10.	Move:	the **highlight** to the "relative to" field.
11.	Press:	**M** to choose Margins. Margins is chosen to fix the position of the banner between the left and right margins.

Note: *In the "relative to" field opposite "horizontal frame position," the margins refer to left and right margins. In the "relative to" field opposite "vertical frame position," margins refer to top and bottom margins.*

12.	Move:	the **highlight** to the "vertical frame position" field.
13.	Press:	**F1** to display the choices.
14.	Move:	the **highlight** to "Top."
15.	Press:	**F1** to return to the menu.
16.		Leave the "relative to" field set at "Margins." If you specified "Page" in this menu, the heading would be placed at the top edge of the page, not at the top margin.
17.	Move:	the **highlight** to the "frame width" field.
18.	Press:	**F1** to display the choices.
19.	Move:	the **highlight** to "Double column."

Note: *Setting the "frame width" field for "Double column" is necessary to position a paragraph over two columns.*

20.		Leave the remaining field, "distance from text," at the default.
21.	Press:	**Enter** to return to the document. The banner will be positioned to print over both columns at the top of the page.

<u>To center and type the text in all caps:</u>

22.	Press:	**Alt C** and **Caps Lock**.
23.	Type:	**THE KTECH CORPORATION QUARTERLY**.
24.	Press:	**Shift Enter** twice. (If **Enter** were pressed, a second box would be displayed.)

25.	Type:	**MARCH 1990**, press the **space bar** to the right edge of the box, and type **VOLUME 1**.
26.	Move:	the **highlight** between the date and the Volume number, and press the **space bar** enough times to move each entry to the ends of the line. (This is necessary because center formatting is still in effect.)
27.	Press:	the **End** key to move the **highlight** to the end of the line.
28.	Press:	**Enter** and **Alt P** to return to normal paragraph formatting.

Note: *Alt P not only returns to normal paragraph formatting, but it also returns the Format pOsition menu to single column for the frame width, and "in line" for the vertical frame position.*

To enter the heading in column 1:

```
NEW COURSE OFFERINGS
```

1.	Type:	the column heading **NEW COURSE OFFERINGS** centered in column 1 and in all caps.
2.	Press:	**Enter** and **Alt P** to return to normal paragraph formatting.
3.	Press:	**Caps Lock** to return to lowercase, and **Enter** again to insert a blank line.

To create and position the box at the left side of column 1:

This box, shown below, should be typed directly <u>above</u> the paragraph (text) appearing with it in the column.

```
KTech
Training
Dept.

456-7890
```

1.	Press:	**Esc**, and choose **Format, Border, Box**, and press **Enter**.
2.	Type:	**KTech Training Dept.** and **Shift Enter** twice. Use Shift Enter to keep the text formatted as one paragraph.
3.	Type:	**456-7890**.

<u>To position the paragraph:</u>
(Be sure the **highlight** is located at any position within the paragraph.)

The only change in the menu will be in the "frame width" field.

4.	Press:	**Esc** and choose **Format, pOsition** to display the menu.
5.	Set the fields as follows:	

horizontal frame position: Left

relative to: Columns
 (the default response)

vertical frame positions: In line
 (the default response) This means that the paragraph frame will remain with the following paragraph text. It will not be at a fixed position vertically on the page.

Using Microsoft Word Advanced Functions, Part 3

relative to: Margins
(the default response)

frame width: 1.2"
This is changed to create the small box within the column.

distance from: 0.167
(the default response) This refers to the amount of space between the frame edges and the surrounding paragraph text.

6. Press: **Enter** to return to the document.
7. Press: **Enter** again and press **Alt P** to return to normal paragraph.
8. Type: the remaining text in column 1 which is shown in the box below.

```
With so much to know about the fast changing world of
business automation, the least of your worries should be
learning how to take command of your personal computer.
At KTech Corporation, we want to help you take charge.

We have classes that help the new user get started.  If
you are just beginning, we will steer you in the right
direction with "Word Processing for Beginners" which is a
new class offered this month.  All of our courses are
offered on a regular basis.

Call the KTech Training Department for further information
on course offerings and to register for classes scheduled
this month.

Register early to get into the class of your choice.

All courses are hands-on, one person to a computer, unless
otherwise specified.
```

9. Press: **Ctrl F9** to go to the Print preView screen to view the output.
10. Choose: **Exit** to return to the document screen.

To create and position the box in the center of the page:

The text is shown on the following page.

1. Position the **highlight** on the line below the last line of text in column 1. Since it is going to be at a fixed position, this paragraph may be entered any place on the page and then positioned using the Format pOsition menu. When a paragraph has to stay with corresponding text (as with the box in column 1), then the paragraph has to be entered above the text appearing with it.

2. Press: **Esc** and choose **Format, Border, Box** to format the paragraph mark with a border.
3. Press: **Enter** to return to the document.

To position the paragraph:
4. Press: **Esc** and choose **Format, pOsition** to display the menu.
5. Set the fields as follows:

    horizontal frame position: Centered
        (Either type the word "centered" or press **F1** to display the list of choices.)

    relative to: Margins

    vertical frame position: Centered
        (Either type the word or press **F1**.)

    relative to: Margins

    frame width: 1.7
        (This measurement may be whatever you choose to make it.)

    distance from text: 0.167
        (the default response)

6. Press: **Enter** to return to the document.
7. Type: the text as it appears in the box below. Remember to press **Shift Enter** to end lines and to insert blank lines.

```
INSIDE:

What's
Happening at
KTech This
Month.

Looking Back--
Where are They
Now?
```

8. Press: **Enter** at the end of the text.
9. Press: **Alt P** to return to normal paragraph formatting.

To enter a column break and type the text for column 2:

On the line below the box:
1. Press: **Ctrl Alt Enter** A row of dots will appear at the end of column 1 indicating the end of column 1 and the beginning of column 2.

2. Type: all of the text for the **DID YOU KNOW?** section for column 2 on the following page. Center and type the heading in all caps. Do not add a box for this text.

The text is shown in the box below.

```
DID YOU KNOW?

In 1960 IBM began installing its first commercial
electronic computer system:  the 1401 processor with 1.2K
to 16K RAM.  The standard was 8K RAM at the time.  Few
customers needed 16K.

This early system was quite different from computer
systems in use today.  There was no magnetic storage or
operating system.  Programs and data were stored on punch
cards.

Once a week, service technicians powered down the system
for about two hours to do preventive maintenance.
```

3. Press: **Enter** at the end of this text.

To create and position the PROMOTIONS paragraph:

The text is shown in the box below. This paragraph will <u>not</u> be formatted in a box, but with a single line above "PROMOTIONS FOR APRIL."

```
PROMOTIONS FOR APRIL
─────────────────────

Joan Smith, Vice President,
Sales

Benjamin MacDonald, Vice
President, Accounting

Jeffrey Baldwin, Secretary,
Corporate Investments

Molly Adams, Administrative
Counsel
```

To use the Format Border menu to add the line above the paragraph.
1. Press: **Esc** and choose **Format, Border, Lines**.
2. Move: the **highlight** to the "above" field.
3. Press: **Y** to choose "Yes."
4. Press: **Enter** to return to the document. A line appears above the paragraph mark.

To position the paragraph:
5. Press: **Esc** and choose **Format, pOsition** to display the menu.
6. Set the fields as follows:

> **horizontal frame position**: Left (The horizontal frame position is in relation to the column; therefore, left is appropriate.)

relative to: Column

vertical frame position: Bottom
 (This will fix the position of the paragraph at the bottom of the column regardless of other text which may be added above or below it.)

relative to: Margins

frame width: Single column
 (It will expand or contract to fit with the column margins.)

distance from text: 0.167

7. Press: **Enter** to return to the document.
8. Type: **PROMOTIONS FOR APRIL** in all caps and double-underlined (press **Alt D** for double-underline).
9. Press: **Alt space bar** to return to normal character formatting, **Caps Lock** to return to lowercase, and **Shift Enter** twice.
10. Type: the remainder of the text on the previous page. Remember to use **Shift Enter** to insert line ends and blank lines.
11. Save the document. Name it **newsltr**.

To view the document as it will look when printed:

1. Press: **Ctrl F9** or **Esc,** and choose **Print, preView**.

Note: *If the text isn't positioned correctly, you may then return to the document screen and make necessary adjustments. It takes some experience working with graphics layout to get the results you want. The text in the columns does not fill the entire space. If you wish to add more text, do so. Maybe type a paragraph a second time, or make up text on your own.*

The example of the final output was shown on page 45 so you may compare text.

2. Choose: **Exit** to return to the document.

USING SHOW LAYOUT TO DISPLAY THE TEXT ON THE SCREEN IN TWO COLUMNS

When you are in show layout mode, you may edit the text, which you cannot do when you are in Print preView. This exercise will show you how to move the **highlight** from one column to the next, or from one object (graphic/positioned paragraph) to the next. The **highlight** moves more slowly in show layout mode, so you probably won't want to work in this mode all the time. Also, the ruler line display will be discussed.

1. Press: **Alt F4**. An **LY** is displayed in the status line and the columns appear side by side on the screen as they will look when they are printed.
2. Press: **Ctrl Page Up** to move the **highlight** to the top of the document. Then move the **highlight** down into the first column.

Using Microsoft Word Advanced Functions, Part 3 53

To jump to the next object or column:

Object is a term Word uses to identify the positioned paragraphs or frames which may contain text or graphics.

1. Press: **Ctrl Keypad 5** and the **right arrow**. Keypad 5 is the 5 on the numeric keypad at the right side of the keyboard. Also, press the right arrow on the keypad when the Keypad 5 is being used. This is more efficient than using the arrow keys located between the alphabet keys and the numeric keypad on an enhanced keyboard.

To jump to the previous object or column:

1. Press: **Ctrl Keypad 5** and **left arrow**.

Experiment with these moves in order to get used to viewing the screen in show layout mode.

To display and view the ruler line:

If the ruler is not displayed:
1. Press: **Esc.**
2. Choose: **Options.**
3. Move: the **highlight** to the "show ruler" field
4. Press: **Y** to choose "Yes."
5. Press: **Enter** to return to the document.

Note: *As you move the **highlight** from one column or object to another, the ruler line adjusts so the left measurement always begins at 0. This shows the width of each column or object.*

6. Move the **highlight** around in the document, and look at the ruler line change as you move from column to column.

7. Press: **Alt F4** to leave the show layout mode.

8. Save the edited document.
9. Print the document.
10. Clear the screen.

Note: *If you press Alt P within a paragraph positioned at a specific point, you will lose the Format pOsition formatting and return to the default position discussed on page 46.*

Note: *In this document, you used nearly all of the possible choices in the vertical and horizontal frame position fields in order to demonstrate the possibilities of placing paragraphs in text. Positioning paragraphs outside or inside margins was not discussed; however, these options will be covered in the following section of this chapter.*

POSITIONING PARAGRAPHS OUTSIDE THE MARGINS

The document used in this exercise contains paragraphs positioned outside the margins. This type of formatting is used to add emphasis to the contents of the corresponding paragraphs within the margins. An example of how pages 2 and 3 of the document will look when printed is displayed below in the Print preView screen image.

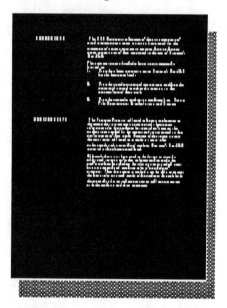 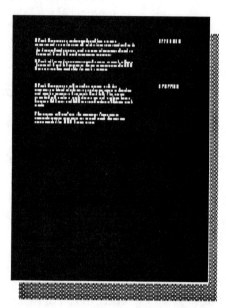

Use the "outside" position in the "horizontal frame position" field when you want to create a document with mirror margins. Mirror margins are used for facing pages in text to be printed double sided (in a book, for example). If your document is not going to be printed double-sided, then use side-by-side paragraph formatting to achieve a similar effect. For example, if you always wanted the "outside" paragraphs to be on the left on every page, you would use side-by-side paragraphs to position the paragraphs rather than the Format pOsition menu.

To create a title page:

1. Type: the text below in any vertical position on the first page. Use any font name and size that seems appropriate, and center the text vertically and horizontally on the page. Also, use the default margins for this page.

```
          PROPOSAL FOR TRAINING

                   FOR

              ABC CORPORATION
```

To set mirror margins for pages 2 and 3:

1. Press: **Enter** at the end of the last line of the title, and press **Alt P** to return to normal paragraph.
2. Press: **Ctrl Enter** to enter a new division mark at the bottom of page 1. You must do this so that the formatting for page 1 will not be changed.
3. Move: the **highlight** below the new division mark. It may already be there.
4. Press: **Esc** and choose **Format, Division, Margins**.

Using Microsoft Word Advanced Functions, Part 3   55

5.   Make the following changes in the Margins menu:

   left: at 1"
   right: at 3.25"
   mirror margins: Yes

Note: *These are the margins for the odd-numbered pages printed on the right. The margins will be reversed for the pages printed on the left; however the formatting for the outside paragraphs will always be the same regardless of the page on which they appear.*

6.   Press: **Enter** to return to the document.

To create and position the first paragraph on page 2:

The paragraph "BACKGROUND" is to be positioned "outside" and must be entered directly above the paragraph containing the corresponding text. The box below displays the text for this section.

```
BACKGROUND      The ABC Corporation, because of their
                intensive use of word processing computer
                programs, has a need for the provision of
                training services in assisting them in the
                on-going preparation of their personnel in
                the use of Microsoft Word 5.0.

                The services required include, but are not
                necessarily limited to:

                1.  Providing basic training in using
                Microsoft Word 5.0 at the beginning level.

                2.  Providing applications and user
                training enabling the personnel trained to
                utilize the program in the various facets
                of their work.

                3.  Providing specific application needs
                such as:  merge, file management, graphic
                layout, and macros.
```

1.   Type: in all caps, the word **BACKGROUND**.
2.   Be sure the **highlight** is in the paragraph.
3.   Press: **Esc** and choose **Format, pOsition** to display the menu.
4.   Make the following changes in the menu:

   horizontal frame position: Outside
      (Press **F1** to display the list of choices or type "outside.") If you pressed **F1** to display the list, press **F1** a second time to return to the menu to make further changes.

   relative to: Page
      This is essential. The paragraph will not be positioned correctly if either of the other options is chosen.

> **vertical frame position**: In line
>
> **relative to**: Margins
>
> **frame width**: 3" This measurement must be slightly less than the right margin, which was set at 3.25".
>
> **distance from text**: 0.167

5. Press: **Enter** to return to the document.

Note: In this exercise, you are instructed to type the text before positioning the paragraph. This is not mandatory. You may position the paragraph mark first, then type the text.

6. Press: **Enter** again to go to the next line.
7. Press: **Alt P** to return to normal paragraph.

If the **highlight** is on the division mark, press **Enter** and move the **highlight** up to the blank line.

To type the corresponding text within the margins:

8. Move: the **highlight** to the line below BACKGROUND.
9. Type: the text corresponding to BACKGROUND.
10. Press: **Enter** three times after the last paragraph.

The text for the remaining paragraphs on page 2 are shown below. REQUIREMENTS will be outside the margins, the same as BACKGROUND was in the previous exercise.

```
REQUIREMENTS    The Training Program will need to be
                comprehensive in the sense that it must
                encompass not only beginning information
                for the students, but must also focus on
                the applications needed by the corporation
                and its personnel in the performance of
                their work.  Because of this requirement,
                the contractor will need to provide a
                trainer who understands and is capable of
                teaching Microsoft Word 5.0 material at the
                above stated level.

                Although there may be a need in the future
                to provide additional training to further
                enhance and upgrade the staff's working
                knowledge, the information provided must be
                so organized and taught as to be a "stand
                alone" program.  Thus the trainer provided
                must be able to convey the basic
                informational needs of the students through
                both theoretical and practical instruction
                as well as interacting with the students
                and their questions.
```

To format the paragraph REQUIREMENTS and the corresponding text on page 2:

1. Type: **REQUIREMENTS** in all caps.
2. Press: **Esc** and choose **Format, pOsition**.

3. Make the following changes:

    horizontal frame position: Outside
    (Press **F1** to display the list of choices or type "outside.") If you pressed **F1** to display the list, press **F1** a second time to return to the menu to make further changes.

    relative to: Page

    vertical frame position: In line

    relative to: Margins

    frame width: 3"
    This measurement must be slightly less than the right margin, which was set at 3.25".

    distance from text: 0.167

4. Press: **Enter** to return to the document.
5. Press: **Enter** again and **Alt P** to return to normal position.

<u>On the line below the word REQUIREMENTS:</u>
6. Type: the two paragraphs corresponding to REQUIREMENTS.

Insert a page break at the end of the last paragraph to be entered on page 2:
7. Press: **Ctrl Shift Enter** to insert a new page mark and go to page 3.

To format the paragraphs on page 3:

The text is shown below.

```
KTech Corporation understands and has          APPROACH
trainers experienced in performing all
of the functions involved with the
design, development, and training of
courses related to Microsoft Word 5.0
word processing program.

KTech will provide an experienced trainer
to teach a Basic Microsoft Word 5.0
course to the six or seven people
ABC Corporation has available for such
training.


KTech Corporation will provide a trainer      STAFFING
with the appropriate blend of education
and experience to develop and teach a
course in Microsoft Word 5.0.  The
trainer provided will perform work
during normal working hours between
8:00 a.m. and 5:00 p.m. and within a
40-hour work week.

The trainer will perform the necessary
functions to research, create, organize,
write, and teach the various items
needed for ABC Corporation.
```

Instructions for positioning APPROACH and STAFFING outside the margin will be the same as the instructions for BACKGROUND AND REQUIREMENTS. The fields in the Format pOsition menu will be set exactly the same because the Format Division Margin menu was set for mirror margins.

1. Type: **APPROACH.**

2. Go to the **Format pOsition** menu, and set "horizontal frame position" at "Outside"; "relative to" at "Page"; and "frame width" at 3. Press **Enter** to return to the document.

3. Press: **Enter** and **Alt P** to return to normal position.
4. Type: the corresponding paragraphs, and press **Enter** three times at the end of the second paragraph.

5. Type: **STAFFING**, and repeat the formatting as listed in step 2 above.

6. Type: the remaining paragraphs.

7. Save the document. Name it **proposal**.

Using Microsoft Word Advanced Functions, Part 3   59

To view the document:

1.   Be sure the **highlight** is positioned in either page 2 or page 3.
2.   Press: **Ctrl F9** to go to Print preView.
3.   Choose: **Options.**
4.   Choose: **Facing-pages.**

Note: *If the text isn't positioned as you would like it, return to the document and make any necessary adjustments. You will be instructed to center the text in each outside paragraph.*

5.   Choose: **Exit** to return to the document.

6.   The four paragraphs "Outside" the margins should be centered in their frames to enhance their appearance on the page. Move the **highlight** to each paragraph, and press **Alt C** to center.

7.   Go to Print preView again to view the change.

8.   Save the edited document.
9.   Print the document.
10. Clear the screen.

USING THE CAPTURE.COM PROGRAM

The Capture.COM program enables the user to save a screen image from Word or from any other DOS program. The Library Link Graphic menu is then used to import the graphics file into a Word document. In this section, you will learn how to capture a screen image in Word and to import it into a Word document. The advantage of saving a screen image in Word, rather than having it as part of the text of the document, is that you may use the Library Link Graphics menu to resize the screen image.

The Capture.COM program is located on the Word Utilities Disk 3. If you are using a dual disk drive system, this disk will have to be inserted in Drive A to load the program. If you are using a hard disk drive system, the program was copied to the Word 5 directory when the Word 5.0 was installed.

If you have not used the Capture.COM program before, you will want to set it up first.

To set up the Capture.COM program:

If you are using a dual floppy disk drive system:
At the **A:>** prompt:
1.   Insert the Utilities Disk 3 in Drive A.
2.   Type: **capture/s.**
3.   Press: **Enter** to display the Capture Setup menu.

If you are using a hard disk drive system:
4.   Press: **Esc.**
5.   Choose: **Library, Run.**

Note: *The Library Run menu is used to go directly to DOS and enter any DOS commands or commands to run other programs, as you will be doing here.*

6.   Type: **capture/s.**
7.   Press: **Enter** to display the Capture Setup menu.

The Capture Setup menu displays the options discussed below.

To change the setup:

Changes in the Capture.COM setup menu depend upon the type of monitor you are using. Ask your instructor for assistance in this section if you are uncertain about the characteristics available to you.

Note: *When you display the screen corresponding to each option discussed below, an explanation is shown at the top of the screen to help you make the correct choices.*

1. Press: the letter corresponding to each option listed below, read the information displayed on the screen, and make the recommended changes if they are appropriate for your monitor.

    to select a display adapter press D
    Specifies the type of screen display for your computer. You will probably not have to make any change in this menu.

    to enable/disable text screen as picture press T
    Capture can save a screen in text mode; however, you are will not be able to change screen boundaries in text mode. Graphics mode allows the user to change the screen boundaries, and displays text as it will be printed--for example, italic formatting will appear in italic on the screen--the screen will be in black and white generally. <u>Leave this setting at "no"</u>--you will not be able to save a screen image in text mode; however, when you want to save a screen image, you will press Alt F9 in Word 5.0 to change the screen to graphics mode. This allows you to use your color monitor, but to change to graphics mode when you want to save a screen image, and you will also be able to clip the boundaries if you set the menu below to "enable" clipping.

    to enable/disable saving in reverse video press V
    In reverse video, black will be saved as white, and white will be saved as black. Change to save in reverse video.

    to enable/disable clipping press P
    Clipping allows you to change the boundaries of the screen image. You cannot clip a Microsoft Windows screen; however, and must disable clipping if you are using Windows. If you are <u>not</u> using Windows, set this menu to enable clipping.

    to enter the number of text lines per screen press N
    No change is necessary in this menu.

    to quit and save settings press Q
    Press **Q** to save and return to the screen.

2. Press: any key to return to the Word 5.0 screen.

To create the graphic to be saved as a screen image:

<u>To change the line draw character:</u>
1. Press: **Esc** and choose **Options**.
2. Move: the **highlight** to "line draw character" field.
3. Press: **F1** to display the list of available characters.
4. Select a wide shaded character if one is available.
5. Press: **Enter** to return to the screen.

To use line draw:

1.	Press:	**Ctrl F5** to go to Line Draw mode.
2.	Press:	the **right arrow** to draw the first line as shown below, from position 0 to 4.4 (look at the ruler line to confirm the numbers) to correspond to 44%.
3.	Press:	**Ctrl F5** to leave line draw, and press **Enter** three times.
4.	Press:	**Ctrl F5** to go to line draw, and draw the second line from position 0 to 2.9.
5.	Press:	**Ctrl F5** to leave line draw, and press **Enter** three times.
6.	\\	Draw the third line from position 0 to 2.1, leave line draw, and press **Enter** three times.
7.	\\	Draw the fourth line from position 0 to 0.6, leave line draw, and press **Enter** once.
8.	Move:	the **highlight** to the end of the first bar, press the **Tab key** to correspond to position 5 displayed on the ruler line, and type **JAPAN**.
9.	Press:	the **down arrow** and press **Tab** enough times to go to position 5.
10.	Type:	**44%**
11.	\\	Following steps 8 through 10 for the remaining bars in order to enter the information at the end of each bar.

The screen will look similar to the chart below.

12. Before saving the screen image, go to the Options menu and set "show non-printing symbols" at "None", and set "show style bar" at "No."

To capture a screen image:

Note: *If you set "Enable/disable text screen as picture" at "No" (which means you won't be able to save a screen displayed in text mode), then press Alt F9 to go to the graphics display mode. Otherwise leave the screen as is. If you remained in text mode, you will not be able to clip your image.*
  Also, if you have a color monitor, you may have to change the background color to black if you are saving in "reverse video," in order to get a better graphic image. Go to the Options menu, move the **highlight** *to the "color" field, and press F1 to display the list of options. Select "black" and press* **Enter** *to return to the document.*

To change to graphics mode:
1. Press: **Alt F9** or press **Esc** and choose **Options**.

Note: *If you use the Options menu to go to graphics mode, move the highlight to "display mode" field. Press F1 to display the list of available options--this list varies depending upon the type of printer being used. Select "graphics mode."*

2. Press: **Shift Print Screen** to begin the capture program. A filename is displayed at the top of the screen. You may either accept this filename, or give the image an eight-character name of your own. The program automatically adds an extension **.SCR** for graphics screen images, or **.LST** for text screen images.

3. Press: **Enter** to accept the file name "capt0001.scr." This will be the first file name available. If you wish, you may enter your own eight-character filename.

To clip the screen image:

Note: *If you enabled clipping in the Capture Setup, you may then use the direction keys to change the boundaries of the screen. The term clipping refers to changing the outside boundaries of the screen to save a specified section of the screen.*

press	to
Direction (arrow) keys	move the lines to a new boundary
Tab	enable the direction keys to move the bottom and right lines to clip the image
Plus (+) on the keypad and then the arrow keys	move the lines in larger increments
Minus (-) on the keypad and then the arrow keys	move the lines in smaller increments
Insert and then press the arrow keys	move the top and bottom lines simultaneously
Delete	return to single line control

1. Experiment with clipping using the keys listed above to change the boundaries of the screen image. Move the boundary lines so the menu is eliminated.

To save the clipped image:

1. Press: **Enter**. The system will beep when the image is saved. It may take a while to save.

2. Clear the screen. You do not need to save the graphics on the screen since it was saved in the Capture program.

3. Press: **Alt F9** to return to text mode. Most users prefer to work in text mode, as it is faster than graphics.

4. Go to the Options menu and set "show non-printing symbols" at "Partial," and "show style bar" at "Yes."

To load the capture program the next time after setup:

Use these instructions the next time you want to use the Capture.COM program. Once you have changed the choices in the setup menu as discussed on page 60, those choices will remain until you change them again.

<u>If you are using a dual floppy disk drive system:</u>
At the **A:>** prompt:
1. Insert the Utilities disk 3 in Drive A.
2. Type: **capture** to load the program.

<u>If you are using a hard disk drive system:</u>
1. Press: **Esc.**
2. Choose: **Library, Run.**
3. Type: **capture** to load the program.

USING THE LIBRARY, LINK, GRAPHICS MENU

The Library, Link, Graphics menu is used to import graphics; not only Word screen images, such as you have just done, but also from other programs. Programs from which graphics may be imported were listed on the first page of this section. Also refer to the README.DOC on the Word Utilities disk 1 for complete information about the graphics packages Word supports.

In addition to importing graphics file, another important function of the Library, Link, Graphics menu is that it allows you to <u>resize</u> the graphic image to better fit your document. You may reduce or change the proportions of the imported graphics. If you find when the graphic is printed that the size needs to be revised, move the **highlight** into the graphics paragraph, display the Library, Link, Graphics menu, and change the measurements in the "graphics width" and "graphics height" fields. You will learn how to do that in this section.

To create a document containing a graphic image:

1. Type: the following sentence and press **Enter** twice.

```
The following chart presents an interesting display
of world-wide investments.
```

To import the graphic saved with Capture.COM:

<u>If you are using a hard disk drive system:</u>
1. Press: **Esc.**
2. Choose: **Library, Link, Graphics** to display the menu.
3. Type: **c:\word5\capt0001.scr** or see the note below if you are working in some other directory.

Note: *The Capture files are saved in the Word5 directory. If you are working in a different subdirectory, you must type the path as displayed above.*

Go to step 4 shown on the following page unless you are using a dual disk drive system.

<u>If you are using a dual disk drive system:</u>
1. Press: **Esc.**

2. Choose: **Library, Link, Graphics** to display the menu.
3. Type: **A:capt0001.scr.**
4. Move: the **highlight** to "alignment in frame:" field.

Note: *When you moved the* **highlight***, the word "capture" appeared in the "file format" field. This is the name of the program which generated the graphics image.*

To set the "alignment in frame" field:

1. Press: **F1** to display choices.
2. Move: the **highlight** to Centered and press **F1** to return to the menu.

To change the measurements of the graphic:

1. Move: the **highlight** to "graphics width."
2. Type: **4"** to change the width of the image.
3. Move: the **highlight** to the "graphics height" field.
4. Type: **2"** to change the height.

5. Leave the two remaining fields as is. These fields are similar to the "space before" and "space after" fields in Format, Paragraph menu used to set a space before or a space after a paragraph.

6. Press: **Enter** to display a paragraph on screen in the position where the graphic image is to be imported when the document is printed. The paragraph should resemble the following:

```
.G.C:\WORD5\CAPT0001.SCR;4";2";CAPTURE
```

Note: *The .G. indicates the text is formatted as hidden text and instructs the program to import the graphic when the document is printed. The path and filename indicate the graphic file to be imported, the dimensions show the size of the graphic, and the word "CAPTURE" names the program used to generate the graphic image. If .G. are not shown on the screen, go to the Options menu and set "show hidden text" at "Yes." The .G. will then be shown on the screen.*

To add a caption to the graphic:

1. Move: the **highlight** to the line directly below the graphics paragraph. If it is on the "end mark," press **Enter**, then move the **highlight** up to the blank line.
2. Type: **World Market Capitalization** and press **Alt C** to center.
3. Press: **Ctrl F9** to go to Print preView, choose **Options,** choose **1-page** to display the graphic as it will look in the document.
4. Choose: **Exit** to return to the document screen.

To add a box around the graphic:

1. Move: the **highlight** to any position in the graphics paragraph.
2. Press: **Esc** and choose **Format, Border, Box**.
3. Press: **Enter** to return to the screen. The box extends from the left to the right margin.

Using Microsoft Word Advanced Functions, Part 3

To indent the left and right margins to fit the box around the graphic:
4. Press: **Esc** and choose **Format, Paragraph**.
5. Set "left indent" at 1.
6. Set "right indent" at 1.

Note: Because the graphic width was set at 4" in the Library Link Graphics menu, indenting the box 1" from each margin will reduce it to fit around the image.

7. Press: **Enter** to return to the document.

8. Press: **Ctrl F9** again to go to Print preView to see how the changes will look when printed.

9. Save the document. Name it **chart.**

To print a document containing a graphic:

You may wish to change the graphics resolution in the print options menu; however, you may have some problems with this because of memory limits. Some printers cannot print large graphics, or they may print only a portion of the graphic. If this happens, you may have to decrease the size of the graphic.

To change the graphics resolution:
1. Press: **Esc** and choose **Print, Options**.
2. Move: the **highlight** to the "graphics resolution" field.
3. Press: **F1** to display the list of choices available on your printer. DPI refers to "dots per inch."
4. Move: the **highlight** to your choice.
5. Press: **F1** to return to the menu.
6. Move: the **highlight** to the "draft" field.

7. If "draft" is set at "Yes," your graphics will not be printed. This field must be set at "No."

8. Press: **Enter** to return to the Print menu.
9. Choose: **Printer** to begin printing. If the message to "Download fonts" appears, respond to it by pressing "A" to download all fonts or "Y" to download new fonts.

10. After printing the document, clear the screen.

Note: Graphics paragraphs may be positioned within your document, the same way other paragraphs are positioned. Graphics within paragraph frames may be resized using the Library Link Graphics menu.

CHAPTER 7

FORMS

PREVIEW

In this chapter you will learn to use Microsoft Word to produce a form and to fill it in manually. Many organizations create their own invoice forms, requisitions, or application forms. This section will show you how to do that. You will also learn how to create a guide for filling in preprinted forms; for example, forms you might buy at an office supply store.

The following steps are a preview of what you will be doing. Do not actually do this now.

The steps in creating a form are:

(The form you will be creating is shown on page 68.)

a. Position and type the various labels, such as "date," "first name," "last name," "address," etc. Lines or boxes may be added following each label, or you may leave blank spaces for the fill-in information. You may use the Format Border menu to add lines above or below the labels or to add boxes around labels; or you may use the Format Character menu to add underlining to tab marks. You could also draw boxes with line draw and position them at appropriate points for fill-in information, or format a tab set with the leader character set at underscore to draw lines.

b. When filling in a form, in order to move easily from one label to the next, enter a chevron (press **Ctrl]**) following each label. This chevron must be formatted as hidden text. When entering information at each label, press **Ctrl >** to jump to the next chevron, or press **Ctrl <** to jump to the previous chevron.

c. Save the document.

The steps in filling in a form are:

a. Load the form document as a "read only" document. This prevents you from altering the original form.

b. Press **Ctrl >** to jump to the first chevron.

c. Type the information appropriate for the label.

d. Repeat for each of the remaining labels.

e. Print the document.

f. If you want to save the document with the blanks filled in, save it with a new name.

The steps in creating a guide for filling in a preprinted form are:

a. Type the text for each label appearing in the preprinted form, and press **Ctrl]** to add a chevron following the label.

b. Format the label and the chevron as hidden text.

c. Position the label to correspond to the exact position in the preprinted form.

To use the guide for filling in a preprinted form:

a. Load the guide as a "read only" file.
b. Press **Ctrl >** to go to each label position.
c. Type in the appropriate information.
d. Print it on the preprinted forms, making sure the forms are fed into the printer the same way for each document.

Creating and filling in forms is quite easy using Word; however, it does take some experimenting to determine the character formatting for labels, headings, and titles, the layout which is most effective, and the type of lines to be used. You may be limited as far as the type of lines used by the printer which you are using. Determine what your printer will do with linedraw, for instance, before you spend too much time drawing boxes.

Chapter 9, Using Merge, will include more instructions on forms by showing you how to use merge to fill in a form automatically.

CREATING A FORM

You will create the form shown in the box below.

```
                    KTECH CORPORATION
                    PREREGISTRATION FORM
                    Fall Training Seminar
```

Last Name»	First Name»	MI»
Social Security Number»		
Company Name»		
Work Phone»	Ext»	
Mailing Address»		
Branch/Department»		
Title or Function»		
Days Attending: 1 @ $200»_____ 2 @ $400»_____ 3 @ $600»_____ Amount Due »_____ Amount Rec'd »_____		

This form was created using the Format Border menu to add the boxes and using vertical tabs to add the vertical lines within the boxes.

Before creating the form, follow the instructions below to go to the Options menu and set "show hidden text" at "Yes," and set "show non-printing symbols" at "All." This will allow you to view the tab marks as they are entered and format the ones in the box at the bottom of the form with the underline character. It will also allow you to see the chevrons when they are formatted as hidden text.

To change the screen display:

1. Press: **Esc.**
2. Choose: **Options**.
3. Move: the **highlight** to "show hidden text" field, and select "Yes."
4. Move: the **highlight** to "show non-printing symbols" and select "All."
5. Press: **Enter** to return to the document.

To enter the heading and title of the registration form in a box:

1. Press: **Esc.**
2. Choose: **Format, Border, Box.**
3. Press: **Enter** to display the box.
4. Press: **Alt C** to center.
5. Type: **KTECH CORPORATION** in all caps and press **Shift Enter**. You must press Shift Enter to retain the paragraph formatting for a box.
6. Type: the next two lines shown on the previous page, pressing **Shift Enter** at the end of each line.

Note: *If you wanted to enhance the appearance of the heading text, format it with a point size of 14 or 18.*

7. Press: **Enter** to display a second box.

8. Go to the Format Paragraph menu and set the "alignment" field at "left". If you press Alt P to return to left alignment, you will loose the box.

To format and type the labels in the first line of the form:

<u>To set vertical tabs and left flush tabs:</u>
1. Press: **Alt F1** to go to the Tab Set menu.
2. Type: **2.9** and **V** to set a vertical tab.
3. Type: **3** and **L** to set a left flush tab.
4. Repeat step 2 to set a vertical tab at 4.9.
5. Repeat step 3 to set a left flush tab at 5.
6. Press: **Enter.**
7. Type: **Last Name.**
8. Press: **Ctrl]** to type the chevron.
9. Press: **Tab** to go to position 3.
10. Type: **First Name** and press **Ctrl]**.
11. Press: **Tab** to go to position 5.
12. Type: **MI** and press **Ctrl]**.
13. Press: **Enter** to go to the next line.

To reset all tabs and type the labels in the second and third lines:

1. Press: **Esc.**
2. Choose: **Format Tab Reset-all** to remove the vertical tabs and the left flush tabs.
3. Type: **Social Security Number** and **Ctrl]** to insert the chevron.
4. Press: **Enter** to go to the next line.
5. Type: **Company Name** and a chevron.
6. Press: **Enter** to go to the next line.

To set the tabs for the line containing Work Phone:

1. Press: **Alt F1** and set tabs as follows:
   Vertical tab at 3
   Left flush tab at 3.1
2. Press: **Enter** to return to the document.
3. Type: **Work Phone** and a chevron.

4.	Press:	**Tab**.
5.	Type:	**Ext** and a chevron.
6.	Press:	**Enter**.

To reset all tabs and type the labels in the next three lines:

1.	Press:	**Esc** and choose **Format Tab Reset-all**.
2.	Type:	**Mailing Address** and a chevron.
3.	Press:	**Enter**.
4.	Repeat steps 2 and 3 for "Branch/Department" and "Title or Function."	

To format the box and type the labels "Days Attending," "Amount Due," and "Amount Received":

1.	Press:	**Alt F1** and set tabs as follows: Left flush tab at 2 Left flush tab at 3.4 Vertical tab at 3.5
2.	Press:	**Enter** to return to the document.
3.	Type:	**Days Attending:** and press **Shift Enter**.
4.	Press:	**Tab**.
5.	Type:	**1 @ $200** and a chevron.
6.	Press:	**Tab**.

To format the tab mark with the underline character:

7.	Press:	the **left arrow** to move the **highlight** to the tab mark.
8.	Press:	**Alt U** to format with the underline character.

Note: Adding the underline formatting will draw the lines in the box at the bottom of the form.

9.	Press:	the **right arrow** to go to the end of line.
10.	Press:	**Shift Enter** twice.
11.	Repeat:	steps 4 through 10 for the next two lines of text.
12.	Type:	**Amount Due,** press the **Tab key,** and type a chevron.
13.	Press:	**Tab** and format this tab mark with an underline, move to the paragraph mark on the right.
14.	Press:	**Shift Enter** twice.
15.	Repeat:	for **Amount Rec'd**.

To format the chevrons as hidden text:

1.	Press:	**Ctrl Page Up** to go to the top of the document.
2.	Press:	**Ctrl >** to jump to the first chevron.
3.	Press:	the **left arrow** to move the **highlight** on the chevron.
4.	Press:	**Alt E** to format as hidden text.
5.	Press:	**Ctrl >** to jump to the next chevron.
6.	Press:	the **left arrow** to move the **highlight** on the chevron.
7.	Press:	**F4** to repeat the edit (formatting).
8.	Repeat:	steps 5 through 7 for the remainder of the chevrons.
9.	Save the document. Name it **regisfrm**.	

To print 3 copies:
10. Go to the Print Options menu and set "copies" field at "3," press **Enter**, and choose Printer to print three copies. The extra copies will be used as preprinted forms and filled in as part of the exercise on page 75.

11. Clear the screen.

FILLING IN THE FORM

In this section, you will load the document as a "read only" file in order to prevent changing the original form. When a document is loaded as "read only," it cannot be changed. Any edits made to the document have to be saved with a different file name.

To load the document:

1. Press: **Esc** and choose **Transfer, Load**
2. Type: **regisfrm.**
3. Press: **Tab** to go to the "read only" field.
4. Press: **Y** to set at "Yes."
5. Press: **Enter** to load the document.

Note: *An asterisk is displayed on the screen in front of the file name indicating that it is in "read only" form.*

To fill in the form:

Since you marked each label with a chevron, you will use **Ctrl >** to jump quickly to each mark.

With the **highlight** at the top of the document:
1. Press: **Ctrl >** to go to the space following the "Last Name."
2. Press: the **space bar** once to insert a space.

Note: *The space bar separates the information from the label, which is advisable in this exercise, since the font will be the same for both. You wouldn't have to do this if there was a difference in font name or size.*

3. Type: your last name.

4. Repeat: for each of the remaining labels, typing in your own information appropriate to each label.

At "Days attending," type an X on whatever line you choose.

At "Amount Due" type in the amount corresponding to the days attending, and repeat for "Amount Rec'd."

At the end of filling in the form:
5. Press: **Ctrl F9** to go to Print preView to see the final output.
6. Choose: **Exit** to return to the document.

7. Save the document with a new name--**form1** which replaces ***regisfrm.doc** on the screen. The document **regisfrm.doc** still exists in its original format.

To print the document:

8. Go to the Print Options menu, and reset the "copies" field at "1," press **Enter**, and choose Printer to print.

9. Clear the screen.

Note: *When you use the form repeatedly, you may fill it in on the screen, and print it without saving to a new file.*

If you have a printer that supports multiple fonts, you could change the font names for the labels, which would enhance the appearance of the form.

CREATING AND USING A GUIDE FOR FILLING IN A PREPRINTED FORM

In this exercise, assume you have preprinted the form created in the first lesson of the chapter. You wish to use it to either fill it in with pen, or as you will learn in this section, you may use Word to fill in information.

You will create a guide by typing the labels and the chevron, each in its own paragraph, formatted as hidden text. You will then use the Format pOsition menu to specify the exact position where you wish the information following each label to be entered in the preprinted form. After creating the guide, you will use it to enter and print information in the preprinted form.

To create the guide:

The document will resemble the text in the box below.

```
Last name»
First Name»
MI»
Soc.Sec.#»
Company name»
Work Phone»
Ext.»
Mailing Address»
Branch/Dept.»
Title/Function»
1 @ $200»
2 @ $400»
3 @ $600»
Amount Due»
Amount Rec'd»
```

1. Type: each of the labels on a line by itself followed by a chevron (press **Ctrl]**).

To position each label so that the text to be entered for it is printed in the correct position:

This may take some experimenting with positions when you do this on your own. You will be instructed for the correct measurements to enter in the Format pOsition menu in this exercise.

When you are creating and filling in a form of your own, it is helpful to use a ruler to measure the form in order to determine the horizontal and vertical frame positions. The distance from the left margin to the space following a specific label, is the measurement to be entered in the "horizontal frame position" field, and the distance from the top margin down to a specific label is the measurement to be entered in the "vertical frame position" field.

<u>To position the paragraph for the label "Last Name":</u>
1. Move: the **highlight** to any position in "Last Name."
2. Press: **Esc** and choose **Format, pOsition** to display the menu.

The only fields which will be changed are the "horizontal frame position" and "vertical frame position."

3. Set the fields as follows:
   horizontal frame position: 1.1"
       This position is selected because the actual information will be printed 1.1" from the left margin.
   vertical frame position: .9"
       This will position the entry .9" from the top margin of the document.

4. Press: **Enter** to return to the document.
5. Move: the **highlight** to the paragraph containing "First Name."

6. Go to the Format pOsition menu to set the fields as follows:
   horizontal frame position: 4.1"
   vertical frame position: .9"

7. Press: **Enter** to return to the document.

8. Repeat for the remaining labels, entering the measurements listed below in the "horizontal" and "vertical frame position" fields.

"MI"	**horizontal**	5.3"
	vertical	.9"
"Soc.Sec.#"	**horizontal**	2.5"
	vertical	1.3"
"Company Name"	**horizontal**	1.5"
	vertical	1.6"
"Work Phone"	**horizontal**	1.5"
	vertical	1.9"
"Ext."	**horizontal**	3.5"
	vertical	1.9"
"Mail.Address"	**horizontal**	2"
	vertical	2.3"

"Branch/Dept."	horizontal	2"
	vertical	2.6"
"Title/Funct."	horizontal	2"
	vertical	2.9"
"1 @ $200"	horizontal	3"
	vertical	3.4"
"2 @ $400"	horizontal	3"
	vertical	3.7"
"3 @ $600"	horizontal	3"
	vertical	4.1"
"Amount Due"	horizontal	2"
	vertical	4.4"
"Amt Rec'd."	horizontal	2"
	vertical	4.7"

After positioning all the labels, and before formatting as hidden text, go to Print preView to see how the positions look. If you format the labels as hidden text before going to Print preView, you will not see anything on the screen. Hidden text is not displayed in Print preView.

9. Press: **Ctrl F9.**
10. Choose: **Exit** to return to the document and make any adjustments that you think may be needed. (You are not really going to be able to know until you print whether or not the settings are correct.)

To format each label and chevron as hidden text:

1. Move: the **highlight** to "Last Name" and "select" the words and the chevron. Do not "select" the paragraph mark.
2. Press: **Alt E**
3. Repeat: for the remaining labels. Be sure you don't format the paragraph mark following each label as hidden text. Use **F4** (repeat edit) to repeat the formatting.

4. Save the document. Name it **guide.**
5. Clear the screen.

To enter the information for each label:

To load the document **guide** as a "read only" file:
1. Press: **Esc** and choose **Transfer, Load.**
2. Type: **guide.**
3. Move: the **highlight** to the "read only" field and set at "Yes."
4. Press: **Enter** to load the document.

To enter the appropriate information:
5. Press: **Ctrl >** to jump to the end of the first label "Last Name."
6. Type: your last name.

7. Repeat steps 5 and 6 for the remaining labels. Type your own information, as you did in the preceding exercise. Be sure that the text you are entering is not formatted as hidden text. If it is, it will not be printed.

To view the entered information:

1. Press: **Ctrl F9** to go to Print preView.

Note: *Only the information is displayed--not the labels.*

2. Choose: **Exit** to return to the document.

Note: *You might test the printing on a blank sheet of paper, rather than using one of the preprinted forms. Then compare the copy to the form to see if the fields fit.*

To print the text on a preprinted form:

1. Load the printer with the extra forms printed on page 71. Be sure that the paper is positioned correctly and that the printer is on-line.

2. Press: **Esc** and choose **Print Options.**
3. Confirm that the "print hidden text" field is set at "No."
4. Press: **Enter** and choose **Printer** to print.

Note: *If the text is not printed accurately and the positions have to be changed, remember you loaded the document "guide" as a "read only" file. You will have to clear the screen and reload it with the "read only" field set at "No" in order to make any changes to the file.*

5. Clear the screen without saving the filled in form.

6. Go to the Options menu, set "show hidden text" field at "No," and set the "show non-printing symbols" field at "Partial" if those choices have been changed.

REINFORCEMENT EXERCISES

FUNCTIONS REVIEWED

Chapter 5:
    Formatting paragraphs with borders--boxes and/or lines.
    Using tabs to draw horizontal lines.
    Using vertical tabs to insert vertical lines in tables.
    Using linedraw mode to draw boxes and lines.

Chapter 6:
    Using the Format pOsition menu to place paragraphs.
    Using the Capture.COM program to save screen images.
    Using the Library Link Graphics menu to import graphics into Word.

Chapter 7:
    Creating a form.
    Filling in the form.
    Creating and using a guide for filling in a preprinted form.

RECALL QUESTIONS

Answers to recall questions are on page 81.

1. List four different ways to draw lines in text.

2. Name the menu used to add gray shading to a box.

3. What menus may be used to change the size of a box?

4. Name the menu used to change the font name or font size.

5. What is the speed key that moves the highlight directly to the "font name" field?

6. When positioning paragraphs "outside" margins, what setting must you make in the Format Division Margins menu?

7. When you position a paragraph "outside" the margins, the horizontal frame position must be set as relative to what--Columns? Margins? or Page?

8. Name the menu used to import a graphic from another program.

9. How can you change the size of an imported graphic?

10. What character is set that enables the user to go quickly to a label in a form?

11. What keystrokes are used to type the character referred to in question 10?

12. What keystrokes are used to go quickly to the mark following a label?

13. List the steps in creating a guide for filling in a preprinted form.

14. What is meant by loading a document as a "read only" file?

15. How can you tell that a document is a "read only" file when it is displayed on the screen?

DOCUMENT 3: USING FORMAT BORDER AND THE FORMAT POSITION MENU TO CREATE A NEWSLETTER

1. Create the document shown on the following page.

2. The logo is in capital letters, Times Roman 14 point. Use another point size if 14 point is not available.

3. Format the heading and the date line in a box.

4. Format the columns with a line between and lines around as shown in the example.

5. Position the paragraphs in boxes as they are shown in the example. Use a different font name and size that is available to you for the text in the boxes.

6. Run a spell check.

7. Go to Print preView to see how the document will look when it is printed. Make any necessary adjustments to the text. If the text in column 2 appears to be to close to the vertical line between the columns, format each paragraph in column 2 with a 0.1" paragraph indent. Use the Format Paragraph menu for the first paragraph and repeat the formatting by using the F4 key.

8. Save the document as **position**.

9. Print a copy of the document.

KTECH CORPORATION QUARTERLY

September 1990 _____ Volume 3

Summer Summary:

All conference attendees did a tremendous job reporting on the conference sessions and sharing their valuable expertise with others at KTech. Thank you for the time you took to write complete and informative reports from which all of us can profit.

DAY CARE

KTECH Day care Proposal Accepted by Management!

Day care facilities are now provided at KTech Corporation. Temporary facilities are in the old conference room at the East end of the building.

Many requests have been submitted during the past year, and it was recently the management's decision to happily report that the Corporate Board approved our proposal to include day care facilities for working parents at KTech.

New facilities will be built at the south end of the parking lot and will include a small cafeteria, playground, and classroom/playroom for children ages six months to five years.

Expense Reports:

Most of you have been doing a commendable job in turning in your Expense Reports on time.

We do, however, have some reports still out from the summer conference held in San Francisco.

Please submit all reports by the two week deadline. If you still have a report out, turn it in as soon as possible.

Thank you for your cooperation.

Meetings

The following meetings and in-house seminars are coming up next week.

Additional meetings this month are posted next to the personnel office.

Monday: MIS Departmental Procedure Changes at the MIS department. 3 p.m.

Get Reimbursed for education. Call Personnel

Tuesday: Question and Answer session on Payroll changes and deduction. In Accounting. Noon

Wednesday: Looking to the year 2000. A report from Management. In the President's office. 4:30 p.m.

DOCUMENT 4: CREATING A FORM

1. Create the form document shown on the following page. Try to duplicate the form as nearly as possible; however you might be limited by the fonts available to you.

2. Use the Format Border Box menu and vertical tabs for the first six lines asking for information.

3. For the "Training Received" section, use the vertical tab for drawing the vertical lines within the box, and use the tab with the underscore as a leader character to draw the horizontal lines. You should also set a left flush tab immediately following the vertical tab in order to begin the horizontal line. If you don't do this, the horizontal line will extend from the word preceding it, rather than from the vertical line. Press Shift Enter at the end of each line to format the entire paragraph in a box.

4. The three remaining sections are paragraphs with two extra lines in each (press Shift Enter to create the two lines). Each paragraph is formatted with a box.

5. Enter a chevron formatted as hidden text following each label so the form may be filled in later.

6. Save the document as **survey.**

7. Use Print preView to see the layout before printing. Make any adjustments necessary.

8. Print a copy of the form and clear the screen.

KTECH	

Please Return This Form by January 15.

KTECH CUSTOMER SURVEY

Survey No.:	Date:

Company Name:

Company Street Address:

Department:

City:	State:	Zip:

Date of most recent service from KTech:

Training Received:	Word Processing Database Spreadsheet MIS Structure Networking Communications Other: Please State:	_____ _____ _____ _____ _____ _____ _____

How did you hear about KTech?

Requests for Additional Service:

Other Comments:

Training	**Consultations**	**Expert Advice**	**Data Flow Diagrams**

Using Microsoft Word Advanced Functions, Part 3

ANSWERS TO RECALL QUESTIONS

1. Use Format Border menu to add lines above, below, right or left of paragraphs, or to format text in boxes.

    Use Tabs set with the underscore as a leader character.

    Use Vertical tabs to draw vertical lines.

    Go to line draw mode--Ctrl F5 and draw lines with the direction keys.

2. Format Border menu.

3. Format Border and Format pOsition menus.

4. Format character.

5. Alt F8.

6. You must set "mirror margins" at "Yes."

7. Page.

8. Library Link Graphic.

9. Go to Library Link Graphic menu and change "graphic width" and "graphic height" fields.

10. Chevron formatted as a hidden character.

11. Press Ctrl].

12. Ctrl >.

13. a. Type each label following by a chevron.

    b. Format both as hidden text.

    c. Use the Format pOsition menu to set the horizontal and vertical positions for each label. The horizontal position should be in relation to the left margin. The vertical position is in relation to the top margin.

14. Edits or changes to the document will not be saved without changing the document name.

15. An asterisk precedes the file name in the lower right corner of the screen.

PART 4

CHAPTER 8　　USING MERGE　　　　84

    Merging a Form Letter with a Data Document　　84
    Using SET and ASK Variables in a Form Letter　　87
    Using Merge to Produce Labels in a Single Column　　90
    Using Merge to Produce Labels in Multiple Columns　　91
    Merging Addresses with Different Numbers of Lines　　94
    Using IF/ENDIF Instructions　　96
    Using the INCLUDE Instruction　97
    Using Merge to Fill in a Form　　99

CHAPTER 9　　SORTING TEXT　　　　102

    Sorting Paragraphs　　102
    Sorting the Lines of a Table　　105
    Sorting Columns in a Table　　105
    Sorting Records in a Data Document　　106

REINFORCEMENT EXERCISES　　　　107

CHAPTER 8

USING MERGE

PREVIEW

The merge program is used to produce personalized form letters. The form letter (Word uses the term "main document") contains the standard text plus the field names where individual data is to be automatically inserted during the merge process. A data document is created containing the information pertaining to each individual to whom the form letter is to be sent. Then the Print Merge command is used to combine the two files to produce the personalized letters. This merge process may be tailored so that letters are sent to only specified individuals in your data document. Or you can set up a standard form letter which allows you to enter data from the keyboard rather than from a data document.

The merge function may be used to produce labels, either in single columns, in multiple columns, on continuous feed labels, or on single cut sheets.

Merge is also used to produce documents containing boilerplate or standard paragraph text. Many organizations--for example, law firms, real estate companies, or financial planners--use boilerplate paragraphs when preparing documents for individual clients. The boilerplate documents are saved in separate files, and an INCLUDE instruction is used in the main document to specify the documents to be merged into one final document tailored to the client's particular needs.

Finally, the merge function may be used to fill in forms such as applications, invoices, or registration forms.

MERGING A FORM LETTER WITH A DATA DOCUMENT

In this section you will learn how to use the merge function to produce personalized form letters. The procedure involves three basic steps:

a. Create a main document containing the standard text that will appear in every letter, plus the field names typed in the position where the variable information is to be inserted during merge.

b. Create a data document containing the variable information or data for each individual to whom the form letters will be sent.

c. Use the Print Merge menu to combine the main document with the data document to produce the personalized documents.

To create the main document (the form letter):

The first item entered in the main document is the DATA instruction telling Word which data document to use in the merge. That instruction must be on the first line of the document as shown on the following page. It consists of the word "DATA" plus the name of the data document, and it must be enclosed in chevrons. Following that instruction is the text of the document, plus the field names also enclosed in chevrons. The field names are entered at the positions in the document where you want the variable information to be inserted during the merge process. You will include spacing between the field names as is appropriate, plus any required punctuation.

Using Microsoft Word Advanced Functions, Part 4

The text for the main document is shown in the box below.

```
«DATA MAILLIST.DOC»

today's date


«title» «fname» «lname»
«street»
«city», «state»   «zip»

Dear «title» «lname»:

The enclosed note represents a dollar amount you
invested, plus interest through «month».

The quarterly interest payment due «paydate» will be
added to the principal amount.

Very truly yours,

Your Name
Vice President

Enclosure
```

To type a DATA instruction as the first paragraph of the document:

Note: *This instruction names the file which contains the data to be combined (merged) with the main document. The filename must be an exact match. If your merge isn't successful, this is one of the first items to check for accuracy.*

Note: *Press* **Ctrl [** *and* **Ctrl]** *to type the chevrons.*

1. Type: **«DATA MAILLIST.DOC»**

Note: *If you have saved the data document in a different directory or drive, specify that directory or drive in the DATA instruction by typing the path preceding the data filename.*
Example: DATA C:\WORD5\DATA\MAILLIST.DOC.

2. Press: **Enter** four times to move the **highlight** to line 5 (if the line numbers are displayed in the status line).

Note: *If you were preparing the main document to be printed on letterhead paper, you would want to move the date line to the point where it would be printed below the letterhead.*

3. Type: today's date at the left margin.
4. Press: **Enter** five times.

To enter the field names at the positions where variable information is to be entered during the merge:

5. Type: «title» and press the **space bar**.
6. Type: «fname» and press the **space bar**.

7.	Type:	«lname» and **Enter**.
8.	Repeat:	for each of the remaining field names.
9.	Type:	the text for the main document, including field names and punctuation in paragraphs at the appropriate positions.

Note: *Field names are entered at the position where corresponding data is to be inserted during the merge process. Also, enter the appropriate punctuation, such as the comma following «city», in the main document.*

10.		Save the document. Name it **letter**.
11.		Clear the screen.

To create the data document:

The data document containing the variable information to be combined with the main document consists of a header record followed by data records.

Header record
The first line is called a header record and contains the names of the fields entered in the form document. These words must be an exact match with the words entered in the main document in order for the merge to be successful. Each field name is separated by a comma with no spaces between the name and the commas. The field names may be up to sixty-four characters long, and they must begin with a letter. They may contain only letters, numbers, or the underscore character. A field name appearing in the main document must also be entered in the data document; however, field names in the data document do not necessarily have to be used in the main document. Field names may appear in the main document any number of times, and they do not need to be in the same order as the field names in the data document.

Data records
The remaining lines of the data document are called the "Data records" and contain the information pertaining to each individual to whom the main document is going to be sent. Each item in the data record must be in the same order as the corresponding field name in the header record. For example, if the title is the first field in the header record, then "Mr." must be the first field in the data record. Also, the items in the data record are separated by commas with no spaces. If an item in the data record contains a commas, then the field must be set off with quotation marks around it, followed by a comma. Press **Enter** only at the end of each record. Do not insert a blank line at the end of the last record--Word will think this is another record and will try to merge it (unsuccessfully obviously).

An example of the data document you will create is shown below.

Header record ──────▶ `title,fname,lname,street,city,state,zip,month,paydate¶`

Data records ──────▶
```
Mr.,Allen,Baker,5894 Winter
Street,Austin,TX,78746,July,October 30th¶
Mr.,John,Stone,8700 Valley
Road,Bellevue,WA,98008,August,November 30th¶
Ms.,Alice,Parker,909 N.
Wilson,Seattle,WA,98118,June,September 30th¶
```

1.	Type:	the first line as it appears with each field name separated by commas. Press **Enter** at the end of the line.
2.	Type:	each of the following records, with each field separated by a comma. Press **Enter** at the end of each record. Let the data record wrap as shown above.

Note: *When entering information in the data document, fields may be separated by tabs instead of commas. This type of entry would facilitate sorting.*

3. Save the document. Name it **maillist**.
4. Clear the screen.

To merge the main document with the data document:

In this exercise, you will merge the final output to a new file, rather than sending the output directly to the printer. This will allow you to view the output to see if the merge was successful. Once you get proficient at the use of merge, you will want to send the final merge to the printer and not take up disk space with the third document, particularly if you have a large number of letters to be merged.

To merge to a new document file:
1. Press: **Ctrl F7** and load the main document **letter**.

Note: *The main document must be displayed on the screen in order to perform the merge function.*

2. Press: **Esc.**
3. Choose: **Print, Merge, Document.**
4. Type: **final1** as the name for the new document.
5. Press: **Enter** to begin the merge.

Note: *A message will be displayed in the lower left corner of the screen indicating the merge is in process and which record is being merged.*

6. Clear the document **letter** from the screen, and load the new document **final1** to view the final output.

Note: *If there were errors in the merge--for instance, if the name of the city appears where the state should be printed, then you probably made an error in your data document--you may have placed the commas incorrectly. Clear the screen and load the data document to look for the error.*
  If the field names in the main document are not an exact match with the field names in the header record in the data document, your merge will not be successful. Check both the main document and the data document.
  If you merge the files a second time, use the same filename, "final1." You will have to respond to a message to press Y to overwrite the file "final1."

7. Clear the screen.

USING SET AND ASK VARIABLES IN A FORM LETTER

The merge function of Microsoft Word allows the user to enter information from the keyboard during the merge process. You might want to use this when only one or two letters are to be sent at one time; however the main document is a standard letter that is used repeatedly. In this exercise a letter informing a customer of an overdue account is used. This would be the same text which is sent to everyone in similar circumstances; however only one or two of these letters might be sent at any given time.
  The **SET** instruction will set information which will be the same in every document during the merge procedure--a date, for example.
  The **ASK** instruction allows information to be entered which will vary from document to document--name, address, account number.

The steps in using this feature are as follows:
1. Create a main document containing the standard text plus the SET and ASK instructions.

2. Run the Print Merge Document command which allows you to enter data from the keyboard during the merge process, and save it as a second document. (If you want to print the document, instead of saving it to another file, run Print, Merge, Printer command.)

To create the main document:

1. Type: each SET and ASK entry as displayed in the box, using **Ctrl [** and **Ctrl]** to enter chevrons.

Note: *The text following the "?" is a message which will be displayed at the bottom of the screen during the merge prompting the user to type specific information.*

Note: *A field name must be set in the text which corresponds to the SET or ASK field name--«date», «name», «street», for example--and the field names must match exactly the field names typed in the SET and ASK instructions--case, as well as spelling, must be the same.*

2. Type: the text including the field names as shown in the box below.

```
«SET date=?Type today's date»
«ASK name=?Type name»
«ASK street=?Type street»
«ASK city=?Type city»
«ASK state=?Type state»
«ASK zip=?Type zip»
«ASK account=?Type account number»
«ASK overdue=?Type overdue date»

«date»

«name»
«street»
«city», «state»   «zip»

Re. Account Number «account»:

Your account has remained unpaid since «overdue».

Let us assist you in developing a payment schedule to
deal with your account.

Your name
Your title
```

3. Save the document. Name it **form.**

Using Microsoft Word Advanced Functions, Part 4

To use the SET and ASK instructions in a merge:

If the form document **form** were not already on screen, it would have to be loaded.

1. Press: **Esc.**
2. Choose: **Print, Merge, Document.**
3. Type: a new filename for the final output--**final2**.
4. Press: **Enter** to begin the merge.

At the first prompt (displayed at the bottom of the screen):
5. Type: today's date and press **Enter.**
6. Repeat for the remaining items, and press **Enter** after each entry. The remaining information to be inserted is in the box below.
7. Repeat the procedure for another document, using the second name and data information in the box below to respond to the ASK variables.

Note: *After the first document, the date message will not be displayed, but the other ASK messages, beginning with "Type name," will be repeated.*

```
Mr. Wm. W. Mayers
301 Culver Street
Phoenix, AZ   85004

Acct. No.:  67038
Overdue Date:  September 28, 1989
-----------------------------------------------------------
Ms. Nancy Smith
3816 Northern Ave.
Phoenix, AZ   85028

Acct. No.  68930
Overdue Date:  November 30, 1989
```

8. After entering the information for Ms. Smith, press **Esc** to display the message "Enter Y to continue or Esc to cancel."
9. Press: **Esc** again to return to the screen.
10. Clear the screen and load the document **final2** to confirm the accuracy of the merge.
11. Save any edits and clear the screen.

USING MERGE TO PRODUCE LABELS IN A SINGLE COLUMN

The procedure for using merge to address labels is basically the same as the procedure for producing form letters; however the main difference is that the margins have to be set to reflect the size of the labels. Each label is considered a separate page.

The steps in this procedure are as follows:

a. Create a main document which contains the address fields (name, street, city), as well as margins and page length adjusted for the size of the label.

b. Create a data document (if you don't already have one), containing the variable information to be entered in the fields during the merge process.

c. Use Print Merge to combine the main document and the data document.

To create the main document:

1. Type: the DATA instruction and enter the field names exactly as they appear in the box below. Press **Ctrl [** and **Ctrl]** to insert the chevrons. You will use the same data document you used in the first merge exercise in this chapter.

```
«DATA MAILLIST.DOC»«title»  «fname» «lname»
«street»
«city», «state»   «zip»
```

<u>To set the margins to fit a label:</u>
2. Press: **Esc.**
3. Choose: **Format, Division, Margins**.

4. Set the following menu fields:
   - top = 0
   - bottom = 0
   - left = 0.5
   - right = 0
   - page length = 1.25" (This will have to be adjusted to fit your labels.)

5. Press: **Enter**.
6. Save the document. Name it **label1**.

To produce the labels:

(You do not have to create another data document since you are using **maillist** which you created in the first merge exercise.)

The final output will be printed to a document, rather than to the printer.

1. Press: **Esc.**
2. Choose: **Print, Merge, Document**.
3. Type: a document name **final3** and press **Enter** to begin the merge.

Using Microsoft Word Advanced Functions, Part 4

4. Load the document **final3** to check the output. (If a document is currently on the screen, you will have to press N in response to the message line to lose edits.) If there are errors, check the main document and the data document as you did for the first merge exercise.

5. Clear the screen.

USING MERGE TO PRODUCE LABELS IN MULTIPLE COLUMNS

Producing labels in multiple columns on single cut sheets is a slightly more complex than producing labels in a single column. You will have to set up a full page of forms for the labels; however, instead of typing the form repeatedly, you will type the form once, and then copy the form as many times as there are labels in the one column. Then copy the entire column to the remaining columns in your sheet of labels.

To create the main document for multiple-column labels:

The basic steps are as follows:

1. Set the margins to fit the cut sheet of labels.

2. Type the label field names in their correct positions once, and then copy it as many times as there are labels in one column.

3. Set Format Division Layout menu for the number of columns you need.

4. Select the first column, plus the division mark and copy to the second column, and then repeat for the third column if necessary.

The main document includes a NEXT instruction at the beginning of each label form (except the first one) which tells the program to print the next label at that position.

Your main document will be similar to the form in the box below; however, it will have two columns with probably nine label forms in each column.

```
«DATA MAILLIST.DOC»«title» «fname» «lname»
«street»
«city», «state» «zip»

«NEXT»«title» «fname» «lname»
«street»
«city», «state» «zip»

«NEXT»«title» «fname» «lname»
«street»
«city», «state» «zip»
```

To set the margins:
1. Press: **Esc.**
2. Choose: **Format, Division, Margins.**
3. Set the top and bottom margins at 0, and the left and right margins at .5. (These settings may have to be adjusted to your specific needs.) Leave "page length" at 11 and "width" at 8.5.
4. Press: **Enter.**

To type the label forms:
5. Move: the **highlight** above the Division Mark.
6. Type the first form with the DATA instruction plus the field names in their correct positions as shown in the example below.

```
«DATA MAILLIST.DOC»«title» «fname» «lname»
«street»
«city», «state»   «zip»
```

7. Press: **Enter** twice after typing «`zip`».
8. Type: «NEXT».

To copy the label form:
9. "Select" all of the field names beginning with title (do not include the DATA instruction and the NEXT instruction) and press **Alt F3** to copy to scrap.
10. Move: the **highlight** to the space following «NEXT».
11. Press: **Insert** key to copy.
12. "Select" the second copy of the form, including the NEXT instruction, press **Alt F3** to copy to scrap, and press **Insert** to copy. Repeat pressing **Insert** enough times to fill one column for a total of nine labels. Your first column should resemble the document on page 91.

To set column layout:
13. Press: **Esc.**
14. Choose: **Format, Division, Layout.**
15. Set "number of columns" at 2.
16. Set "space between columns" at 0.
17. Set "division break" at "Column" and press **Enter.**

To copy the forms in the first column to the second column:
18. "Select" the column of forms (not including the DATA instruction) <u>plus the division mark</u>.
19. Press: **Alt F3** to copy to scrap.
20. Move: the **highlight** below the division mark.
21. Press: **Insert** key to copy.
22. Press: **Alt F4** to go to show layout mode so you can see how the columns will be printed. You may need to press **Ctrl Page Up** to go to the top of the document.
23. Press: **Alt F4** again to leave show layout mode.
24. Save the document, name it **label2**.
25. Clear the screen.

To create the data document:

A new data document will not be created. Use the **maillist** document and add names to it.

1. Retrieve the data document, **maillist**, created in the first exercise in this section on page 86, and add the names shown below at the end of that file. Your lines may wrap differently these. Be sure to press **Enter** only at the end of the each record, and do not have an extra **Enter** after the last record.

> Ms.,Beth,Lee,1567 2nd Ave.,Kirkland,WA,98034,April,July 15th
> Mr.,Eldon,Jones,Park Ave. S.,Des Moines,IA,50315,May,August 15th
> Ms.,Ruth,Swanson,3rd Pl. N.E.,Chicago,IL,60633,October,December 30th
> Ms.,Janet,Miller,15 Estes St.,Denver,CO,80226,October,December 16th
> Mr.,Marvin,Master,5 Southport Dr.,Juneau,AK,99802,June,October 10th
> Ms.,Elsie,Brown,1302 2nd Ave.,Los Angeles,CA,90019,April,June 15th
> Mr.,George,Huff,15 Kiowa Dr.,Boise,ID,83709,March,May 30th
> Mr.,Harry,Conley,152 Broad St.,Seattle,WA,98121,July,August 30th

2. Check the text on the screen for comma placement. Also be sure you have the same number of fields in each record.

3. Save the edited document and clear the screen.

To produce the labels:

1. Load the main document, **label2**.
2. Press: **Esc.**
3. Choose: **Print, Merge, Document** to send the final output to a document file.
4. Type: a document name, **final4** and press **Enter.**

Note: *Watch the status line as the merge is proceeding. If there is an error in a record, a message will be displayed, and you can then go to the data document and make the correction in the corresponding record.*

5. Retrieve the document **final4** to check the output.
6. Press: **Alt F4** to go to show layout mode to view the labels in two columns side by side. You will have only two addresses in column 2.

Note: *When applying these instructions to your own work, you may have to adjust the margins to fit the type of labels you are using, but the basic concepts will be the same.*

Note: *If you are using a laser printer to print the labels, you will have to adjust the top and the bottom margins to two rows down from the top, and two rows up from the bottom. Laser printers automatically insert margins around text and will not print in those areas.*

7. Press: **Alt F4** to leave show layout mode.
8. Clear the screen.

MERGING ADDRESSES WITH DIFFERENT NUMBERS OF LINES

In the preceding exercises, each of the data documents obligingly contained the same number of lines; however, in the real world things aren't always so tidy. Some individuals have two line addresses, plus a company name, so the records have to be dealt with accordingly. This section will show you how to accommodate those variances in two ways.

The first exercise uses one field name for the entire address in the main document. In the data document, each line of the address is ended with a **Shift Enter** which indicates one field.

The second exercise shows how to use IF and ENDIF instructions to avoid blank lines caused by empty fields. These instructions tell the program to print certain fields if they are not empty. If the field is empty, the blank line or space will be omitted. If you don't enter these instructions and a field is empty, then the process will leave a blank line or space where the field should be printed.

To create the main document:

1. Type the form document as it appears in the box below. Notice that only one field name is used for the address.

```
«DATA CLIENT.DOC»
«SET date=?Type today's date»

«date»


«address»

Dear «name»:

Here is the information you requested.

Sincerely yours,


Your name

Enclosure
```

2. Save the document. Name it **maindoc**.
3. Use the Window, Split, Horizontal menu to split the screen horizontally at line 11 and to set "clear new window" at "Yes." Your **highlight** will be in window 2.

Note: *Sometimes it is convenient to use two windows when preparing documents to be used in the merge process. It helps to see the field names in the main document in order to confirm the match with the field names in the header record in the data document.*

Using Microsoft Word Advanced Functions, Part 4   95

To create the data document:

1. Type the text as it appears below. Press **Shift Enter** at the end of each line in the address rather than **Enter**. Press **Enter** at the end of each record. The address field must be enclosed in quotes (" ") since it contains a comma.

Note: *A screen print is displayed to show the down arrows representing new lines.*

```
address,name¶
"Mr. Alfred Brown↓
941 132nd St. E.↓
Bronx, NY 10454",Mr. Brown¶
"Ms. Joan Bannister↓
ABC Corporation↓
16079 S. W. Olive Way↓
Seattle, WA  98102",Ms. Bannister¶
"Mr. R. B. Krebs↓
2499 Medical Annex↓
17 Oldford Dr.↓
San Diego, CA  92111",Mr. Krebs¶
"Mr. Jeffrey Acton III↓
3492 Highland Rd.↓
Dallas, TX  75228",Mr. Acton¶
```

2. Save the data document. Name it **client**.

3. Clear the screen
   Or
4. Press: **F1** to move the **highlight** into the screen containing the main document--
                    maindoc--if you are using a split screen.

To merge only specified records (1 and 3):

1. Load the main document if it is not displayed on the screen.
2. Press: **Esc.**
3. Choose: **Print, Merge, Options.**

In the Print, Merge, Options menu:
4. Set: "range" field at "Records."
5. Move: the **highlight** to "record numbers" field.
6. Type: **1,3** to specify merging only records 1 and 3.
7. Press: **Enter** to return to the Print Merge menu.
8. Choose: "Document" field.
9. Type: **final5** as the name of the document to contain the final output.
10. Press: **Enter.**

When the "RESPONSE" menu is displayed at the bottom of the screen:
11. Type: the current date to set the date in the merged output. Remember you used a
                    SET instruction for the date.
12. Press: **Enter** to merge and wait as all records are merged.
13. Clear the screen.

14. Load the document **final5** to view the merged output. Only letters to Brown and Krebs should be merged.

Note: *This is an easy way to handle addresses with varying numbers of lines if you do not want to use your data document for any other purpose. However, most businesses prefer to construct a data document similar to the "maillist" file with fields separated by commas or tabs. In this case, you need to use IF/ENDIF instructions, as shown in the next section, in order to handle records with varying numbers of lines (fields).*

15. Clear the screen.

16. Go to the Print Merge Options menu, reset the "range" field to "All," and press **Enter**, then **Esc,** to return to the screen. If you don't do this, the next merge will merge only records 1 and 3.

USING IF/ENDIF INSTRUCTIONS

IF/ENDIF instructions are included to eliminate blank lines when certain fields are empty. For example, if some addresses contain one line instead of two, the blank line in the final output will be avoided if an IF/ENDIF instruction is included in the main document. Any time an `IF` instruction is used, a corresponding `ENDIF` instruction must be entered.

The following is an example of how these statements are used in a main document.

```
«DATA CUSTOMER.DOC»«name»
«IF streeta»«streeta»
«ENDIF»«streetb»
«city», «state»   «zip»
«IF country»«country»«ENDIF»
«IF streeta=""»«ENDIF»
```

To create the main document:

1. Type: the fields as they are shown in the box above.

Note: *The last line in the box above is entered to insert an extra blank line at the end of the address if there is no streeta. This would be used when setting up the form document for labels when the line spacing needs to be controlled because of label size.*

2. Save the document. Name it **address**.
3. Clear the screen, or split the window.

To create the data document:

This section will show you how to set up a data document with each field separated by a tab, rather than by a comma.

1. Use the Format, Division, Margins menu to set the Left and Right margins at 0" so each record can be typed entirely on one line on the screen. This makes it easier to proofread the records.
2. Press: **Enter** to insert a blank line above the division mark, and move the **highlight** to the line above the division mark.

Using Microsoft Word Advanced Functions, Part 4 97

To set the tabs:
3. Press: **Alt F1** to go to the Tab Set menu.
4. Set: left flush tabs at 1.7, 2.7, 4.5, 5.7, 6.4, and 7. (To set the tabs, type the position number and an L for each tab.)
5. Press: **Enter** to return to the document.

To enter the data:
6. Type: the data shown below (displayed in a screen print in order to show the tab sets). The last field at position 7 is "country". Mr. Waters record includes Canada in this field. Be sure to insert the tab marks in the empty fields, as shown in the display. Press **Enter** at the end of each line.

```
[·········1·········2·········3·········4·········5·········6·········7·····]
name→         streeta→  streetb→        city→     state→ zip→   coun
Ms.·Janet·Mills→ Suite·2→ 456·N.·10th→  Bellevue→ WA→    98008→ USA¶
Mr.·John·Meyer→  →        450·North·Walnut→ Des·Moines→ IA→ 50317→ ¶
Mr.·Adam·Waters→ →        514·14th·St.→ Calgary→  AB→    T2P·0W8→Cana
```

7. Save the document. Name it **customer**.
8. Clear the screen.

To produce the final output:

1. Load the main document **address**, or move the **highlight** to the window displaying **address.doc** if you have split the window.

2. Press: **Esc**.
3. Choose: **Print, Merge, Document.**
4. Type: **final6** to name a new document for the final output.
5. Press: **Enter** to begin the merge process.

To view the final output:
6. Clear the screen.
7. Load the document **final6**. Check each merged document to see if the blank lines were eliminated at the appropriate positions.
8. Clear the screen.

USING THE INCLUDE INSTRUCTION

The INCLUDE instruction is used to produce a document which merges several documents in one document. This is often used to combine boilerplate text into one document.

The steps in using the INCLUDE instructions are as follows:
1. Create the documents containing the standard text.
2. Create the main document containing the INCLUDE instructions.
3. Use the print merge command to produce the final output.

To create the standard (boilerplate) paragraphs:

1. Type: the paragraph in the box below.

   > According to our records, your invoice is currently 30 days past due.

2. Press: **Enter** once at the end of the paragraph.
3. Save the paragraph. Name it **file1**.
4. Clear the screen.
5. Repeat: steps 1 through 4 for the remaining paragraphs shown below, naming each **file2, file3,** and **file4**. Remember to press **Enter** once at the end of each paragraph.
6. Clear the screen when finished.

Note: *A quick way to save and clear the screen, is to use the Transfer, Clear, All command, press Y at the message requesting you to save, type the filename, and press* **Enter**.

> Most of our customers appreciate a friendly reminder because they understand the importance of a good credit record.

> Please give this matter your prompt attention. Send us your check as soon as possible.

> If you have recently taken care of your account, please disregard this notice.

To create a main document with INCLUDE instructions:

1. Type the text in the box below entering the INCLUDE instructions as shown.

   ```
   (Use glossary "date"--type the word date and press F3
   to expand the entry.)

   Mr. Alden H. Smith
   156 South First Ave.
   Seattle, WA  98106

   Dear Mr. Smith:

   «INCLUDE file2»
   «INCLUDE file1»
   «INCLUDE file4»
   Sincerely yours,

   Your name
   ```

2. Save the file, name it **notice**.

Using Microsoft Word Advanced Functions, Part 4

To use the print merge command to produce the final output:

Be sure the main document **notice** is displayed on the screen.
1. Press: **Esc.**
2. Choose: **Print, Merge, Document.**
3. Type: **final7** and press **Enter.**

The merge will be completed.

4. Clear the screen and retrieve the document **final7** to check the merged document.

Note: *If the spacing between the paragraphs is inaccurate, check the main document first to see if you have entered extra lines (which should not be there) between the INCLUDE instructions. Then check each of the "paragraph" files to see if you have entered a paragraph mark (which should be there) at the end of each file.*

If you have time, repeat the procedure for each of the following names. Use the SET and ASK statements learned in the merge exercise beginning on page 87 to insert the names and addresses.

```
Ms. Amanda Jones
148 N. E. 8th Ave.
Bellevue, WA  98007

Include paragraphs 1, 2, and 3
```

```
Mr. Lee Richards
1569 Seco Pl. S.
Tucson, AZ  85710

Include paragraphs 1, 3, 2, and 4
```

USING MERGE TO FILL IN A FORM

Now that instructions have been given for using merge, you will learn how to apply those instructions to filling in a form. The concepts are the same as those used in any type of merge. A main document (the form) is created which includes a DATA instruction, and field names are entered following each of the labels. A data document similar to the previous data documents is created. The merge process is run using the Print Merge commands.

To create the main document:

A very simple boxed form will be created, and you will format the field names and the tab marks with the underline character to draw the horizontal lines following each label.

A screen print of the form is shown in the box below in order to see the lines drawn when the field names and the following tab marks are formatted with the underline character. You also can see the down arrows representing the new lines.

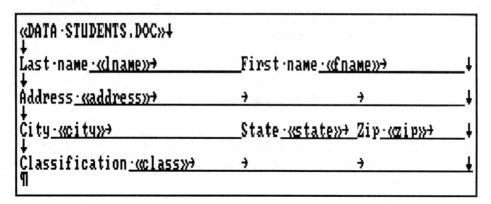

To create the form:
1. Press: **Esc.**
2. Choose: **Format, Border, Box.**
3. Press: **Enter** to return to the document.

To type the DATA instruction at the top of the document:
4. Type: **«DATA STUDENTS.DOC»** This is the name of the data document which will be created to use in this exercise.
5. Press: **Shift Enter** twice to begin a new line and insert a blank line. **Shift Enter** must be pressed at the end of each line in the form in order to preserve the box format.

To set tabs for the labels "First name," "State," "Zip," and for the right side of the form:

The tab has to be set for the right side of the form in order for the tabs formatted with the underline character to draw the lines to the right margin.

6. Press: **Alt F1** to go to the Tab Set menu.
7. Set: left flush tabs at 3, 4.5, and 5.9.
8. Press: **Enter** to return to the document.

To enter the labels and the field names:
9. Type: **Last name** (space) **«lname»**.

Note: Adding a space between the label and the field name makes the final output easier to read.

10. Press: the **Tab** key to position 3.
11. Type: **First name «fname»**.
12. Press: the **Tab** key to position 5.9
13. Press: **Shift Enter** twice.
14. Repeat for the remaining lines of the form.

To format the field names and the tab marks with the underline character:
15. Go to the Options menu and set the "show non-printing symbols" field at "All," so you can see the tab marks and the dots representing spaces.
16. Move: the **highlight** to the chevron preceding **lname**.

17. Press: **F6** and then **F8** three times to "select" the field name and the following tab mark.
18. Press: **Alt U** to format.
19. Move: the **highlight** to the chevron preceding **fname**.
20. "Select" the field name and the following tab mark as instructed in steps 16 and 17.
21. Press: **F4** to repeat the editing. (The underline formatting will be repeated.)
22. Repeat: for the remaining field names and following tab marks in the form.
23. Save the document. Name it **classfrm**.
24. Split the window horizontally at line 11 and set "clear new window" field at "Yes."
25. Press: **F1** to move the **highlight** to window 2 to create the data document.

To create the data document:

1. Type: the data document shown below.

> lname,fname,address,city,state,zip,class
> Sullivan,Roger,1501 Seneca,Seattle,WA,98101,Junior
> Voges,Jan,1015 Olivero Rd.,Modesto,CA,95351,Senior
> Miles,Ronda,879 Bohl St. E.,Phoenix,AZ,85044,Freshman

2. Check the data document for accuracy.
3. Save the document. Name it **students**.

To use Print Merge to fill in the form:

1. Move: the **highlight** into Window 1.
2. Press: **Esc**.
3. Choose: **Print, Merge, Document**.
4. Type: **final8** to name the output document.
5. Press: **Enter** to merge.
6. Clear all screens--use **Transfer, Clear, All**.
7. Load the document **final8** to check the final output.
8. Use the Print preView screen to see the underlining in the form.
9. Print the forms.

In this chapter, you learned all of the basic merge functions. They may have seemed cumbersome to you; however, as you work with them and fully understand the concepts involved in each step, they become quite easy to use. Once a main document and a data document have been created, and you know that the field names and data are entered correctly, the merge process can save you an immense amount of time in producing the types of documents discussed in this chapter.

CHAPTER 9

SORTING TEXT

PREVIEW

The sort function allows you to rearrange text in paragraphs, in lists, or in tables alphabetically, either in ascending (A to Z) or in descending (Z to A) order. You may also sort names and addresses in data documents used in merge functions, and numbered items can be sorted either in ascending or descending order.

When text is sorted, the following guidelines determine the basis for the sort.

* If a punctuation mark (" for example) is at the beginning of a paragraph, that paragraph will come before paragraphs beginning with numbers.

* Paragraphs beginning with numbers come before paragraphs beginning with letters.

* Uppercase letters come before lowercase letters if "case" field is set at "Yes." Otherwise case is ignored when you sort.

* International characters are sorted as they appear in the alphabet.

The Library Autosort menu is used for sorting text. An example of the menu is displayed below.

```
LIBRARY AUTOSORT by: Alphanumeric Numeric   sequence:(Ascending)Descending
                case: Yes(No)           column only: Yes(No)
    Select option
```

As previously noted, the sort may be either alphanumeric or numeric. Also it may be in either ascending or descending order. The "case" field allows you to sort uppercase words before lowercase, and you may set "column only" field at "Yes" to sort a column in a table.
    Text to be sorted must first be "selected."

SORTING PARAGRAPHS

In this exercise you will be sorting a list of terms in a document. Each entry in the list must end with a paragraph mark, and the entire list must be "selected" in order to be sorted.

1. Press: **Enter** several times to insert a buffer between the text and the end mark. If the end mark is "selected" as part of the sort, it may cause two items to appear on the same line.

2. Move: the **highlight** to the top of the screen, and type the text in the box below.

Note: *While these terms are not "paragraphs" in a grammatical sense, Word considers each entry a paragraph since a paragraph mark is inserted at the end of each line.*

```
The following are some terms used in computer
courses:

Software
Hardware
Data entry
Disk storage
Integrated programs
```

To sort the terms in alphabetical order:

1. Save the document. Name it **terms.**

Note: *The sort program requires a large amount of memory; therefore, always save the document before running the sort program in order to avoid the possibility of losing edits because of insufficient memory.*

To "select" the list:
2. Move: the **highlight** to the "**S**" in "**Software.**"
3. Press: **F6** to go to extend mode.
4. Press: the **down arrow** to "select" the remaining terms.

To sort:
5. Press: **Esc.**
6. Choose: **Library, Autosort** to display the menu.
7. Leave all of the fields as they are shown.
8. Press: **Enter** to sort. The list should appear as follows:

```
The following are some terms used in computer
courses:

Data entry
Disk storage
Hardware
Integrated programs
Software
```

9. Save the edited document. Clear the screen.

To sort the paragraphs in alphabetical order:

There may be times when you want to submit a list of terms or individual's names, such as the list of candidates shown in the box below. It is convenient to type the items as you think about them, then sort them alphabetically later. In this exercise you will be creating a slate of candidates and then alphabetizing them.

1. Type: the text in the box below. Press **Shift Enter** following each name in order for the name and the following text to be formatted as one paragraph. Press **Enter** twice at the end of each paragraph following the individual's name to end the paragraph and to insert a blank line.

```
Fowler, Horace
     Age 56, currently serving as mayor of Arlington,
Washington.  He previously served two terms in the
state legislature.

Dawson, David
     Age 29, currently serving as chairperson of the
Downtown Business Association in Tacoma, Washington.

Brown, Beryl
     Age 49, currently serving as chairperson of the
City Council in Redmond, Washington.

Green, Grace
     Age 35, currently serving as a member of the
Metro Council and as the committee chairperson for
Sharon Precinct in King County.
```

2. Save the document--name it **slate**.

3. Press: **Shift F10** to "select" the entire document.
4. Press: **Esc.**
5. Choose: **Library, Autosort.** The alphanumeric response is highlighted.
6. Press: **Enter** to sort the paragraphs in alphabetical order.

To sort the paragraphs in numeric order:

The paragraphs must be numbered.

Note: *Numbering paragraphs will be discussed in the chapter on outlining. The Library Number menu is used to <u>renumber</u> paragraphs which have already been numbered; however, it cannot be used to add numbers to text except in outline view.*

1. Type: a number in front of each paragraph in the following order: **4, 1, 3, 2.**
2. Press: **Shift F10** to "select" the document.
3. Press: **Esc.**
4. Choose: **Library, Autosort.**
5. Press: **N** or the **space bar** to choose "Numeric."
6. Press: **Enter** to sort.
7. Save the edited document **slate**, and clear the screen.

Using Microsoft Word Advanced Functions, Part 4

SORTING THE LINES OF A TABLE

In this exercise you will sort the lines of the table on the basis of the last names listed in the first column.

To create the list:
1. Press: **Alt F1** and set left flush tabs at 2, 3.7, and 4.2.
2. Press: **Enter** to return to the document.
3. Type the text in the box below. The names are to be entered at the left margin. Press **Enter** at the end of each line. Do not press **Shift Enter**, since each line must be a separate paragraph in order to be sorted.

```
Baker, Allen        Austin          TX    78746
Stone, John         Bellevue        WA    98008
Parker, Alice       Seattle         WA    98105
Adams, Joan         Anchorage       AK    99508
Corwin, Milton      Fairbanks       AK    99701
Freeman, Helen      Santa Barbara   CA    93101
Gerber, Elliott     San Francisco   CA    94104
```

4. Save the document and name it **list**.

To sort the list in ascending alphabetical order:

1. Press: **Shift F10** to "select" the entire list.
2. Press: **Esc.**
3. Choose: **Library, Autosort.**
4. Set: "by" field at "Alphanumeric."
5. Press: **Enter** to sort the list alphabetically by the last name. (The sort will be on the basis of the first word of each paragraph.)

To sort the list in descending alphabetical order:

1. Press: **Shift F10** to "select" the entire list. (It may already be selected.)
2. Press: **Esc.**
3. Choose: **Library, Autosort.**
4. Move: the **highlight** to "sequence" field and set at "Descending."
5. Press: **Enter** to sort.

SORTING COLUMNS IN A TABLE

You may sort the lines of a table on the basis of items in a single column--not necessarily the first word in each line. To do this, you will use Column Select (**Shift F6**) to "select" the column to be sorted.

To sort the table by zip code:

1. Move: the **highlight** to the first character in the zip code column.
2. Press: **Shift F6** (column selection).
3. Press: **right arrow** and the **down arrow** to "select" the entire column.
4. Press: **Esc.**
5. Choose: **Library, Autosort.**
6. Press: **N** or **space bar** to choose "Numeric."

7. Set: "sequence" field at "Ascending."
8. Press: **Enter** to sort.

Practice another sort on your own. Sort the cities in alphabetical order.

Note: *You were not required to set the "column only" field at "Yes" in the Library Autosort menu, since you sorted each line of the table on the basis of information in one column. If this field had been set at "Yes," then the corresponding information in other columns would not have been moved--only the information in the selected column would have been sorted.*

9. Save the edited document. Clear the screen.

SORTING RECORDS IN A DATA DOCUMENT

The critical part of sorting records in a data document is to remember that sorting is based on the first word in each paragraph. Therefore, if the fields are separated by commas, the "field" to be sorted must be moved to the beginning of each record. If fields are separated by tabs, then the column containing the field to be sorted would be "selected" and then sorted.

1. Retrieve the document named **maillist**.

2. To sort the records by last name, you must move the <u>last name plus the following comma</u> to the beginning of each record. To do this:
    a) "Select" the name and comma.
    b) Press **Delete**.
    c) Press the **Home** key to move the **highlight** to the beginning of the line.
    d) Press **Insert** to move the name.

<u>After moving the names:</u>
3. Move: the **highlight** to the first record. (Do not include the header record at the top line.)
4. Press: **F6** to go to extend mode.
5. Press: **down arrow** and **End** key to "select" the rest of the records.
6. Press: **Esc.**
7. Choose: **Library, Autosort**.
8. Set: "by" field at "Alphanumeric."
9. Set: "sequence" at "Ascending."
10. Press: **Enter** to sort.

Note: *If you wished to sort the data document by zip codes, the zip codes must be moved to the <u>beginning</u> of each record, then proceed with the sort function as in previous exercises.*
     If you anticipate sorting records in a data document, give some thought to the way the records are entered in order to eliminate the time-consuming task of moving entries. You may create your data document with fields separated by tabs rather than by commas in order to facilitate sorting the records.

11. Save the edited document with a new name **maillist1** so that the original is not changed for future merges. Clear the screen.

More practice: retrieve the document named **table** created in chapter 5, Editing a Table, and practice sorting the names and numbers.

Clear the screen.

REINFORCEMENT EXERCISES

FUNCTIONS REVIEWED

Chapter 8:
- Merging a form letter with a data document
- Using SET and ASK variables in a form letter
- Using merge to produce labels in a single column
- Using merge to produce labels in multiple columns
- Using IF/ENDIF instructions
- Using INCLUDE instructions

Chapter 9:
- Sorting paragraphs
- Sorting numbers
- Sorting columns in a table
- Sorting records in a data document

RECALL QUESTIONS

The answers to the recall questions are on page 112.

1. List the two types of documents combined in a merge process.

2. Describe the information contained in each type of document used in a merge.

3. What are the two ways you may separate fields in a data document?

4. Name the menu used to produce the merged output.

5. What is the purpose of the Print Merge Document menu?

6. What information is included in a DATA instruction?

7. What is the purpose of using an ASK instruction in a merge?

8. What is the purpose of using an IF instruction in the main document?

9. What instruction must always accompany an IF instruction?

10. Name the merge instruction used to combine several document files into one document automatically.

11. Name the menu used to sort a list of terms alphabetically.

12. List the steps necessary to sort a column of zip code numbers in a table.

13. What is the first step in preparing to sort a data document containing fields separated by commas?

14. Name the keystrokes used to "select" all paragraphs in a document in order to sort them.

15. In what order does Word sort characters?

PRACTICE DOCUMENTS 5 AND 6:   MERGE AND SORT

1. Merge the letter displayed on page 109 with the data file document is shown beginning on page 110. Follow the steps listed below.

2. Use the glossary entry "dateprint" to insert the current date in your form letter when it is printed.

3. Create your own field names. You do not have to use the ones displayed in the form letter. Enter IF/ENDIF instructions to eliminate blank lines for the addresses that contain less than four lines. Before creating the main document, study the information in the data document to determine how you want to set up the main document.

4. Create the data document separating the fields either by commas or tabs; however, you will be asked to sort the fields in the data base by zip code and by last name, so it would probably be easier to set up the fields in a table separated by tabs. If you do this, be aware of your page limitations. You will have to change your page width and the font size to accommodate the records. Set the page width for 11 inches and use a font size of 10 points, if that is available to you.

5. Remember to enclose a field containing commas in quotes --several of the "date" entries have commas in them.

6. Choose your own document names for saving the main document and the data document.

7. Sort the data document on the basis of zip code in ascending order.

8. Use Print Merge menu to produce the merged form letters.

9. Set up a form for producing single column labels and use Print Merge to print the 10 labels. If you don't have labels available, assume the label size is 1.5" long by 3" wide, and print each label on a separate page as you would if you were using actual labels.

10. Set up a form for producing name tags for each name in the data document. The main document for the name tag should be similar to the form shown below. The size of the name tag is 2.5" long by 3.5" wide. Use a large font size for the name--14 point, if possible--and 12 point for the company name and for KTECH CORPORATION SEMINAR, if these are available to you.

```
«DATA CLIENTS.DOC»

            «NAME»



«IF COMPANY»«COMPANY»«ENDIF»



    KTECH CORPORATION SEMINAR
```

11. Use the Format pOsition menu, "frame width" field to set the width of the box.

12. Copy the form two times to display three boxes on the page. Remember to use a NEXT instruction at the beginning of the second and third forms. It is not necessary to retype the DATA instruction in the second and third forms.

13. Enter an IF/ENDIF instruction for the company name.

14. Use the Print preView menu to display the form before merging.

15. Sort the data document by last name in ascending alphabetical order. (Hint--use the "lname" field, or whatever you named the field to be used for the name in the salutation, for sorting the last name.)

16. Merge the form for the name tags with the data document.

```
(dateprint)



(Name)
(Company)
(Address)
(City), (State)   (Zip)

Dear (Name):

We are pleased that you will be attending our
(days_attend)-day Fall Training Seminar on (date).

Our software seminars are designed for the business
professional and include presentations on word processing,
spreadsheets, and database programs.

Your time will be spent in a productive environment with a
computer available for each participant.  In addition to
hands-on instruction, there will be plenty of time for
class discussion concerning application of the various
programs.

We look forward to seeing you on (date).

Sincerely yours,



Amelia Randolph
Training Director
KTech Corporation
```

Data document:

John Gates 415 Beryl Ave. San Diego, CA 92109 two October 14 and 15
Emory Bailey A & R Industries 4310 Paradise Dr. Carmichael, CA 95608 three October 14, 15, and 16
Larry VanCort Harrison Mills 6130 Goodland Ave. North Hollywood, CA 91606 one October 14
William Barnett P. O. Box 167 Lake Oswego, OR 97034 two October 14 and 15
Margaret Bain Toys Unlimited 2346 Eagle Ave. Bremerton, WA 98310 three October 14, 15, and 16

```
George Fabrezis
Royal Industries
25 Westmere Ave.
Everett, WA  98201

three

October 14, 15, and 16
```

```
Kenneth Archer
904 Powell Blvd.
Portland, OR 97202

one

October 14
```

```
Lucy Ross
Armada Assoc.
1590 Lynn Ave.
Medford, OR 97501

one

October 14
```

```
Karen Balduchi
P. O. Box 1470
1506 Empire Ave.
Spokane, WA 99206

two

October 14 and 15
```

```
Thomas Klemmer
Mansfield Motors
1595 South 72nd Street
Tacoma, WA 98408

three

October 14, 15, and 16
```

ANSWERS TO RECALL QUESTIONS

1. A main document (form letter) and a data document.

2. Main document contains:
   >DATA instruction
   >field names
   >standard boilerplate text

   Data document contains:
   >header record which is a list of the field names
   >data records for each individual containing the information corresponding to the fields listed in the header record

3. Fields may be separated by commas or by tabs.

4. Print Merge menu.

5. The Print Merge Document menu allows the user to save the final output of the merge to a separate document file.

6. The DATA instruction consists of the word DATA and the filename of the data document to be merged with the main document. A path name may have to be included with the filename if the data document is located in a directory different from the main document.

7. The ASK instruction allows the user to enter data directly from the keyboard during the merge process.

8. The IF instruction is used in a main document to tell the computer that "if" the field named in the IF instruction has information in it, then it should be printed. If the field is empty, then the space should be skipped, and the next field should be printed in that position. It is used to avoid blank lines in addresses.

9. ENDIF instruction must be included to end the IF instruction.

10. INCLUDE instruction.

11. Library Autosort.

12. Use Shift F6 to go to column select mode.
    "Select" the column of numbers.
    Use Library Autosort menu.
    Set the "by" field at "Numeric."
    Press Enter to sort.

13. Move the field to be sorted to the beginning of each record.

14. Shift F10.

15. a. Punctuation marks are sorted first, if they are typed at the beginning of the paragraph.
    b. Numbers come before letters.
    c. Uppercase letters if "case" is set at "Yes," otherwise case is ignored.

PART 5

CHAPTER 10   USING MATH   114

    Add   114
    Subtract   115
    Multiply   115
    Divide   116
    Totaling a Column in a Table   116
    Percentages   118
    Percentage   118
    Creating a Table and Performing Multiple Calculations   119

REINFORCEMENT EXERCISES   123

CHAPTER 10

USING MATH

PREVIEW

The math function of Microsoft Word allows you to add, subtract, multiply, divide and calculate percentages.

Operators must be entered with the numbers to instruct Word to perform the various types of calculations. The operators are:

Function:	**Operator**
Addition	+ or no operator
Subtraction	− or parenthesis ( ) around the negative number
Multiplication	*
Division	/
Percent	%

More than one operator may be used in a calculation. If an operator is not entered, the system assumes "addition" is the function.

Other points to know about Math:

* When numbers containing commas are calculated, the commas are included in the results.

* When multiple calculations are made, Word calculates percentages first, then multiplication or division, and then addition or subtraction. For example: 2+3*4=14 and 2*3+4=10.

* If any number in the calculation contains more than 1 or 2 decimals, the result will be displayed with the maximum number of decimals used in the expression. However, if all of the numbers in the expression are integers, the calculation will be displayed with the lowest number of decimal places required by the result.

ADD

To add two numbers:

1.	Press:	**Enter** several times to create a buffer, and move the **highlight** to the top of the screen.
2.	Type:	**123**.
3.	Press:	**Enter**.
4.	Type:	**456**.
5.	Press:	**Enter**.

To "select" the two numbers:

6.	Move:	the **highlight** to the first digit in the first number.
7.	Press:	**F6** to go to extend mode.
8.	Press:	the **down arrow** to "select" both numbers.

Using Microsoft Word Advanced Functions, Part 5

To calculate the total:

9.	Press:	**F2** to calculate. The result (579) is displayed in scrap.
10.	Press:	**F6** to leave extend mode.
11.	Move:	the **highlight** to the point where the result is to be inserted. (Press the **down arrow**.)
12.	Press:	**Insert** key to move the answer from scrap to the text, and press **Enter** to go to a new line.

To add several numbers in a sentence:

1.	Type:	**25 shirts, 13 pairs of shoes, and 1 coat make a total of.**
2.	Press:	**F9** or **Shift F9** to "select" the paragraph (line).
3.	Press:	**F2** to calculate the total and display it in scrap.
4.	Move:	the **highlight** to the end of the sentence and press the **space bar** to enter a space.
5.	Press:	**Insert** to insert the total "39" from scrap, and type a period.
6.	Press:	**Enter** to go to a new line.

SUBTRACT

The operator used to subtract is the minus sign or the parenthesis. If a number is enclosed in a parenthesis (5) it is a negative number and will be subtracted; however, if an expression (2+3) is enclosed in parenthesis, this does not make the expression a negative. In this case, a minus sign would have to be inserted in front of the expression − (2+3).

To subtract two numbers:

1.	Type:	**156 books - 45 books =**.

To select the text:

2.	Press:	**F9** or **Shift F9** to select the paragraph (line).
3.	Press:	**F2** to calculate and display the result in scrap.
4.	Move:	the **highlight** to the end of the line.
5.	Press:	**Insert** key to move the answer (111) into the text.
6.	Press:	**Enter** to go to a new line.

MULTIPLY

The operator used to multiply is the asterisk (*). After performing the various calculations, delete the operators if you do not wish to have them displayed in text.

To multiply the following:

1.	Type:	**5 automobiles @ *$24,598 ea. =**.

To select the line of text containing the numbers:

2.	Press:	**F9** or **Shift F9** to select the paragraph (line).
3.	Press:	**F2** to calculate.
4.	Move:	the highlight to the end of the line.

5.	Press:	**Insert** key to insert the answer (122,990) at the appropriate point.
6.	Type:	a dollar sign ($) in front of the answer, and delete the asterisk.
7.	Press:	**Enter** to go to a new line.

DIVIDE

The operator used to divide is the slash (/). Again, delete the operators after performing the calculations, if you do not wish them to appear in the final document.

To divide:

1.	Type:	**690 lines of text with /54 lines per page =**.

To select the line of text containing the numbers:

2.	Press:	**F9** or **Shift F9** to select the paragraph (line).
3.	Press:	**F2** to calculate.
4.	Move:	the highlight to the end of the line.
5.	Press:	**Insert** key to insert the answer (12.78) at the end of the line.
6.	Type:	**pages.** after the number to complete the statement.
7.		Clear the screen. You do not need to save the document.

TOTALING A COLUMN IN A TABLE

Retrieve the document named **table** created in chapter 5 and shown below.

```
Thermometer           $     7.50      250
Oscilloscope              2,999.99     62
Electrocardiograph        3,255.95     21
Hemostat                     12.50     15
One liter beaker              4.95    175
Balance                     950.00     73
```

To add a column of numbers:

1.	Move:	the **highlight** to the first symbol in the first line of column 2 ($).
2.	Press:	**Shift F6** to turn on Column Select.
3.	Press:	**right arrow** eight times, and the **down arrow** five times to "select" the entire column.
4.	Press:	**F2** to calculate (the total will appear in "scrap" in the status line at the bottom of the screen).
5.	Move:	the **highlight** to the bottom line of the table, and press **Shift Enter**. (This will carry the correct tab sets to the line below the last line of the table.)
6.	Press:	**tab** key to move to column 2.
7.	Press:	**Insert** key to insert the answer from scrap.

To add underlining:

1. Add the word "Total" at the beginning of that same line, and add a $ sign in front of the total amount.
2. Add underlining under 950.00 and double-underlining under the total amount.

Note: *To add double-underlining, "select" the total amount, and press Alt D to format.*

To calculate the product of each line of the table:

To multiply the number in column 2 by the number in column 3:
1. Insert an asterisk (*) in front of each number in column 3. (Move the **highlight** to the first digit in each number and type *.)

To "select" the numbers in columns 2 and 3:
2. Move: the **highlight** to the first number in column 2 (7).
3. Press: **F6**.
4. Press: **right arrow** or the **End** key to "select" both the numbers in column 2 and the numbers in column 3.

To calculate:
5. Press: **F2** to calculate (the total 1875.00 appears in scrap).
6. Press: **F6** to leave extend mode.
7. Press: **right arrow** or the **End** key to move to the "down arrow" displayed at the end of the line.
8. Press: **Insert** key to insert the calculation from scrap.
9. Repeat for the remaining lines in the table.

10. To add a $ in front of the first number in column 4, move the **highlight** to "1," type $, press the **space bar** three times.

11. "Select" and add column 4. Insert the total 326,653.08, and add a $ sign in front of it.

12. Delete the * from each of the numbers in column 3, and "select" and add the column.

13. Add underlining and double underlining for each total.

A screen image of the table is shown below.

```
{·········1·········2·········3·········4·········5·········]·
        Thermometer         $    7.50    250    $    1875.00↓
        Oscilloscope         2,999.99     62       185,999.38↓
        Electrocardiograph   3,255.95     21        68,374.95↓
        Hemostat                12.50     15           187.50↓
        One liter beaker         4.95    175           866.25↓
        Balance                950.00     73         69350.00↓
↓
-       Total               $7,230.89    596       $326,653.08¶
```

14. Save the edited document and print it.
15. Clear the screen

PERCENTAGES

To calculate with a percentage:

Calculate a commission of 7% for each of the following items.

RATE	GROSS AMOUNT	COMMISSION	NET AMOUNT
7%	*$7,748.30		
7%	*1,355.40		
7%	*4,672.50		

To enter the text shown in the box above:
1. Set decimal tabs at 1.5, 3.5, 5.5.

2. Type the column headings <u>after</u> the numbers have been entered. Use the space bar to position them manually--do not use the tab sets, as they will not be aligned correctly--or set different tabs for the line containing the headings.

3. Type: the numbers in the box above. The items in the RATE column are entered at the left margin. The asterisks must be entered in order to multiply each number by 7%.

Note: You may press either **Shift Enter** *or* **Enter** *twice at the end of each line.*

To calculate:
4. Move: the **highlight** to 7% in the first line.
5. Press: **Shift F9** to select the numbers in the first line.
6. Press: **F2** to calculate.
7. Press: the **right arrow** once, then the **left arrow** to return the **highlight** to the line, and press the **tab** key to move to column 3 (COMMISSION).
8. Press: **Insert** key to insert the answer from scrap.
9. Repeat steps 4 through 9 for the remaining two lines.

To subtract the amount of each commission from the total amount of the item:
10. Type: − a minus sign in front of each amount in the COMMISSION column.

To calculate:
11. Move: the **highlight** to the first number in GROSS AMOUNT column (do not include the asterisk).
12. Press: **F6** to go to extend mode, and press the **End** key to "select" the numbers in both columns.
13. Press: **F2** to calculate.
14. Press: **F6** to leave extend mode, and press the **right arrow**, then the **left arrow** to return the **highlight** to the line.
15. Press: **Tab** to move the **highlight** to the last column (NET AMOUNT).
16. Press: **Insert** key to insert the answer from scrap.
17. Repeat steps 11 through 16 for each of the remaining lines.
18. Delete the asterisks and the minus signs in columns 2 and 3.

19. Calculate a total of each of the columns and insert the total on the line below each column. Remember to use Column Select (Shift F6) to "select" each column. Add underlining and double-underlining at appropriate positions.

Your final document should look like the table shown in the screen image below.

RATE	GROSS AMOUNT	COMMISSION	NET AMOUNT
7%	$7,748.30	542.38	7,205.92
7%	1,355.40	94.88	1,260.52
7%	4,672.50	327.08	4,345.42
	13,776.20	964.34	12,811.86

20. Save the document. Name it **table2**.
21. Clear the screen.

CREATING A TABLE AND PERFORMING MULTIPLE CALCULATIONS

In this exercise, you will create the table shown in the box below, total the columns, calculate the "Full-time" figures by subtracting "Part-time" numbers from the "Combined Part- and Full-time" numbers. Then calculate the percent of increase for both the "% of Increase Full-time" column and the "% of Increase Part-time" column, and determine the student/teacher ratio.

To create the table:

The table is shown in the screen image below with the ruler line displayed to show the tab sets.

Student	Combined Part- & Full-time	Part-time	Full-time	% of Increase Full-time # x 5%	% of Increase Part-time # x 7%
Freshmen	4,823	1,248			
Soph.	3,941	951			
Junior	2,643	898			
Senior	2,103	795			
Total					
Student/teacher ratio:					

To format the table in a box:
1. Press: **Esc**, choose **Format Border Box**, and press **Enter** .

To set the tabs:

2.	Press:	**Alt F1** and set tabs as follows:
		Decimal tabs at 1.6, 2.6, 3.6, 4.6, and 5.6. Vertical tabs at 0.9, 1.9, 2.9, 3.9, and 4.9.
3.	Press:	**Enter** to return to the document.
4.	Type:	the headings as they appear on the previous page, using the <u>space bar</u> to move one space to the right of each vertical line. Type the first line across the table, press **Shift Enter** to begin a new line, then type the second, and so on. Don't use the tab key to move to various positions when typing the heading. Your text won't be aligned correctly, if you do.
5.	Press:	**Enter** following "# x 7%," in the last column on the right, to repeat the formatting for the box.
Note:		*The screen print on the previous page shows the new line marks (down arrows) and the paragraph marks.*
6.	Press:	**Ctrl F9** to go to Print preView to see if the headings are aligned correctly.
7.	Press:	**Ctrl F9** or choose **Exit** to return to the document.
Note:		*Courier 10 was used to create this document. If you are using a font name or size different from that, the alignment and underlining instructions in this exercise may not produce the same results.*

To enter the items in the columns:

8.	Type:	**Freshmen**.
9.	Press:	**Tab**.
10.	Type:	**4,823**.
11.	Press:	**Tab**.
12.	Type:	**1,248**.
13.	Press:	**Shift Enter** twice to go to a new line and insert a blank line.
14.	Repeat:	for the remaining lines of the table.

To type the last line without the vertical tabs:

15	Press:	**Enter** after typing the word "Total" to repeat the formatting for the box.
16.	Press:	**Esc** and choose **Format, Tab, Reset-all** to return to the default tab sets and remove the vertical lines.
17.	Type:	**Student/teacher ratio:**.
18.	Save the document. Name it **study**.	

To total columns 2 and 3:

1.	Move:	the **highlight** to the **4** in the first line of column 2.
2.	Press:	**Shift F6** to go to column selection mode.
3.	Press:	the **right arrow** four times.
4.	Press:	the **down arrow** six times to "select" the numbers.
5.	Press:	**F2** to calculate the total and display the answer in scrap.
6.	Press:	the **down arrow** to move the **highlight** to the paragraph mark following the word "Total."
7.	Press:	the **Tab** to tab to column 2.
8.	Press:	**Insert** to enter the total at the end of column 2.
9.	Repeat:	steps 1 through 8 for column 3, move the **highlight** to the **1** in the first line of column 3 to begin the process.

To calculate the entries for "Full-time" column:

The entries in column 3 must be subtracted from the entries in column 2.

To add a minus sign in front of each entry in column 3:
1.	Move:	the **highlight** to the **1** in the first line of column 3.
2.	Type:	−.
3.	Repeat:	steps 1 and 2 for the remaining entries in column 3.

To subtract each entry in column 3 from each entry in column 2:
4.	Move:	the **highlight** to any point in the "Freshmen" line.
5.	Press:	**Shift F9** to "select" the line.
6.	Press:	**F2** to calculate.
7.	Press:	the **right arrow**, then the **left arrow** to move the **highlight** to the "down arrow" symbol following "1,248."
8.	Press:	**Tab** to move to column 4.
9.	Press:	**Insert** to insert the result.
10.	Repeat:	steps 4 through 9 for the remaining lines including the "Total" line.

To calculate the "percent of increase forecasted" for columns 5 and 6:

To enter the percentage and format as hidden text.

Note: *The percent will have to entered on the line below each number. It will be formatted as hidden text, copied to scrap, and inserted on each of the remaining blank lines. Then the numbers to be calculated will be "selected," press F2 to calculate, move the highlight to column 5 and press Insert to insert the result.*

1.		Before beginning this part of the exercise, go to the Options menu, and set "show hidden text" field at "Yes."
2.	Move:	the **highlight** to the "down arrow" symbol on the line below "Freshmen."
3.	Press:	the **Tab** key 3 times to move to column 4.
4.	Press:	**Alt E** to begin hidden text formatting.
5.	Type:	***5%.**
6.	Press:	**Alt space bar** to end hidden text formatting.
7.		"Select" ***5%** and press **Alt F3** to copy to scrap.
8.	Move:	the **highlight** to the line below 2,990.
9.	Press:	**Insert** to copy the percent formatted as hidden text from scrap.
10.		Repeat for the remaining lines in column 4.

To multiply the entries in column 4 by 5% and insert the result in column 5:
11.	Move:	the **highlight** to the first number in column 4.
12.	Press:	**Shift F6** and move the arrow keys to "select" 3,575 and *5%. Be sure the % sign is "selected."
13.	Press:	**F2** to calculate.
14.	Move:	the **highlight** to the "down arrow" symbol following 3,575.
15.	Press:	the **Tab** key to go to column 5.
16.	Press:	**Insert** to insert the result.
17.	Repeat:	steps 1 through 6 for the remaining entries in column 5.

<u>To calculate the entries for column 6, multiply the entries in column 3 by 7%:</u>

18. Delete the minus signs in front of each entry in column 3.

19. Insert ***7%** formatted as hidden text in each blank line following each entry in column 3. Use the same procedure used to enter ***5%** in column 4; however, you have already inserted the tab marks, so you won't have to do that. Just move the **highlight** to the tab marks in column 3 and press **Insert** to insert the 7% copied in scrap to the correct position in each line.

20. Calculate the percentage of increase for each entry, and insert the result in column 6. Follow the same procedure used in the previous steps for the entries in column 5; however, to go to column 6, move the **highlight** to the "down arrow" symbol following the entries in column 5 and press the **Tab** key, then press **Insert** to enter the result.

To calculate the student/teacher ratio:

Divide the total number of part-time and full-time students by 358 faculty members, which was the number given in a recent survey.

1. Move: the **highlight** to the **3** in **3,892** of column 3.
2. Press: **F6** to go to extend mode.
3. Move: the **highlight** to the right until both total numbers in columns 3 and 4 are selected.
4. Press: **F2** to add.
5. Move: the **highlight** below the table to any position.
6. Press: **Insert** to enter the result.
7. Type: **/358** which is the number of faculty.
8. "Select" both numbers and press **F2** to calculate.
9. Move: the **highlight** to the space following "ratio"--last line in the table.
10. Press: **Insert** to insert the result--37.74.
11. Go to the Options menu and set "show hidden text" field at "No."

Your document should look like the screen image shown below.

Student	Combined Part- & Full-time	Part-time	Full-time	% of Increase Full-time # x 5%	% of↓ Increase↓ Part-time↓ # x 7%
Freshmen	4,823	1,248	3,575	178.75	87.36↓
Soph.	3,941	951	2,990	149.5	66.57↓
Junior	2,643	898	1,745	87.25	62.86↓
Senior	2,103	795	1,308	65.4	55.65↓
Total	13,510	3,892	9,618		
Student/teacher ratio:37.74¶					

12. Save the edited document, and print.
13. Clear the screen.

Using Microsoft Word Advanced Functions, Part 5

REINFORCEMENT EXERCISES

FUNCTIONS REVIEWED

Chapter 10:
Using Math to Add, Subtract, Multiply, and Divide
Using Math to Calculate Percentages

RECALL QUESTIONS

Answers to recall questions are on page 128.

1. List the "operators" used in each type of math calculation?

2. Numbers must be in what mode in order to be calculated?

3. What key is pressed to perform the calculation?

4. Name the operators used to multiply a number by a percent.

5. Where does the answer appear when a calculation is performed?

DOCUMENTS 7 AND 8:   MATH

Document 7:

You will be doing the Budget Forecast for KTech Corporation shown on the following page.

1. Set up the document shown on the following page, inserting all numbers that are shown on the sheet. Use a font size of 10 point, if possible. You may have to reset margins to 1/2 inch.

2. Set decimal tabs for the number columns.

3. Compute the following totals:

    a. The Total amount of Cost for each month.
    b. The gross profit by subtracting the Total Cost from the Sales.
    c. The percentage of the gross profit distributed among departments to be used by department managers for all expenses other than payroll:

    Multiply the gross profit times the following percentages for EACH month per department:

Personnel:	5%
Research:	10%
Accounting:	5%
Management:	8%
Sales:	15%
Staff:	5%

    d. The percentage of increase in gross profit by dividing last year's gross profit figure, 1,500,000 by this year's total gross profit.

4. Align all numbers in each of the columns using a right flush tab or a decimal tab.

5. Save the document as **forecast**.
6. Print a copy of the document.

		BUDGET FORECAST KTECH CORPORATION FIRST AND SECOND QUARTERS					
		January	February	March	April	May	June
Sales		1,120,000	1,200,000	1,150,000	1,105,000	1,160,000	1,180,000
Cost							
	Material	120,000	121,500	122,290	120,105	123,800	122,780
	Labor	50,102	150,250	150,500	150,110	150,800	150,250
	Overhead	140,200	142,500	143,100	144,250	140,890	141,750
	Total						
Gross Profit							
Breakdown:							
Personnel							
Research							
Accounting							
Management							
Sales							
Staff							
Percentage of Increase in Gross Profit							

Document 8:

You are to compute the forecasted percentage of services or materials that make up the total gross sales for each month based on the Budget Forecast just completed.

Based on past sales of both services and materials, the following predictions have been made:

Service/Materials:	January	February	March	April	May	June
		Percentage				
Word Processing	10%	10%	8%	8%	10%	10%
Database:	8	10	9	10	11	12
Spreadsheet	25	26	28	28	28	30
MIS Structure	15	15	16	16	17	15
Networking:	20	20	18	19	22	20
Communications:	5	6	7	6	7	8
Other:	17	13	15	13	5	5

1. Create the document shown on the following page. Set decimal tabs for the month columns.

2. Insert the Percentage of Gross Sales amounts for each service by multiplying the percentage shown above by the Gross Sales.

    Hint: Calculate the percentage in an area above or below the table, then insert the result in the appropriate position.

    Hint: Use the Copy command to repeat entering the gross amount for each item in the appropriate monthly column, enter the % below it, calculate the amount of the percent, insert the result, then delete the gross amount and the percent.

3. Save the document as **percent**.

4. Print a copy of the document.

KTECH CORPORATION Predicted Percentage of Gross Sales by Service or Materials January through June						
Services/ Materials:	January	February	March	April	May	June
Word Processing						
Database						
Spreadsheet						
MIS Structure						
Networking						
Communi- cations						
Other						

ANSWERS TO RECALL QUESTIONS

1. Add = +
   Subtract = -
   Multiply = *
   Division = /
   Percent = %

2. The number must be "selected."

3. F2.

4. The asterisk (*) and the percent (%) sign.

5. In Scrap.

PART 6

CHAPTER 11   USING MACROS   130

    Using the Supplied Macros   130
    Creating a Macro   131
    Running a Macro Using Control Codes   133
    Editing a Macro 134
    Deleting a Macro   135
    Writing a Macro Containing a SET Instruction   135
    Writing a Macro Containing Several Macro Instructions   139

REINFORCEMENT EXERCISES   145

CHAPTER 11

USING MACROS

PREVIEW

Macros are series of keystrokes which are saved and given a name. These keystrokes may be either text, Word commands and function keys, macro instructions, or a combination of all three. They are stored in the glossary and may be used similar to the way glossaries are used. You may go to the **Insert** menu, press **F1** to see the list of macros, and select the one you want to run, or you may use the control code which is a combination of the **Ctrl** key plus alphabet keys to automatically run the macro.

The purpose of macros is to make your word processing work more efficient by storing often-used combinations of keystrokes and using a macro to enter those keystrokes when you want to use them. Not only is this a faster way of working, but it is also more accurate. Once the macro has been created, you don't have to think about hitting the wrong keys in order to perform some function.

Microsoft Word has created a number of macros and included them in the software package. This chapter will show you how to use these supplied macros, as well as how to create and use your own macros.

USING THE SUPPLIED MACROS

The user-supplied macros are located in a file named MACRO.GLY. When the software is installed, this file is copied to the directory which contains the Microsoft Word program; however it is not ready to be used immediately. In order to use the supplied macros for the first time, they must be merged with your glossary files. You will only need to do this one time.

To merge the supplied macros:

Press **Esc**, choose **Insert**, and press **F1**. If you see a list of macros, it means that the macros have already been merged, and you may skip the following instructions. Press **Esc** to return to the document.

If you have a hard disk:
1. Press: **Esc.**
2. Choose: **Transfer, Glossary, Merge**.
3. Type: **c:\word5\macro** If your program has been installed in a directory other than "word5" type that directory name.
4. Press: **Enter** to merge.

If you have a floppy disk system:
1. Insert the Microsoft Word Utilities disk into Drive B.
2. Press: **Esc.**
3. Choose: **Transfer, Glossary, Merge**.
4. Type: **macro.**
5. Press: **Enter.**

Note: *If you run the file named README-FIRST from the Insert menu and print it out, you will have a list of the supplied macros, plus the control codes used to run the macros.*

Using Microsoft Word Advanced Functions, Part 6

To run a supplied macro using the Insert menu:

1. Press: **Esc.**
2. Choose: **Insert**.
3. Press: **F1** to display the list of macros.
4. Move: the **highlight** to the macro "**mailing_label.mac.**"
5. Press: **Enter** to run.

6. Respond to the screen prompt to set the number of columns at 3. You will then see label forms displayed on the screen. Since you do not have a data file to be used with this form document, press **Esc** to cancel the macro.

7. Clear the screen without saving.

To run a supplied macro using the control code:

The control code consists of the keys used in combination with the **Ctrl** key to run the macro.

In this exercise you will run the macro "MEMO_HEADER" which will create a memo with appropriate fields.

1. Move: the **highlight** to the position where the memo is to be created--top of the screen.
2. Press: **Ctrl MH** (do not press the space bar between M and H).

The macro will automatically begin running on screen.

Note: *Fill in the memo with appropriate entries, print the document, and clear the screen without saving.*

CREATING A MACRO

There are two ways of creating a macro:

1. Recording a macro. Press **Shift F3** to go to "Record Macro" mode and record keystrokes as they are typed.

2. Writing a macro. Type representations for various keystrokes.

In this exercise, you will create two macros by recording keystrokes. In the exercises beginning on page 135, you will create macros by writing them.

To record (create) a macro for a heading:

You will record the keystrokes used to type the return address displayed in the box below. The glossary entry "dateprint" will be used to print the current date.

```
                    R. L. Stevens
                 3110 West Allen Street
                   Seattle, WA 98145
                      (dateprint)
```

1.	Press:	**Shift F3** to begin recording. RM will be displayed in the status line.
2.	Press:	**Alt C** to go to the center point.
3.	Type:	and center each line of the return address.

At the (dateprint) line:
4.	Type:	**dateprint** without typing the parenthesis.
5.	Press:	**F3** to expand the glossary--parenthesis will be added.

Note: *The current date will be inserted at this point only when the document is printed*

6.	Press:	**Enter.**
7.	Press:	**Alt P** to return to normal paragraph.
8.	Press:	**Enter** four more times to insert blank lines.

Note: *Entering four blank lines positions the highlight at the point where text will be entered when the macro is used in a letter.*

9.	Press:	**Shift F3** to stop recording keystrokes. A message will be displayed: "COPY to: ( )."

To name the macro and assign control codes:
10.	Type:	**letterhead.mac^<Ctrl L>H.**

Note: *The caret (**Shift 6**) followed by greater than (>) and less than (<) symbols assigns the keys **Ctrl LH** to be used to run the macro. The L and H do not have to be typed in caps.*

Note: *Macro names may contain thirty-one characters including control codes. You can use the underscore and period in the macro, but no spaces.*

11.	Press:	**Enter** to save. (This macro will be used later.)

To record a macro for a closing:

In this exercise you will record the keystrokes used to set a tab stop at 3" and to type the text for a standard closing for letters. The text is shown in the box below.

```
                              Sincerely yours,


                              Your name
                              Your title

ABC/(your reference initial)
```

1.	Press:	**Shift F3** to begin recording. An RM is displayed in the status line.
2.	Press:	**Alt F1** to set tab.

In the tab menu:
3.	Type:	**3** and **L** to set a left flush tab at 3" from left margin.
4.	Press:	**Enter** to return to the document.
5.	Type:	the text for the closing as displayed above. Remember to press the **Tab** key to move to the tab set for each line except the last.

Using Microsoft Word Advanced Functions, Part 6

<u>At the end of the text:</u>
6.   Press: **Shift F3** to end the recording.

<u>At the message "COPY to ( )":</u>
7.   Type: **closing.mac^<Ctrl C>L.**
8.   Press: **Enter** to save.

9.   Clear the screen. Press **N** to not save the changes to the <u>document</u>, but press **Y** to save the glossary at the "Save changes to the glossary" message.

RUNNING A MACRO USING CONTROL CODES

In this section, you will use both macros in the letter shown in the box below.

To run the macro containing the letterhead:

1.   Move: the **highlight** to the position where the macro for the letterhead is to be inserted (top of the document).
2.   Press: **Ctrl LH** to run the macro.

3.   Type: the inside address, salutation, and the text for the letter.

```
(insert the macro for the letterhead)
Ms. Virginia Howard
3309 West Seventh Street
Fort Worth, TX 76107

Dear Ms. Howard:

Thank you for your interest in the new word
processing program which we are writing.

You may have a demonstration of this program at any
time.  Just mail the enclosed card.

(Insert macro for closing--see instructions below)

Enc.
```

To run the macro for the closing:

1.   Move: the **highlight** to the point where the closing is to be entered.
2.   Press: **Ctrl CL** to run the macro for the closing.

3.   Save the document, name it **howard**, and print the letter.
4.   Clear the screen.

EDITING A MACRO

In order to edit a macro, it must be displayed on the screen as a written macro. The screen print below shows the "closing.mac" in "written" form.
    In this exercise you will change the closing entries so they are flush left, and delete the word "yours" in the complimentary close.

To display the macro as a "written" macro:

1. Press: **Esc.**
2. Choose: **Insert**.
3. Press: **F1** to display the list of glossary entries and macros.
4. Move: the **highlight** to the macro "closing.mac^<Ctrl C>L."
5. Type: ^ (**Shift 6**) If you don't type the caret, the macro will be run, rather than displayed as a written macro.
6. Press: **Enter.**

Note: The "written" macro is shown in the screen print below.

```
<alt f1>3l<enter><tab>Sincerely
yours,<enter><enter><enter><enter><tab>Your
name<enter><tab>Your title<enter><enter>ABC/ps¶
```

To make revisions:

To remove the tab at 3":
1. Move: the **highlight** to the < symbol preceding **Alt F1 >**.
2. Press: **F6** then press **F8** enough times to "select" the command plus 3l<**Enter**><**Tab**>.
3. Press: **Delete.**
4. Delete all the remaining Tab codes <tab>.

To delete "yours":
5. Move: the **highlight** to "yours."
6. Press: **F8** to "select."
7. Press: **Delete**. Also delete the extra space between "Sincerely" and the following comma.

To "select" and save the edited macro:
8. Press: **Shift F10** to "select" the entire macro.
9. Press: **Esc.**
10. Choose: **Copy** or **Delete** to display message "Copy to" or "Delete to."
11. Press: **F1** to display the list of macros.
12. Move: the **highlight** to "**closing.mac.**"
13. Press: **Enter.**

At the message "Press "Y" to overwrite Glossary, etc. . .":
14. Press: **Y** to overwrite the macro.

Note: You could type the name instead of viewing the list, if you were certain how it was typed originally.

15. Clear the screen if you chose the Copy command. Respond with a "No" to the "Save change to document" message, but "Yes" to the "Save Changes to the Glossary" message.

Using Microsoft Word Advanced Functions, Part 6

DELETING A MACRO:

To delete the macro "letterhead.mac":
1. Press: **Esc.**
2. Choose: **Transfer, Glossary, Clear.**

Note: *At this point, you could type in the names of several macros, each separated by a comma; however, you will delete only one macro at this time.*

3. Press: **F1** to see the list of macros.
4. Move: the **highlight** to "letterhead.mac."
5. Press: **Enter** to display the message "Enter Y to clear glossary names."
6. Press: **Y** to delete the macro.

Note: *When quitting Word, press Y at the prompt to save the glossary changes in order to delete the macro permanently.*

WRITING A MACRO CONTAINING A "SET" INSTRUCTION

The advantage of writing a macro is that the user may enter a variety of instructions in addition to text and commands. For example, SET and ASK instructions may be written, IF and ENDIF statements may be entered, or instructions to PAUSE or add COMMENTS may be included.

In this section, you will be instructed to write a macro which sets a header consisting of the title of a manual, plus the chapter number, and the "page" glossary entry. The macro will include a SET instruction enabling you to set the chapter number. This type of macro could then be used in several different files, and the appropriate chapter number could be entered for each file.

An example of how the running head will appear when it is printed is displayed below.

<u>KTech Corporation Training Manual, Chapter 1   2</u>

An example of the written macro is shown below.

```
<Alt F1>6R<Enter>¶
KTech Corporation Training Manual, Chapter «SET number
=?Enter chapter number»«number»<Tab>page<F3>¶
<Ctrl Esc>fbl<Tab 6>y<Enter>¶
<Ctrl F2>¶
```

There are certain conventions which must be observed in writing macros.

* When you are writing representations of keystrokes <u>other</u> than alphabet or number keys, enclose the names of those keys in < >. For example, to specify using the Enter key, write **<Enter>**.

* When direction keys--Tab, Shift Tab, Enter, Escape, Insert, Delete, Backspace, and the arrow keys--are to be repeated, you may enter the keyname the desired number of times or you may enter a number after the keyname. For example if you wish to enter the instruction to press the tab key six times, type **<tab 6>**. The arrow keys are identified by typing **right, left, up,** or **down**.

*   Text is written the same way text is written in a document.

*   Variables must be enclosed in chevrons « » which are typed by pressing Ctrl [or Ctrl]. For example, the variable, "number," in the macro displayed on page 135 must be typed «number».

*   Macro instructions such as ASK, SET, IF, ENDIF, COMMENT, and PAUSE must be enclosed in chevrons.

*   It is recommended that each part of the macro be on a separate line. Since Word does not recognize Enter, Shift Enter, or Tabs unless they are "written," the user may press **Enter** to end a line of instruction and to insert a blank line between parts of the macro.

To write the instructions for setting a right flush tab at position 6:

You should have a clear screen at this point.

1. Type: `<Alt F1>` which represents the keystrokes for displaying the Tab Set menu.
2. Type: 6R which tells Word to set a tab at position 6, and set the alignment at (Right).
3. Type: `<Enter>` which is the instruction to press **Enter**.
4. Press: **Enter** to go to the next line.

To type the text for the header:

1. Type: `KTech Corporation Training Manual, Chapter.`

To write the SET instruction:

1. Type: `«SET number =?Enter chapter number».`

Note: *Remember to use Ctrl [and Ctrl] to type the chevrons. The text "Enter chapter number" will be displayed at the bottom of the screen when the macro is run, to prompt the user to type the chapter number.*

To write the variable, "number":

1. Type: `«number»`. The variable will contain the number typed in response to the SET instruction.

To write the instructions for the tab and the glossary entry "page":

1. Type: `<Tab>page<F3>`. The F3 instruction following the word page, expands the glossary name "page." Page numbers will be automatically inserted in this position when the document containing this header is printed.
2. Press: **Enter** to go to the next line.

To write the instructions to format the header with a line below:

1. Type: `<Ctrl Esc>`. This instruction accesses the command menu.

Note: *You need to add "Ctrl" before "Esc" to avoid leaving the command menu if the macro happens to be run when the highlight is in the command menu.*

2.	Type:	`fbl`. These are the keystrokes used to choose Format, Border, Line.
3.	Type:	`<Tab 6>`. The Tab key must be pressed six times to get to the "below" field in the Format Border menu.
4.	Type:	`y` to set the "below" field at "Yes."
5.	Type:	`<Enter>` --the instruction to press the **Enter** key.
6.	Press:	**Enter** to go to the next line.

To write the instruction to format the text as a header:

1.	Type:	`<Ctrl F2>`. This is the speed key to format text as a header.

To save the macro and assign control codes:

1.	Move:	the **highlight** to the beginning of the macro text `<Alt F1>`.
2.	Press:	**F6** to turn on Extend.
3.	Move:	the **highlight** to the end of the macro to "select" it.
4.	Press:	**Esc.**
5.	Choose:	**Copy** or **Delete**.

To enter the macro name:
6.	Type:	**running_head.mac^<Ctrl R>H**.
7.	Press:	**Enter** to save.
8.	Clear the screen.	

To test the macro step by step:

Ctrl F3 is the Step Macro function key. When you are in Step Macro mode, the macro is run step by step. You must press any key to go from one step to the next. This allows you to view carefully the results of each keystroke recorded in your macro.

If there is an error in your macro, leave Step Mode when the macro is ended, display the macro in written form--see page 134 for instructions--make the correction, "select" the entire macro, and save it again, using the same name. You will have to press Y at the message to overwrite the macro.

With your highlight at the top of the screen:
1.	Press:	**Ctrl F3** An ST is displayed in the status line, and will remain there until **Ctrl F3** is pressed a second time.
2.	Press:	**Ctrl RH** --the control code used to run this macro.
3.	Press:	any key other than **Esc** or **Ctrl F3**, to view the first keystroke. The Tab Set menu will be displayed. Continue pressing any key several times to display the remaining keystrokes.

At the Set message:
4.	Type:	**1** to set the chapter number at 1.
5.	Press:	**Enter** and then any key to continue to the end of the macro.

Your screen should resemble the screen print shown below.

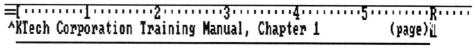

6. Press: **Ctrl F3** to leave Step Macro mode.

7. Clear the screen without saving the document. At the prompt to save the glossary, press **Y**.

To run the macro:

Move the highlight to the top of the screen.
1. Press: **Ctrl RH**.
At the Set message to "Enter chapter number":
2. Type: any number to indicate a chapter number.
3. Press: **Enter** to continue running the macro.

4. Clear the screen without saving. If the prompt to save the glossary is displayed, press **Y**.

Using Microsoft Word Advanced Functions, Part 6

WRITING A MACRO CONTAINING SEVERAL MACRO INSTRUCTIONS

In this section you will learn how to write a macro which includes the following macro instructions: PAUSE, IF, ENDIF, ELSE, SET, and ASK.

This exercise will provide a review of previous functions learned. First, you will create an invoice form. Next, you will fill it in, and use math to calculate amounts in each line. Then you will write a macro that calculates a subtotal of the amounts, figures the sales tax if the tax is applicable, and calculates and inserts the total amount. After writing the macro, you will use Step Macro mode to test it, then run it again to be impressed with how well it works.

While it takes a considerable amount of time and thought to write macros, once they are written correctly, they save a great deal of time and contribute to the accuracy of your work.

To create the invoice form:

The form is shown in the box below. Instructions for creating the form are listed below the box.

```
                       KTECH CORPORATION
              P.O. BOX 167, KIRKLAND, WA 98034

                           INVOICE

DATE:          (dateprint)

BILLED TO:     »

P.O.NUMBER:    »
_____

DESCRIPTION                    QUANTITY      COST     AMOUNT
_____

»
»
»
»
»
»
»
                                       Subtotal         »
                                      Sales tax         »
                                          Total         »
```

1. This is a fairly simple invoice form. Type the title and guide words "DATE," "BILLED TO," and "P.O. NUMBER." Use the glossary entry "dateprint" as shown above--type **dateprint** and press **F3** to expand. Set »'s as markers, and format them as hidden text, as you did in the exercise in chapter 7 on forms.

2. Format the paragraph mark at the end of the "DESCRIPTION. . ." line with lines above and below. Use the Format Border menu for this. Position the headings using the space bar rather than the tab key. They may have to be adjusted after you set your tabs.

3. On the line below "DESCRIPTION . . .", press **Alt F1** to set tabs as follows:
   Right flush tab at 3.5 for the "Quantity" column.
   Decimal tab at 4.5 for the "Cost" column.
   Decimal tab at 5.5 for the "Amount" column.

4. Enter seven lines (where entries could be typed) with a chevron formatted as hidden text in each, as shown in the example on page 139.

5. Reset All Tabs--Press **Esc** and choose **Format, Tab, Reset-All** on the line below the last chevron at the left margin.

6. Press **Alt F1** to set new tabs for the Subtotal, Sales tax and total section as follows:
   Right flush tab at 4.5 for "Subtotal," "Sales tax," and "Total."
   Decimal tab at 5.5 for the chevrons opposite each of the above.

7. Type "Subtotal," "Sale tax," and "Total" with corresponding chevrons as shown on page 139.

8. Save the document. Name it **invoice1**. Clear the screen.

To fill in the form:

1. Load the document **invoice1** as a "read only" file to avoid changing the invoice form.

The filled-in form is shown below. The instructions for filling in the form are given following the example.

```
                    KTECH CORPORATION
              P.O. BOX 167, KIRKLAND, WA 98034

                         INVOICE

DATE:            (dateprint)

BILLED TO:       »ABC Corporation
                 16079 S. W. Olive Way
                 Seattle, WA  98107

P.O.NUMBER:      »104
_____

DESCRIPTION                QUANTITY        COST       AMOUNT
_____

»Training manuals              10         *25.50
»Data disks                    10         *1.25
»
»
»
»
»
                                       Subtotal         »
                                       Sales tax        »
                                           Total        »
```

2.	Press:	**Ctrl >** to go to the first marker.
3.	Type:	**ABC Corporation** and **Enter**.
4.	Press:	the **Tab** key to move the **highlight** to the line under ABC Corporation to type the address and repeat for the city, state, and zip.
5.	Repeat steps 2 and 3 for the remainder of the form to move to each marker and to type the information as displayed. Do not press **Enter** after typing the amount *25.50. Press **Ctrl >** to go to the next marker.	

To calculate the AMOUNT for each entry:

6.	"Select":	the first row of numbers in the QUANTITY and the COST columns (10 and *25.50).
7.	Press:	**F2** to calculate.
8.	Press:	the **Tab** key to move to the AMOUNT column
9.	Press:	the **Insert** key to insert the answer from scrap.
10.	Repeat:	steps 5 through 8 for the second row.
11.	Save the document. Name it **invoice2**.	
12.	Split the window horizontally at 11. Clear the new window and write the macro in window 2. In this case, using a split window is handy for it enables you to move back and forth between windows to check the keystrokes needed to perform the tasks included in the macro.	

To write the macro:

Writing a macro takes a good deal of planning. Think through what you want to accomplish, and perhaps write down the keystrokes needed to do that. In this section, follow the instructions-- explanations are included as you write each section of the macro.

The written macro is displayed in the box below. Instructions for writing the macro are given following the example.

```
«PAUSE Move the highlight to the first number in the
AMOUNT column»

<Shift F6><right 6><down 6><F2>
<Ctrl . 7><Ins><Ctrl .>

«ASK Tax =?Are these items for resale?»
«IF Tax ="n"»«SET Tax =scrap * .08»«Tax»
«ELSE»«0.00»«ENDIF»

«PAUSE Move the highlight to the first number opposite
Subtotal»

<Shift F6><right 6><down><F2><Ctrl . 2><Ins>
```

Points to remember when writing macros.

* The < > characters are used to enclose keystrokes representing direction and function keys.

* The « » chevrons are used to enclose macro instructions such as PAUSE, ASK, SET, IF, ELSE, ENDIF.

* An IF instruction must always have a corresponding ENDIF instruction.

To write the PAUSE instruction:
1. Type: the first line as it appears above. When you run the macro, this will display the message "Move the highlight..." at the bottom of the screen, and you will have to press **Enter** to end the pause. The word PAUSE does not have to be typed in all caps; however, it helps to type it this way so you can easily see which instruction you are using. Remember to press **Ctrl [** and **Ctrl]** to type the chevrons.

2. Press: **Enter** twice at the end of the PAUSE instruction. It is a good idea to separate the parts of the macro, so they can be more easily read.

To write the instructions for "selecting" and calculating the total of the AMOUNT column, and for inserting the subtotal:
3. Type: `<Shift F6>` the instruction to begin "column select."
4. Type: `<right 6>` the instruction to move the right arrow six times (to the end of the first line of numbers).
5. Type: `<down 6>` the instruction to move the down arrow six times. This highlights the entire column. Although there are just two entries in this particular invoice, this macro would work if there were entries in all seven lines.
6. Type: `<F2>` the instruction to calculate and enter the subtotal in scrap.
7. Press: **Enter** to go to a new line.
8. Type: `<Ctrl . 7>` the instruction to move past seven markers to go to the position where the subtotal amount is to be inserted.

Note: *Because the > symbol is used in writing macro instructions, the period is used instead of the > symbol following the word Ctrl to write the instruction for jumping to the next mark.*

9. Type: `<Ins>` the instruction for inserting the subtotal. Do not type "Insert". The macro does not accept that word as representing the Insert key.
10. Type: `<Ctrl .>` the instruction to move the **highlight** to the "Sales tax" level.
11. Press: **Enter** twice to separate these instructions from the following instructions.

To write the ASK instruction:
12. Type: «`ASK Tax =?Are these items for resale?`». This statement will be displayed at the bottom of the screen. If the answer to this is "no" (which it will be), then the sales tax needs to be calculated. Steps 13 through 17 give the instructions for calculating the sales tax.

To write the IF instruction:
13. Type: «`IF Tax ="n"`».

To write the SET instruction:
14. Type: «`SET Tax =scrap *.08`». This instruction means if the response to "ASK tax" is "no," then sales tax has to be paid. This statement instructs the macro to multiply the amount displayed in scrap by 8%, and to enter the amount in the variable, «`Tax`».

Using Microsoft Word Advanced Functions, Part 6

To write the variable Tax :

15. Type: «Tax». Variables are names of locations where text or numbers may be stored when a macro is running. At this point, the **highlight** is positioned at the end of the "Sales Tax" line; therefore, the amount in the variable «Tax» would be displayed at this position.

To write the ELSE instruction:

16. Type: «ELSE»«0.00». If no sales tax was calculated, this instruction enters 0.00 in the "Sales tax" line.

To write the ENDIF instruction:

17. Type: «ENDIF». If this instruction is not included, the macro would be aborted, since every IF instruction must have a corresponding ENDIF instruction.
18. Press: **Enter** twice.

19. Type the second PAUSE instruction as displayed on page 141 telling the user to move the **highlight** to the subtotal number.

20. Press: **Enter** twice.

To write the last line of the macro:

21. Type: the line exactly as it appears. It instructs the macro to "select" the "subtotal" and "sales tax" amounts, calculate the total, move to the last mark <Ctrl.2>, and insert the total from scrap.

To save the macro:

1. "Select" the entire macro. If this is the only text in the window (and it should be), press **Shift F10** to "select".

2. Press: **Esc.**
3. Choose: **Copy.**
4. Type: **invoice.mac^<Ctrl I>N** to name and assign a control code to run the macro.
5. Press: **Enter.**

To test the macro in Step Macro mode.

If there is an error in your macro, leave Step Mode when the macro is ended, go to Window 2, make the correction, "select" the entire macro, and save it again, using the same name. You will have to press Y at the message to overwrite the macro.

1. Press: **F1** to move the **highlight** to window 1 where the **"invoice2"** document is displayed. You may want to press **Ctrl F1** to zoom (expand) the window.
2. Press: **Ctrl F3** to display ST in the status line and go to Step Macro mode.
3. Press: **Ctrl IN** and press any other key to begin running the macro step by step.

The first message is "Move the highlight to the first number in the AMOUNT column."
4. Move: the **highlight** as instructed.
5. Press: **Enter** and any other key to continue running the macro.

Watch the screen closely as you run the macro in Step Macro mode. You will need to press any key to move from step to step, and at this point, the highlight is "selecting" the numbers. Each time you press any key, the highlight moves one additional space.

When the message, "Are these items for resale?" is displayed:
6.   Press: **N** to indicate "No."
7.   Press: **Enter** and then press any other key to continue running the macro.

At times during this procedure, you will not see anything happening on the screen. The macro is responding internally to the instructions. Just keep pressing any key to continue to the end of the macro.

Remember to press **Enter** after responding to each PAUSE instruction displayed on the screen.

<u>At the end of the macro:</u>
8.   Press: **Ctrl F3** to leave Step Mode.

9.   Delete all of the entries inserted during the macro so you can run the macro again, not in Step Mode.

To run the macro:

The **highlight** must be in window 1.
1.   Press: **Ctrl IN**.

<u>At the PAUSE instruction:</u>
2.   Move: the **highlight** as instructed.
3.   Press: **Enter** to continue the macro.

<u>At the ASK instruction "Are these items for resale?":</u>
4.   Respond to the ASK instruction with an **N**.

<u>At the next PAUSE instruction:</u>
5.   Move: the **highlight** as instructed at the second PAUSE, and press **Enter** to continue to the end of the macro.

6.   Save the invoice as **invoice2**.
7.   Print the document.
8.   Clear the screen.

This exercise used several of the macro instructions. As noted before, refer to the Word manual for extensive instruction in using macros. They are well worth the time and effort involved in writing them. Take time, also, to look at the description of the supplied macros. These supplied macros are extremely useful and time-saving, and apply to many of the everyday tasks involved in word processing. The README file in the glossary menu contains the list of name and description of the supplied macros.

REINFORCEMENT EXERCISES

FUNCTIONS REVIEWED:

Chapter 11:
> Using the supplied macros
> Creating a macro
> Running a macro using control codes
> Editing a macro
> Deleting macros
> Writing a macro

RECALL QUESTIONS:

Answers to the recall questions are on page 149.

1. Define a macro.

2. Define the control code.

3. Name the menu used to display the list of macros.

4. What function key is used to begin recording a macro? to end recording a macro?

5. What form or mode does a macro have to be in, in order to edit it? How do you display the macro in this form?

6. Describe the "step macro" mode. What is the purpose of the "step macro" mode.

7. What keystrokes are used to go to "step macro" mode?

8. Name the menu used to delete a macro.

9. In a written macro, how would you indicate that the Enter key is to be used?

10. In a written macro, how would you indicate that the Tab key is to be used four times?

DOCUMENT 9: WRITING A MACRO

You recently completed a form for a KTech survey being conducted on customer services--see Practice Document 4 at the end of part 3. It has been decided that this form will also be used to conduct telephone surveys. You will write a macro with instructions for retrieving the form document and pauses that allow you to type in the information at the appropriate positions.

In order to get you started an example of the macro is shown below.

```
<Esc>tlsurvey.doc<Enter>
<Ctrl .>«PAUSE Type survey No.»
<Ctrl .>Date<F3>
<Ctrl .>«PAUSE type company name»
```

1. The first line is the instruction for loading the form called **survey**.

2. The next line is the instruction for using Ctrl . to go quickly to the chevron following the label "Survey No.," plus the PAUSE instruction to display the message "Type survey No" and allow time for the number to be entered.

3. Line 3 is the instruction for using the glossary "date" to enter the current date following the appropriate label.

4. Line 4 is the instruction for moving to the "Company Name" label, plus the PAUSE instruction.

5. Repeat instruction number 4 above for each label in the form as listed below. Make up your own messages for the remaining labels.

    Company Street Address
    Department
    City
    State
    ZIP
    Date of most recent service from KTech
    Training received (This isn't a label so don't include it.)
        Word Processing
        Database
        Spreadsheet
        MIS Structure
        Networking
        Communications
        Other
    How did you hear...?
    Requests...
    Other Comments

6. Save the macro. Name it "survey.mac^<Ctrl K>S" (for KTech Survey).

7. Clear the screen.

8. Run the macro and fill in information for each of the following three responses. In the Training Received section, enter X's in the appropriate line according to the response.

9. Save each filled-in form as a separate document, giving it a name of your choice, and print each of the forms.

Responses:

Survey No. 101
New Seattle Technology, Inc.
1278 S. W. Terry Street, Suite 200
MIS Department
Seattle, WA 98123
02/15/90
Received:
    MIS Structure
    Networking
    Communications
Through the Business Journal
Yes, in advanced programming

Survey No. 102
Alpha Services, Inc.
20000 Mt. Blvd.
Personnel Dept.
Kirkland, WA 98034
6/90
Received:
    Word Processing
    Spreadsheet
    Database
    Communications
Through the local networking organization
No additional service needed at this time
All training has been very useful

Survey No. 103
The Freeland Group, Inc.
The I-90 Business Park Complex
Suite 385
General Management
Issaquah, WA 98027
4/90
Received:
    Networking
From The Dwellings Real Estate Company
Additional training in DBase V will be needed in a couple of months.
No other comments.

DOCUMENT 10: WRITING A MACRO TO CALCULATE A TOTAL

Management has recently decided that the KTech Customer Survey form will be adopted as the standard format for questionnaires used by the Research department; however, the format needs to be changed somewhat for different surveys. In this exercise you will change the format necessary for a survey on the materials purchased and then write a macro that retrieves the document, pauses to allow you to fill in information and calculates the total amount of the cost in a column.

1. Load the document **survey** and make the following changes:

    a. Replace "Date of most recent service from KTech" with "Date of most recent purchase from KTech."

    b. Add the Label "Quantity" on the same line with "Date of most recent purchase..." Place it to the right of center.

    c. Delete "Training Received" section and replace as shown below. Add the word "Total" on the line below "Other."

	Materials Purchased:	Word Processing Manuals
		Database manuals
		Spreadsheet manuals
		MIS Structure Handbook
		Networking diagrams/handbook
		Communications handbook
		Other
		Total

2. Write a macro that will calculate the total of manuals purchased similar to the one in Practice Document 9, and similar to the one included in the instruction section of this part.

3. When filling in the forms, make up your own PAUSE comments, and the information to be filled in.

4. Save the filled-in form and print it.

ANSWERS TO RECALL QUESTIONS:

1. A series of keystrokes which are saved and given a name, then may be run automatically in text at a specific position by press the Control key plus two other keys. The saved keystrokes may be text, keystrokes used to access the command menu, speed keys, or macro instructions.

2. The control code consists of the control key plus two alphabet keys. The control code is used to run the macro automatically.

3. Insert menu. Press F1 to see the list of macros.

4. Shift F3 to begin.
   Shift F3 to end.

5. A macro must be displayed as a "written" macro in order to edit it.

   To display a macro as a written macro:
   a. Press Esc, choose Insert.
   b. Press F1 to display the list of macros.
   c. Highlight the macro to be edited.
   d. Type ^ (Shift 6) to display the macro on the screen as a written macro.

6. In "step macro" mode, a macro is run one keystroke at a time. The user must press any key to run the next keystroke. "Step macro" mode allows you to view the results of your macro. If you have made an error, a message will be displayed telling you where the error is located. The macro may then be displayed as a "written" macro and can be edited.

7. Ctrl F3.

8. Transfer, Glossary, Clear.

9. <Enter>.

10. <Tab 4>.

PART 7

CHAPTER 12   USING THE FOOTNOTE MENU   152

    Entering a Footnote   152
    Revising Footnote Text   153
    Deleting a Footnote   154
    Moving a Footnote   154
    Formatting the Footnote Numbers   155
    Printing Footnotes at the End of the Document   155

CHAPTER 13   USING ANNOTATIONS   156

    Entering an Annotation   156
    Printing Annotations at the Bottom of the Page   157

CHAPTER 14   USING BOOKMARKS   158

    Designating Text as a Bookmark   158
    Using a Bookmark for Cross Referencing   159
    Removing a Bookmark Designation   160

REINFORCEMENT EXERCISES   161

CHAPTER 12

USING THE FOOTNOTE MENU

PREVIEW

The footnote function allows you to enter footnotes in text and to choose whether to print them at the bottom of the same page or at the end of a division. The system automatically numbers the footnotes, and will renumber them if you delete or move a footnote. Or, if you wish, you may enter your own footnote numbers or whatever character you choose to use--perhaps an asterisk (*), or the word "note."

Footnotes are entered with normal character formatting. To format the footnotes in superscript, "select" the footnote number and press **Alt +** or **Alt =**. You also may wish to change the font size of the footnote numbers.

The text you will be typing is shown in the box below. The footnotes to be entered for each paragraph are shown on the following page.

```
     The 1980s were marked by a parade of introductions of
packaged integrated software programs of infinite variety.
In addition, the microcomputer phenomenon was accompanied
by a deluge of user-oriented software packages that
brought end users headlong into a first-hand
acquaintanceship with various software programs.

     The 1980s showed that sophisticated software programs
are no longer applications used by a select group of
computer wizards or programmers.  Business managers to
caterers are finding themselves in contact with or even
actively using integrated software programs and other
sophisticated programs when performing routine, daily
functions.

     There are software packages designed for a wide range
of sizes and capacities of systems.  The knowledge needed
for understanding these packages has increased with the
degree of sophistication of the applications.
```

ENTERING A FOOTNOTE

1. Type: the text for the first paragraph in the box above.

To enter the footnote:

The **highlight** should be in the space following the period at the end of the paragraph.

1. Press: **Esc.**
2. Choose: **Format, Footnote.**

Note: *To number footnotes automatically, leave the "reference mark" field blank.*

3. Press: **Enter** to insert the footnote number, and to go to the typing area where the footnote text is to be typed.

Note: *The typing area for footnotes is located between two end marks at the end of the document. A footnote number is displayed at the left margin, as well as the corresponding footnote number in the text.*

4. Type: the footnote text shown in the box below for the first paragraph. Press the Tab key to indent one tab stop.

```
    S. R. Chapple, Computers in the '80s, (Portland,
Oregon: Campus Publishers, 1988), p. 23.
```

To return the highlight to the footnote number in the text:

1. Press: **Esc.**
2. Choose: **Jump, Footnote** to return the highlight to footnote number 1.
3. Move: the **highlight** to the space following the footnote number, and press **Enter** twice to type the next paragraph.
4. Type: the remaining two paragraphs, inserting the footnotes shown below at the ends of paragraph 2 and paragraph 3.

```
    T. S. Marshall, Introduction to Integrated Programs,
(Bellingham, WA,:  Universal Press, 1989), pp. 51-55.

    R. L. Roberts, "Assessing Software", User's Guide to
Software, (March, 1990):  24-35
```

5. Save the document. Name it **footnote**.

REVISING FOOTNOTE TEXT

To use the Jump Footnote menu:

1. Move: the **highlight** to the footnote number (**1**) at the end of the first paragraph.
2. Press: **Esc.**
3. Choose: **Jump, Footnote** to move immediately to the corresponding footnote text.
4. Make the following revision: Change the year to read 1989.
5. Press: **Esc.**
6. Choose: **Jump, Footnote** to return to the typing area.

Note: *All text is on the same page in this document; however, if you were working with a multi-page document, the corresponding footnote text would not be as apparent, and the Jump Footnote feature would be the quickest way of moving from the footnote area to the text area.*

To use the footnote window to make revisions to footnote text:

Footnotes are stored at the end of documents. In order to display both text and corresponding footnotes, split the window to show the footnote window.

1.	Press:	**Esc.**
2.	Choose:	**Window, Split, Footnote.**
3.	Press:	**F1** to move the **highlight** to the selection bar, and move the **up** or **down arrows** to move the **highlight** to the point where you want the top of the footnote window to appear--preferably in the lower third of the screen.
4.	Press:	**Enter.**

Note: *The top window contains the text. The bottom window (window number 2) displays only the footnotes that correspond to the footnote numbers displayed in window 1.*

5.	Press:	**F1** to move the highlight into the Footnote Window.

To revise footnote text:
6.	Move:	the **highlight** to the year in footnote number 2, and change it to read 1988.
7.	Press:	**F1** to return to Window 1 and to continue editing text.

To close the footnote window:
8.	(Be sure the footnote window is active--if necessary, press **F1** to move to window 2.)	
9.	Press:	**Esc**
10.	Choose:	**Window, Close** and press **Enter.**

DELETING A FOOTNOTE

1.	Move:	the **highlight** to the footnote number (number 2 in the text).
2.	Press:	**Delete** key.

Note: *The footnote number and the footnote text are deleted into scrap. The remaining footnote number is automatically renumbered "2."*

MOVING A FOOTNOTE

A footnote may be moved in the same way any other type of text is moved. Delete the footnote number, move the highlight to the new position, and press Insert to insert the number from scrap. The program will automatically renumber the footnotes.

1.	Move:	the **highlight** to the end of the first sentence in the second paragraph.
2.	Press:	**Insert** key to move footnote number 2 which had been deleted to scrap to this position.

Note: *The system automatically renumbers the footnotes.*

FORMATTING THE FOOTNOTE NUMBERS

1. Move: the **highlight** to footnote number 1.
2. Press: **Alt =** or **Alt +** to format in superscript.
3. Repeat: for the remaining footnote numbers.
4. Press: **Ctrl F10** to save the edited document.
5. Press: **Ctrl F9** to go to Print preView to see how the footnotes will be printed on the page.
6. Choose: **Print** and press **Enter** to print the document.
7. Choose: **Exit** to return to the document.

To insert new page marks between each paragraph:

Insert new page marks, so you can see how the footnotes will be printed when you choose to print them at the end of the document.

8. Move: the **highlight** to the line below paragraph 1.
9. Press: **Ctrl Shift Enter** to insert the new page mark.
10. Repeat: steps 8 and 9 for paragraph 2.
11. Save the edited document.

PRINTING FOOTNOTES AT THE END OF THE DOCUMENT

Footnotes are printed at the bottom of the page corresponding to the footnote number. However, if you wish to print the footnotes at the <u>end</u> of the division or document, follow the instructions listed below.

1. Press: **Esc.**
2. Choose: **Format, Division, Layout.**
3. Type: **E** or press the **space bar** to select "End."
4. Press: **Enter.**
5. Save the edited document.
6. Print the document again to see the change in footnote placement.

Note: *When footnotes are printed at the end of the document, they are not separated by a line as they are when printed on the same page. If you wanted them to be printed on a separate page, insert a new page mark after the last paragraph.*

7. Clear the Screen.

CHAPTER 13

USING ANNOTATIONS

PREVIEW

Annotations are comments added to a document, not necessarily intended to be printed when the final draft is printed. These comments may be reminders to the author, or they may be notes to others who will be viewing and editing the document. This would be particularly useful on a network where several people may be working on the same document.

Annotations are essentially footnotes. The same procedure is used to insert annotations in text as is used for footnotes, except the Format Annotation menu is used instead of the Format Footnote menu. The user has the option of entering the date and the time of the annotation in the Format Annotation menu. The annotations are numbered in the same order as footnotes; for example, if you have two footnotes, then an annotation, and then another footnote, the number for the last footnote will be (4). If you are not going to print the annotations, the annotation reference numbers should be deleted the same way footnote numbers may be deleted. The footnotes would then be automatically renumbered consecutively. Word includes a supplied macro named ANNOT_REMOVE.MAC which can be used to automatically remove the annotations before printing.

ENTERING AN ANNOTATION

1. Retrieve the document named **footnote.**
2. Move: the **highlight** to the paragraph mark at the end of the second paragraph.

To enter an annotation reference mark:

1. Press: **Esc.**
2. Choose: **Format, Annotation.**
3. Type: your initials in the "mark" field.

Note: *Any combination of keystrokes may be used to denote the annotation; however, it is recommended that initials be used if you are working on a network system where several users are going to be entering annotations.*

A maximum of twenty-eight keystrokes may be entered. Word will remember the last entry in the "mark" field and display it as the choice for the next annotation.

4. Move: the **highlight** to the "insert date" field and set it at "Yes." Leave "insert time" set at "No."
5. Press: **Enter**. The **highlight** jumps to the annotation screen area and the annotation number (3), the initials, and the date are displayed between footnotes 2 and 4.

To enter the text for the annotation:

The highlight will be positioned immediately after the date information. Without inserting a space:
1. Type: **Roger, when you read this would you confirm the publication date of <u>Computers in the 80s</u>?**

To return to the document area:

1. Press: **Esc.**
2. Choose: **Jump, Annotation.** The **highlight** returns to the annotation reference number.

To format the annotation reference characters in superscript:

1. Move: the **highlight** to the number in the reference.
2. Select: the number and the initials.
3. Press: **Alt +** or **Alt =** to format the annotation reference characters in superscript.

4. Save the edited document.

PRINTING ANNOTATIONS AT THE BOTTOM OF THE PAGE

1. Press: **Esc.**
2. Choose: **Format, Division, Layout.**
3. Choose: "Same page."
4. Press: **Enter** to return to the document.

5. Print the document so you can see how the annotations will appear.

Note: *Annotations will be printed at the bottom of the corresponding page, unless you choose to specify printing them at the end of the document along with footnotes. They will always be printed where the footnotes are printed--either on the same page or at the end of the document.*

6. Clear the screen.

Note: *Since annotations are actually a different version of footnotes, the annotation reference numbers and characters may be deleted and/or moved, exactly the same way you delete or move footnote reference numbers and text.*

CHAPTER 14

USING BOOKMARKS

PREVIEW

A bookmark is a type of formatting where a block of text may be marked and then used as a placemark for cross-referencing, or to enable you to "jump" quickly to a specified section of text in a long document.

Text formatted as a bookmark is "selected" and then given a name. Nothing appears on the screen to indicate the bookmark; however, the bookmark names are stored along with the first and last character of the "selected" text. A list of the names may be viewed by pressing F1 in the Format bookmarK menu.

In this section, you will retrieve the document used in the previous exercise. Blocks of text will be designated as bookmarks, and page references will be inserted for cross-referencing.

DESIGNATING TEXT AS A BOOKMARK

1. Retrieve the document **footnote.**
2. Add the heading: **Part 1** at the top, left above the first paragraph
3. Repeat: for the remaining two paragraphs, entering the headings "Part 2" and "Part 3."

Your text should look like the text in the box below:

```
Part 1
     The 1980s were marked by a parade of introductions of
packaged integrated software programs of infinite variety.
In addition, the microcomputer phenomenon was accompanied
by a deluge of user-oriented software packages that
brought end users headlong into a first-hand
acquaintanceship with various software programs.1
..............................................................
Part 2
     The 1980s showed that sophisticated software programs
are no longer an application used by a select group of
computer wizards or programmers.2  Business managers to
caterers are finding themselves in contact with or even
actively using integrated software programs and other
sophisticated programs when performing routine, daily
functions.3y1
..............................................................
Part 3
     There are software packages designed for a wide range
of sizes and capacities of systems.  The knowledge needed
for understanding these packages has increased with the
degree of sophistication of the applications.4
```

To select and name text for a bookmark:

1. Move: the **highlight** to the first paragraph (on page 1).

Using Microsoft Word Advanced Functions, Part 7

2. Press: **F9** to "select" the entire paragraph.
3. Press: **Esc.**
4. Choose: **Format, bookmarK** to display the Format Bookmark menu.
5. Type: **software** to name the "selected" text.

Note: Up to thirty-one characters may be used for the bookmark name. The name may not contain spaces or colons. An underscore character may be used, but the name cannot begin with the underscore.

6. Press: **Enter** to return to the document.

To designate a footnote as a bookmark

The footnote number will be selected and named the same way you selected and named the paragraph in the preceding steps.

1. Move: the **highlight** to page 2, footnote number 2.
2. Press: **Esc** and choose **Format, bookmarK.**
3. Type: **user** to name the bookmark.
4. Press: **Enter** to return to the document.

To jump to a bookmark:

1. Press: **Esc.**
2. Choose: **Jump, bookmarK.**
3. Press: **F1** to display the list of bookmark names.
4. Move: the **highlight** to "software." (It may already be there.)
5. Press: **Enter** to go immediately to that bookmark.

Note: The entire block of text is highlighted. This would be an easy way to edit text. For example, if you were not sure you wanted this section of text, mark it as a bookmark, then when you are editing and decide to remove it, just "jump" to it, and press Delete.

USING A BOOKMARK FOR CROSS REFERENCING

The glossary entry (page:bookmark name) may be used to insert a page number reference in text. "Select" and mark the text to be referenced, then at the point where you want to refer to that bookmarked text, type `page:bookmark name`, and press **F3** to expand the entry. The reference will appear as displayed above in parenthesis; and when the document is printed, the page number of the marked text will be printed in this position. If the text is edited and the page number of the marked text changes, the page number will change automatically when the document is printed.

To enter the cross-reference:

1. Move: the **highlight** to page 3 (use **Alt F5**, type **3**, and press **Enter**).
2. Move: the **highlight** to the space following the last footnote at the end of the paragraph.
3. Press: the **space bar** twice.

Type the following sentence:
4. Type: **S. R. Chapple examined this need in the book <u>Computers in the '80s</u> as referred to on page.**
5. Press: **space bar** once.

To use the glossary entry for the reference following the word "page":

6.	Type:	**page:software**.
7.	Press:	**F3** to expand the glossary entry. The entry will appear in parenthesis--(page:software). Add a period at the end of the sentence.

Note: *When the document is printed, the appropriate page number will be printed in this position.*

To cross-reference a footnote number:

In this section, you will enter a reference to footnote number 2 which is on page 2.

1.	Press:	the **space bar** twice.
2.	Type:	**For further information see footnote number.**
3.	Press:	the **space bar** once.
4.	Type:	**footnote:user** and press **F3** to expand the entry, placing it in parenthesis.
5.	Type:	a period at the end of the sentence.
6.		Save the edited document.
7.		Print page 3 to see the cross-referencing. (To print only page 3, go to the Print Options menu, set "range" field at "Page," go to the "page numbers" field and type "3," press **Enter** and choose **Printer**.)

REMOVING A BOOKMARK DESIGNATION

In order to quickly remove a bookmark designation, "select" the text, go to the Format bookmarK menu, and rather than entering a name, leave the "name" field blank by pressing **Enter** and **Y** to delete the bookmark.

To jump to the bookmark "software":

1.	Press:	**Esc** and choose **Jump, bookmarK**.
2.	Press:	**F1** to display the list of bookmark names.
3.	Move:	the **highlight** to "software."
4.	Press:	**Enter** to go to the bookmarked text. The block of text will be highlighted.

To remove the bookmark designation from the paragraph on page 1:

1.	Press:	**Esc**.
2.	Choose:	**Format, bookmarK** to display the menu.
3.	Press:	**Enter**. The message "Enter Y to confirm deletion of bookmark(s)" will be displayed at the bottom of the screen.
4.	Press:	**Y** to delete.

To check the list of bookmark names:

5.	Press:	**Esc** and choose **Format, bookmarK**.
6.	Press:	**F1** to display the list. Only the word "user" will be displayed.
7.	Press:	**Esc** to return to the document.
8.		Save the edited document.
9.		Clear the screen.

REINFORCEMENT EXERCISES

FUNCTIONS REVIEWED

Chapter 12:
: Entering footnotes
Revising footnotes
Deleting a footnote
Moving a footnote
Formatting footnotes

Chapter 13:
: Using annotations

Chapter 14:
: Designating text as a bookmark.
Formatting a footnote as a bookmark
Using a bookmark as a cross-reference
Removing a bookmark designation

RECALL QUESTIONS

Answers to the recall questions are on page 164.

1. Name the menu used to enter a footnote in text.

2. Where is the text for the footnote displayed on the screen?

3. How do you return to the document from the footnote area?

4. List the steps to be followed in moving a footnote.

5. Where are the two positions where footnote text may be printed?

6. What menu is used to set the position where footnotes will be printed?

7. Define an annotation.

8. Name the menu used to format a block of text as a bookmark.

9. What menu is used to move the highlight to a section of text which has been formatted as a bookmark?

10. How do you write the cross-reference to the page where a bookmark is located?

DOCUMENT 11: FOOTNOTES

1. Type the document as it is displayed on the following page.

2. Enter the footnotes as shown in the document with the corresponding text for each.

3. Save the document. Give it a name of your choice.

4. Add an annotation following the footnote number in the first paragraph. Use your initials as the reference, and add the date. Type: Suggest that the last paragraph in the text be moved to the beginning of the document.

5. Format the first paragraph which begins "Vigorous writing. . ." as a bookmark. Name it "Strunk."

6. Insert page end marks to place each paragraph on a separate page.

7. Go to the fourth paragraph and insert the following cross reference at the end of the paragraph, in front of the footnote number: "As William Strunk discusses on page (page:strunk), every word in a sentence is important."

8. Delete the footnote number at the end of the paragraph beginning "An outline should be used. . ." Remove the page end mark separating that paragraph from the following paragraph.

9. Edit footnote no. 3. Type the text for what was originally footnote no. 2, except type "p. 12" at the end.

10. Format footnote numbers in superscript.

11. Save the edited document and print it.

12. Move the last paragraph to the beginning of the document.

13. Change the footnote text for what is now footnote number 2, to read "Ibid. p. 23."

14. Remove the annotation.

15. Save the edits and print the document.

WRITING TIPS FROM PROFESSIONALS

Vigorous writing is concise. A sentence should contain no unnecessary words, a paragraph no unnecessary sentences, for the same reason that a drawing should have no unnecessary lines and a machine no unnecessary parts. This requires not that the writer make all his sentences short, or that he avoid all detail and treat his subjects only in outline, but that every word tell.[1]

An outline should be used when planning and developing a manuscript to help ensure that all the points are covered. But the outline is often abandoned as the manuscript nears completion. Then, an arrangement may suggest itself that is better for the reader. In short, outline and final format frequently are not the same.[2]

The advantage of the conventional outline is that it provides a visible, systematic master plan that can be followed from the start. The disadvantage is that its rigid appearance may discourage the writer from making changes.[3]

Why study grammar? Unless you know the rules and terminology of grammar, you may be unable to identify faults or embarrassing mistakes in your writing. A knowledge of grammar may not prevent these errors, but it will at least help you keep close watch over your sentences.[4]

Endnotes are growing in popularity because (1) they are easier to type and (2) they leave the text pages looking less cluttered and less complicated. They do present one drawback, however: the reader does not know in each instance whether the endnote will contain a comment of substance (which is typically worth reading) or simply a bibliographic reference (which is usually of interest only in special cases).[5]

Writing is, for most, laborious and slow. The mind travels faster than the pen; consequently, writing becomes a question of learning to make occasional wing shots, bringing down the bird of thought as it flashes by.[6]

---

[1] William Strunk, Jr. and E. B. White, <u>The Elements of Style, Third Edition</u>, New York, MacMillan Publishing Co., Inc. 1979, p. 23.

[2] William C. Paxson, <u>The Business Writing Handbook</u>, New York, Bantam Books, 1984, p. 11.

[3] Ibid., p. 12.

[4] Edward A. Dornan and Charles W. Dawe, <u>The Brief English Handbook</u>, Boston, Little, Brown and Company, 1984, p. 2.

[5] William A. Sabin, <u>The Gregg Reference Manual</u>, New York, Gregg Division/McGraw-Hill Book Company, 1985, p. 333.

[6] William Strunk Jr. and E. B. White, <u>The Elements of Style, Third Edition</u>, New York, MacMillan Publishing Co., Inc. 1979, p. 69.

ANSWERS TO RECALL QUESTIONS

1. Format Footnote.

2. At the end of the document between two end marks.

3. Esc, Jump Footnote.

4.
   a. Move the highlight to the footnote number to be moved.
   b. Press Delete key to delete it to scrap.
   c. Move the highlight to the new position.
   d. Press Insert key to insert the footnote number and text from scrap.

5. Same page and end of text.

6. Format Division Layout.

7. An annotation is essentially the same as a footnote; however, is it used primarily to enter comments directed to the user or to other persons who might be working on the document. Frequently, a person's initials are used for the reference characters, and the date and time may also be set to be included in the annotation reference. Annotations are part of the footnote numbering system. If the annotations are removed before printing, the footnote numbers change automatically.

8. Format, bookmarK menu.

9. Jump, bookmarK, and press F1 to see a list of bookmark names.

10. Type page:bookmark_name, press F3 to expand the entry. It looks similar to this: (page:bookmark_name).

PART 8

CHAPTER 15   USING STYLE SHEETS   166

    Changing the NORMAL.STY Style Sheet 167
    Creating a Style Sheet   168
    Using a Style Sheet   172
    Creating a Style Sheet to Use with an Outline   174
    Printing the Style Sheet   176
    Attaching the Style Sheet   176
    Revising the Formatting of a Style   178
    Creating a Style by Example   178

REINFORCEMENT EXERCISES   180

CHAPTER 15

USING STYLE SHEETS

PREVIEW

One of Microsoft Word's most powerful features is the style sheet. It was a new concept in word processing when Word introduced it, and has proven to be a very effective tool for formatting text in a consistent manner.

A style sheet is a file containing several styles; a style is a collection of several formatting commands and may be applied, using the assigned key code, to a character, a paragraph, or a division. For example, one style may contain formatting commands for Helvetica 14 point, uppercase, centered paragraph, plus a "keep follow" command. This style could be used for a title of a chapter. All of these formatting commands, included within one style, may be applied automatically to text by pressing the Alt key plus the key code. The key code consists usually of two alphabet keys that have been assigned to the style and are used to apply the style to text. You do not necessarily have to use two keys for the key code--one key may be used; however it is recommended that two keys be used to avoid confusion or conflict with direct formatting speed keys.

The purpose of a style sheet is to combine all of the styles for a particular document and to save those styles in one file called a style sheet. When creating documents, you generally use several different types of formatting. In a report, for example, you format titles as centered and uppercase, sideheadings would be left aligned and in bold, and footnotes might be formatted in superscript with a different font size. Then when you create that report, attach the style sheet containing the styles appropriate for the document and apply the formatting automatically. This is a very effective way of making your document formatting consistent.

Word automatically attaches a style sheet to your document when you start the program. The filename of that style sheet is NORMAL.STY. (The extension .STY is always used in naming style sheets.) This style sheet includes the default settings for page size, margins, tabs, character formatting, line spacing--all of the character, paragraph, and division formatting commands which are displayed in those specific formatting menus.

In addition to the NORMAL.STY style sheet, Word includes some supplied style sheets for various types of documents. They are:

ACADEMIC.STY for manuscripts and reports used in the classroom.
APPEALS.STY is a style sheet used in legal offices.
FULL.STY is used to create letters using full-block style.
OUTLINE.STY may be used with Word's outline feature.
RESUME.STY contains styles appropriate for resumes.
SAMPLE.STY contains styles for numbered lists, titles , subheads, running heads, and side-by-side paragraphs.
SEMI.STY is used to create letters in semi-block style.
SIDEBY.STY contains five styles for creating side-by-side paragraphs.

The Gallery menu is used to load style sheets, view, edit, or create and add new styles. A style sheet may be attached to a document, either from the Gallery or by using the Format Stylesheet Attach menu.

The exercises in this chapter will show you how to:

* Change the NORMAL.STY style sheet so that every time you start Word you will have margins that fit your own particular style of document

* Create a style sheet.

Using Microsoft Word Advanced Functions, Part 8

* Use a style sheet for document formatting.

* Edit a style.

* Create a style sheet which will be used with the outline feature of Word.

* Create a style by example (record a style).

CHANGING THE NORMAL.STY STYLE SHEET

The NORMAL.STY style sheet consists of the default settings that come with the Word program.

Some of those defaults are:

Character formatting with courier 10 pitch, lowercase.
All lines of paragraphs left aligned and single spaced.
Tabs set every .5".
Top and bottom margins 1" each.
Left and right margins 1.25" each.
Paper size 8.5 by 11 inches.
Running heads .5" from the top/bottom margin.

Preset formats may be changed so that every time you start a word processing session, your normal style sheet automatically applies the new formatting to your text. The Gallery Insert menu is used to create new styles in a style sheet. In this exercise, you will change the top margin from 1" to 1.5".

To go to the Gallery Insert menu:
1. Press: **Esc.**
2. Choose: **Gallery** to go to the area where the styles in a style sheet are displayed.

Note: If this is the first time the NORMAL.STY is changed, the screen will be blank. The filename is displayed in the lower right side of the window.

3. Choose: **Insert** to display the menu.

Note: You do not need to press Esc to go to the Gallery menu.

An example of the Gallery Insert menu is shown below.

```
INSERT key code: [▓]              usage:(Character)Paragraph Division
        variant: 1                      remark:
Enter one or two letter key code for style
```

Note: The fields and the responses available are listed on page 169.

4. Move: the **highlight** to "usage" field and press **D** or the **space bar** to choose "Division" since changing margins is division formatting.
5. Move: the **highlight** to "variant" field and press **F1** to display a list of variants.

Note: *A variant is a preset style which may be included in a style sheet and may be formatted the same way text is formatted in a document.*

(The word "standard" is highlighted.)

6.   Press: **Enter** to display the various formatting commands included in a standard division style.

To change the top margin:

1.   Choose: **Format, Margin**.

"top" is already highlighted.

2.   Type: **1.5** to change the top margin.
3.   Press: **Enter** to make the change in the style.

Note: *In the second line of the style, Top margin now display 1.5".*

<u>To return to the typing area:</u>

4.   Choose: **Exit**.

To delete a style:

Remove the style just entered.

<u>To delete the change to the normal style sheet:</u>

1.   Press: **Esc.**
2.   Choose: **Gallery**.
3.   Move: the **highlight** to the new style just created. It is probably already highlighted.
4.   Choose: **Delete** and **Exit**.

Note: *When you "Quit" Microsoft Word at the end of the session, you will be prompted to save the Style Sheet. Be sure to respond with "yes" to save the edited style sheet.*

CREATING A STYLE SHEET

In this exercise you will be creating a new style sheet different from the NORMAL.STY. After creating the style sheet, you will then attach it to a document, replacing the default style sheet, NORMAL.STY.

A style sheet consisting of four styles will be created:

* A style for division formatting will change the margins.

* A style for paragraph formatting will be used for titles and will include centering, uppercase, and bold.

* A style for paragraph formatting will be used for "note text" and will include characters in italic, hanging indent, and right justified margin.

* A style for character formatting will format footnote numbers in superscript.

Your style sheet will resemble the example below.

```
1   DM  Division Standard                    MARGINS,TOP,L/R
        Page break. Page length 11"; width 8.5". Page # format Arabic. Top
        margin 1.5"; bottom 1"; left 1"; right 1". Top running head at
        0.5". Bottom running head at 0.5". Footnotes on same page.
2   T   Paragraph 1                          TITLE,CTR,BOLD,UPPERCASE
        Courier (modern a) 12 Bold Uppercase. Centered.
3   NT  Paragraph 2                          NOTE TEXT,ITALIC,HANG.IND
        Courier (modern a) 12 Italic. Justified, Left indent 0.5" (first
        line indent -0.5").
4   FR  Character Footnote reference         FOOTNOTE,SUPERSCRIPT
        Courier (modern a) 12 Superscript.
◊
```

To go to the Gallery Insert menu:

1. Press: **Esc.**
2. Choose: **Gallery** which will display "NORMAL.STY."

Note: *If your normal style sheet contains styles, delete them. You won't be losing them, for the new styles will be saved with a different style sheet name, and the deleted styles will remain in the NORMAL.STY style sheet.*

3. Choose: **Insert** to display the style menu.

The following are the fields in the style menu and explanations of the responses.

Field	Response
Key code:	type one or two characters representing the style. (For example: **DM** for division margins.) This key code is used with the **Alt** key to apply the style to a character, paragraph or division in your document.
Usage:	choose the type of formatting to be used--character, paragraph, or division.
Variant:	press F1 to display a list of names and numbers of styles which may automatically be included in the style sheet, or type a number or name to be selected.
Remarks:	type a short descriptive term identifying the style.

To create a style for the division formatting:

The highlight is in the "key code" field.

1. Type: **DM** to specify the key code for Division Margins.

Note: *You may specify any keys you wish for the key code; however, it is helpful if you choose keys that relate to the type of style being used.*

2. Move: the **highlight** to the "usage" field.
3. Press: **D** or the **space bar** to choose "Division."
4. Move: the **highlight** to the "remark" field.
5. Type: **MARGINS, TOP, L/R.**

Note: *Type the remarks in uppercase to make it easier to read them in the style sheet.*

6. Move: the **highlight** to the "variant" field.

7.	Press:	**F1** to display the list of variants.
8.	Move:	the **highlight** to **Standard**. (It should be there.)
9.	Press:	**Enter** to display the preset formatting for the "Standard Division."

Note: *You will now format the style the same way you would format text in a document.*

10.	Choose:	**Format**.
11.	Press:	**M** (Margins).

<u>In the Margins menu, set fields as follows:</u>

12.	Top margin at 1.5".
13.	Left margin at 1".
14.	Right margin at 1".
15.	Press: **Enter** to return to the style sheet screen. Notice the new margins displayed in the style.

To create a style for a title:

1.	Move:	the **highlight** to the page end mark.
2.	Choose:	**Insert** to display the style sheet menu.
3.	Type:	**T** to specify the key code for the Title, Centered.

Note: *The style will be edited later to change the key code to include two characters.*

4.	Move:	the **highlight** to the "usage" field and choose "Paragraph."
5.	Move:	the **highlight** to the "remark" field.
6.	Type:	**TITLE, CTR, BOLD, UPPERCASE**.
7.	Move:	the **highlight** to the "variant" field.
8.	Press:	**F1** to display the list of variants.

Note: *The list of variants is different for each type of usage--Character, Paragraph, or Division.*

9.	Move:	the **highlight** to "1" (located in the fourth column, fifth line).

Note: *Number 1 is selected because this is the first paragraph style to be created; however any number may be selected providing it hasn't been used previously in the same style sheet.*

10.	Press:	**Enter** to display the style.

<u>To format the style for a title:</u>

11.	Choose:	**Format Paragraph**.
12.	Set "alignment" at "Centered" and press **Enter**.	
13.	Choose:	**Format, Character**.
14.	Set "bold" at "Yes," and "uppercase" at "Yes."	
15.	Press:	**Enter**.

While you are still in the Gallery menu:
16. Follow steps 1 through 14 on the previous page to create the "Note Text" style, but make the following changes:

> At "key code," type **NT** for "Note text."
> At "usage," choose "Paragraph."
> At "remark," type **NOTE TEXT, ITALIC, HANG.IND.**
> At "variant," choose **2**. (You do not need to go to the variant list--the number **2** is already displayed in the menu--just press **Enter** to display the formatting.)
>
> Choose **Format Character** to use the character formatting menu to set "italic" at "Yes" and press **Enter**.
> Choose **Format Paragraph** to use the paragraph formatting menu to set "alignment" at "Justified"; set "left indent" at .5" and "first line" at -.5" to format for a hanging indent, press **Enter**.

To create a style to format a footnote in superscript:

1. Move: the **highlight** to the end mark and choose **Insert**.
2. Type: **FR** to specify the key code for the "footnote reference."
3. Move: the **highlight** to the "usage" field and choose "Character."
4. Move: the **highlight** to "remarks."
5. Type: **FOOTNOTE, SUPERSCRIPT.**
6. Move: the **highlight** to the "variant" field and press **F1**.
7. Move: the **highlight** to "Footnote ref (FN)" and press **Enter**.

Note: *By choosing "Footnote ref (FN)" as the variant, when this style sheet is attached to a document, every footnote in that document will be formatted automatically with the characteristics of this style. You will not need to use the key code to apply the style.*

8. Press: **F** to display the Character formatting menu. This is the only option for character formatting.
9. Set "position" field at "Superscript" and press **Enter.**

10. Compare your completed style sheet with the example in the box at the beginning of this exercise. If you need to edit any of the styles, follow the instructions below.

To edit a style:

To change formatting:
1. Move: the **highlight** to the style.
2. Choose: **Format** and choose the menu (character, paragraph, or division) which contains the fields where you want to make changes.
3. Make the formatting changes the same way you did above, and press **Enter** to return to the Gallery screen.

To change "key code," "variant," or "remarks":

In this section change the key code for Title to TC.

4. Move: the **highlight** to style #2.
5. Choose: **Name.**

6.	Move:	the **highlight** to "key code." It is probably already there.
7.	Type:	**TC**.
8.	Press:	**Enter** to return to the Gallery screen.

Note: Choose "Name" in the Gallery menu:
    To change the keys used in the "key code" field.
    To change the terms used in the "remark" field.
    To choose a different variant.

To name and save the style sheet:

1. Choose: **Transfer, Save.**

Note: *The filename NORMAL.STY is displayed.*

2. Type: **report.sty.** (Use the extension ".sty" to specify a style sheet.)

Note: *Choose a name corresponding to the type of document with which the style sheet will be used so it may be easily identified.*

3. Press: **Enter.**

Note: *The style sheet will be saved in your default directory.*

4. Choose: **Exit** to return to the document screen.

USING A STYLE SHEET

In this exercise you will be using the style sheet just created to format the text shown below. Since the style sheet is still displayed on the Gallery screen, it is automatically attached to the document you are going to create. Instructions for attaching a style sheet are on page 176.

FORMATTING A REPORT

Formatting text with a style sheet is referred to as "indirect formatting."[1]

Note: This practice exercise demonstrates how the various styles are created and how the formatting commands contained in a style are applied to text.

---

[1] Peter Rinearson, <u>Word Processing Power With Microsoft Word</u>, Microsoft Press, Redmond, WA, 1986, p. 278.

To show the style bar:

It is recommended that the style bar be displayed in order to see the styles applied to the various sections of text. The key code corresponding to each style will be displayed at the left margin. If your screen does not show these codes, the following instructions may be used to display the style bar.

1. Press: **Esc.**

Using Microsoft Word Advanced Functions, Part 8

2. Choose: **Options**, and set "show style bar" at "Yes."
3. Press: **Enter** to return to the document screen.

To apply the division formatting:

1. Press: **Alt DM.** (A division mark [::::] will be displayed.)
2. Move: the **highlight** to the division mark, (it may already be there) and press **Enter** to insert a blank line.
3. Move: the **highlight** above the division mark to begin typing.

To apply the formatting for the title:

1. Press: **Alt TC.** (Notice the highlight moves to the center of the screen and a "TC" is displayed at the left side of the screen.)
2. Type: **FORMATTING A REPORT.** You do not need to use the **Caps lock** key. Uppercase was selected in the style.
3. Press: **Enter** three times.
4. Press: **Alt XP** to return to normal paragraph formatting. An asterisk will be displayed in the style bar to the left.

Note: *Alt XP will return the formatting to normal paragraph formatting. The X must be pressed, rather than just Alt P, since a style sheet is attached.*

Note: *When the formatting for paragraph text has not been changed from the normal formatting, an asterisk is displayed when the speed formatting keys are pressed.*

5. Type: the first paragraph in the box on the preceding page, "Formatting text with a style sheet is. . ." Do not type the footnote number.

To enter the footnote number:

1. Press: **Esc.**
2. Choose: **Format, Footnote.**
3. Press: **Enter** to enter the number and to go to the footnote screen.

Note: *If you have a color monitor, your footnote number will reflect the change in formatting by appearing in a different color. Because the footnote reference was chosen in the variant menu when the style was created, the formatting characteristics in that style are automatically applied to all footnotes in this text without using a key code.*

4. Type: the footnote text. Do not type the footnote number. Press **Alt XU** to underline and **Alt X space bar** to end underlining.
5. Press: **Esc.**
6. Choose: **Jump, Footnote** to return to the text.
7. Move: the **highlight** to the right of the footnote number and press **Enter** twice.

To apply formatting for "Note" text:

1. Press: **Alt NT.**
2. Type: the text for the note and press **Enter.**
3. Press: **Alt XP** to return to normal paragraph formatting.

4. Save the document. Name it **frmrpt**.
5. Print the document.
6. Clear the screen. Notice when you clear the screen, you are prompted to save the style sheet. Press Y to save the style sheet.

CREATING A STYLE SHEET TO USE WITH AN OUTLINE

In the following exercise, you will create a style sheet using "heading level" paragraph variants that correspond to levels in outline mode. In addition to using the style sheet in this section for the text on page 177, you will also use it in chapter 16 on outlining. When the style sheet is attached to the document created in outline mode, the text in the various outline levels will be formatted automatically corresponding to the heading level style in the style sheet.

An example of the style sheet you will be creating is shown below.

```
    (key
    code) (usage) (variant)                          (remark)

1   SP    Paragraph Standard                   STANDARD PARAGRAPH
          Courier (modern a) 12. Flush left.

2   L1    Paragraph Heading level 1    HEADING CENTER UPPERCASE
          Courier (modern a) 12. Uppercase. Centered, space
          after 1 li (keep with following paragraph).

3   L2    Para. Heading level 2      HEADING FL.L.BLD UPPERCASE
          Courier (modern a) 12 Bold Uppercase. Flush left,
          space before 1 li (keep with following paragraph).

4   L3    Paragraph Heading level 3     HEADING FL.L.UNDERLINE
          Courier (modern a) 12 Underlined. Flush left, space
          before 1 li (keep with following paragraph).

5   HI    Paragraph 1                          HANGING INDENT
          Courier (modern a) 12. Flush left, Left indent
          1.5" (first line indent -1.5").
```

<u>To go to the Gallery:</u>
1. Press: **Esc.**
2. Choose: **Gallery**.

Note: NORMAL.STY will be displayed in the lower right corner of the screen, or if you have just finished the preceding exercise, REPORT.STY will be displayed. If there are styles showing, they should be deleted so that new styles may be created. Refer to page 168 if you need help in deleting styles.

To create a style for STANDARD PARAGRAPH:

1. Choose: **Insert** to display the style menu.

At "key code":
2.	Type:	**SP.**
3.	Move:	the **highlight** to "usage" field and choose "Paragraph."
4.	Move:	the **highlight** to "remarks" field.
5.	Type:	**STANDARD PARAGRAPH.**
6.	Move:	the **highlight** to "variant" field.
7.	Press:	**F1** to display the variants--"Standard" will be highlighted.
8.	Press:	**Enter** to choose the "Standard" variant.

The preset formatting commands for the standard (or normal) paragraph will be displayed on the screen.

<u>To choose a different font:</u>
9.	Choose:	**Format Character.**
10.	Move:	the **highlight** to the "font name" field and press **F1** to display the list of available fonts.
11.	Move:	the **highlight** to a new font. (The selection depends upon the printer which you are using.)
12.	Press:	**Enter** to choose the font and to return to the Gallery screen.

Note: *The font change <u>must</u> be made in "Paragraph" usage, rather than "Character" usage. Character usage would apply to only one character, rather than to all characters in the document.*

To create a style for HEADING CENTER UPPERCASE:

1.	Press:	**down arrow** to move the **highlight** to the end mark.
2.	Choose:	**Insert** to display the menu.

<u>In "key code" field:</u>
3.	Type:	**L1.**

<u>In "usage" field:</u>
4.	Choose:	Paragraph.

<u>In "remarks" field:</u>
5.	Type:	**HEADING CENTER UPPERCASE.**

<u>In "variant" field:</u>
6.	Press:	**F1.**
7.	Move:	the **highlight** to "Heading level 1" (the column at the far right).
8.	Press:	**Enter** to display a preset style.

Note: *Because a "heading level" variant is used for the style, whenever this style sheet is attached to a document which is written using the outline feature, the heading levels will be automatically formatted with the characteristics in the style. The concept is the same as the "Footnote ref (FN)" in the preceding exercise, except this is "Paragraph" usage, and the footnote reference was "Character" usage.*

<u>To format the style for HEADING CENTER UPPERCASE:</u>
(The style must be highlighted.)
9.	Choose:	**Format, Character.**
10.	Set:	"uppercase" field at "Yes" and **Enter.**

11.	Choose:	**Format, Paragraph.**
12.	Set:	"alignment" field at "Centered".
13.	Set:	"space after" field at 1.

Note: Step 13 will ensure that there is always one blank line following a centered heading.

14.	Set:	"keep follow" at "Yes" to avoid a page break immediately following a centered heading.
15.	Press:	**Enter.**

16. Create and format styles for the remaining styles, 3 through 5, shown on page 174.

   a. Move the **highlight** to the endmark and choose **Insert.**
   b. Fill in the "key code," "usage," "remarks," and "variant" fields to correspond to the information shown in the box on page 174.
   c. Format each style with the various characteristics applied to it, as displayed on page 174. You will have to use both the Format Character and the Format Paragraph menus.
   d. For the "HANGING INDENT" style, leave the "variant field" set at "1."

Note: When you go to the paragraph variant menu, notice how the various heading levels are marked as they have been used. This prevents them from being used a second time.

To save the style sheet:

1.	Choose:	**Transfer, Save.**
2.	Type:	**heading**. The extension **.sty** will be added automatically.
3.	Press:	**Enter** to save.

PRINTING THE STYLE SHEET

1.	Choose:	**Print.**

Note: It is convenient to have a copy of the style sheet when working with a document. Make a note of the name of the style sheet on the hard copy.

<u>After printing, exit to the document:</u>
2.	Choose:	**Exit.**

ATTACHING THE STYLE SHEET

1.	Press:	**Esc.**
2.	Choose:	**Format, Stylesheet, Attach.**
3.	Press:	**F1** to display the list of available style sheets.
4.	Move:	the **highlight** to the style sheet named HEADING.STY.
5.	Press:	**Enter** to attach.

Note: The Gallery, Transfer, Load menu may also be used to load a style sheet on the Gallery screen. When Exit is chosen, a message will be displayed "Press Y to attach, N to keep old one, or Esc to cancel."

Note: In either menu (Format, Stylesheet, Attach or Gallery, Transfer, Load) you may press F1 to display a list of the style sheets in your default directory. If you have style sheets in the directory which is the level above the current directory, move the highlight to (..) and press **Enter**; or you may go to Drive A, B, or C from this menu--depending upon the type of system you are using. If you choose "C:," you will go to the "C:\Word5" directory.

To use the styles in a document

The text is shown below.

```
L1                        USING STYLE SHEETS
L2      TERMS TO KNOW

L3      Style Sheets
SP      A style sheet is a file which contains a group of
        styles.  It is attached to a document, and formatting
        commands which are included in the styles may be
        applied to characters, paragraphs, or divisions by
        using the Alt key and a couple key strokes.

L3      Styles
SP      A style contains a group of formatting commands.

L3      The "Insert" menu terms:
HI      1.   Key Code: one or two characters which will
                       represent the style,
                       for  example:  SP for standard
                       paragraph.

HI      2.   Usage:    determines which type of formatting is
                       to be used--character, paragraph, or
                       division.
```

1. In the "Options" menu set "show non-printing symbols" field at "partial" so that the paragraph marks will be displayed, if this is not already set.

2. Set "show style bar" at "Yes" in the Options menu.

<u>To use the style, HEADING CENTER UPPERCASE (heading level 1)</u>
3. Press: **Alt L1** (to begin using the style with the key code "1").
4. Type: **using style sheets** (you do not have to type with Caps lock on since the style carries with it the uppercase formatting command) and press **Enter**.

Note: You do not need to press Alt XP to return to normal paragraph formatting. When you use the next key code the formatting will change.

<u>To use the style, HEADING BOLD UPPERCASE.</u>
5. Press: **Alt L2**.
6. Type: **terms to know** and press **Enter**.

<u>To use the style, HEADING FL.L UNDERLINE:</u>
7. Press: **Alt L3** and press **Enter** to insert extra line.
8. Type: **Style Sheet** and press **Enter**.

9. Use the two remaining styles "SP" and "HI" in the same way--press the key code with the Alt key to begin using the style. Type the text in the box on page 177 using the appropriate styles as indicated. <u>Do not</u> type L1, L2, L3, SP, or HI which are at the left. Those are the characters in the style bar representing the key codes.

REVISING THE FORMATTING OF A STYLE

In this section, add underlining to Style #3--Paragraph Heading level 2--Key Code L2.
1. Press: **Esc.**
2. Choose: **Gallery.**
3. Move: the **highlight** up to style 3--"Paragraph Heading Level 2."
4. Choose: **Format Character.**
5. Move: the **highlight** to "underline" field and set at "Yes."
6. Press: **Enter** to make the changes to the style.
7. Choose: **Exit** to return to the document.

Note: *If the change isn't apparent on the screen, move the highlight to the heading "Items to Know," then go to the Format Character menu, and see if the "underline" field is set at "Yes."*
If you had a multi-page document, think of how efficient this procedure would be. All of the headings at this level in the entire document would be changed automatically.

8. Save the document. Name it **styles.**
9. Print the document.

CREATING A STYLE BY EXAMPLE

In this exercise, you will learn how to create a style by recording the formatting of a paragraph which you have just typed. The paragraph will be indented from both margins and typed in italic.
    The speed key Alt F10 will display the menu quickly, or you may choose Format, Stylesheet, Record to get to the menu.

To format the text:

1. Move: the **highlight** to the end of the document.
2. Press: **Alt Q** to indent one tab stop from both left and right margins. (This is a new speed formatting key in Word 5.)
3. Press: **Alt I** to begin italic.
4. Type: the text shown below. (Assume it is a quote and would be formatted this way.)

> *This text is formatted in italic and indented .5" from both left and right margins. The formatting is going to be recorded and added to a style sheet.*

To record the style:

1. Move: the **highlight** into the paragraph.
2. Press: **F9** or **F10** to "select" the paragraph.
3. Press: **Esc.**
4. Choose: **Format, Stylesheet, Record** or **Alt F10** (the speed key) to display the menu.

At "Key code":
5.   Type: **QI** (for Quote Italic).

Note: *Paragraph usage is automatically chosen because a paragraph was "selected."*

At "Remark":
6.   Type: **QUOTE ITALIC**.

At "Variant":
7.   Press: **Enter** to choose the number displayed and create a style.

Note: *The number displayed in the variant field is the next available number in the list of variants.*

To see the new style in the style sheet:
8.   Press: **Esc** and choose **Gallery.** You now have six styles in the style sheet.
9.   Choose: **Exit** to return to the document.

10.   Save the edited document and print it.

11.   Clear the screen--you will be prompted to save the changes to the style sheet. Press Y to save. If you didn't save the changes to the style sheet in the Gallery menu, then you must save them in the Transfer, Clear menu when clearing the screen.

REINFORCEMENT EXERCISES

FUNCTIONS REVIEWED

Chapter 15:
    Changing the normality style sheet
    Creating a style sheet
    Editing a style
    Using a style sheet
    Creating a style by example

RECALL QUESTIONS

Answers to recall questions are on page 183.

1. Name the menu used to view the style sheet.

2. Define a style.

3. Name the menu used to create a style.

4. List the three types of usages in the Gallery Insert menu.

5. Name the type of usage you would choose, if you wanted to change the font name for an entire document.

6. List the steps in changing the formatting of a style.

7. List the steps in attaching a style sheet to a document.

8. How do you print a style sheet?

9. What happens to text when you change a style in the style sheet attached to the document?

10. List the steps in creating a style by example.

DOCUMENT 12: STYLE SHEET

Frequently you have to input documents for KTech that summarize the outstanding features of KTech services and products. When you type these documents, some paragraphs are itemized with an asterisk in front of each line and others are indented. A sample product sheet is shown in the box below.

PRODUCT SUMMARY SHEET

Product Name: Word Processing Advanced Manual

Functions Reviewed:

* *Creating Form Documents*
* *Designing Tables*
* *Performing Computations*
* *Creating Style Sheets*
* *Creating Macros*
* *Multi-page documentation with Footnotes*
* *Indexes and Tables of Content*

<u>Details</u>:

Main Documents: Form documents are used in a Print Merge function. With a main document, one original can be merged with names in a data file so that literally hundreds of persons can receive an original copy of the same letter without the need to retype hundreds of individual documents.

Creating tables: You can create tables which includes rows of text or figures. The numbers or text in a column may be sorted numerically or alphabetically by "selecting" the column and using the Library Autosort menu.

Math Calculations: Math calculations can be done on columns, rows, or just individual sets of numbers in text. "Select" the numbers and press F2 to calculate. The result is then inserted from scrap.

---

1. Create styles for each of the formats shown in the document above. They are:

    a. A title centered, bold, in uppercase.
    b. A side heading (for "Product Name" and for "Functions Reviewed") in lowercase, bold, aligned at the left margin.
    c. An indented paragraph formatted in italic for the list of items following "Functions Reviewed."
    d. A style for word "<u>Details</u>."
    e. A hanging indent of 1.5" for the "<u>Details</u>" paragraphs.

2. Save the styles, giving the file a name of your choice.
3. Print the style sheet.
4. Type the document displayed in the box using the style sheet.
5. Save the document. Name it **product1**.
6. Print the document.
7. Create a second document using the same style sheet and enter the following information.

> Product Name: Spreadsheet Beginning Manual
>
> Functions Reviewed:
>
> > * Spreadsheet Rows, Columns, and Cells
> > * Review of Menus
> > * Entering Values
> > * Editing Values
> > * Printing the Spreadsheet
>
> Details:
>
> Spreadsheet design: An introduction to the basic design of spreadsheets. Understanding the intersection of a column--the cell. Moving through the spreadsheet and jumping from cell to cell.
>
> Review of Menus: Understanding the logic of spreadsheet menus. The difference between ranges, global settings, worksheet settings, and main and submenus. Understanding terminology so that proceeding through the menus makes sense.
>
> Entering Values: How to enter values, change values, and edit values. The difference between values and labels is discussed.
>
> Editing Values: How to edit values by deleting them, changing them with the F2 key, copying them to other cells and more.
>
> Print the spreadsheet: Deciding how much of the spreadsheet to print. Following the logical pathway to printing the spreadsheet: selecting ranges, setting margins, deciding paper width and character size. The final step to completing a basic spreadsheet.

8. Save the document. Name it **product2**.
9. Print a copy of the document.

ANSWERS TO RECALL QUESTIONS

1. Gallery.

2. A style is a collection or group of formatting commands which may be applied to "selected" text automatically by pressing the Ctrl key and the key code.

3. Gallery Insert menu.

4. Character.
   Paragraph.
   Division.

5. Paragraph usage

6. a. Go to the Gallery menu.
   b. "Select" the style to be formatted.
   c. Choose Format and the desired submenu--character, paragraph, or division depending upon the usage of the style.
   d. Set the fields in the submenu for the responses which will change the formatting of the style.
   e. Press Enter to return to the style sheet screen.
   f. When you Quit the word processing session, press Y at the prompt to save the changes to the style sheet.

7. a. Press Esc and choose Format Stylesheet Attach.
   b. Press F1 to display the list of style sheets, or type the filename of the style sheet.
   c. Press Enter.

8. a. Press Esc and choose Gallery.
   b. Choose Print to print the style sheet which is displayed on the screen.

9. The text formatted with that style takes on the new characteristics with which the style has been formatted.

10. a. Format the text with the characteristics to be saved as a style.
    b. "Select" the text.
    c. Press Alt F10 to go to Record Style or go to the Format Stylesheet Record menu.
    d. Type a key code, select the appropriate usage, type remarks, and type a number for the variant or press F1 to select from a list of variants.
    e. Press Enter to save in the current stylesheet.

PART 9

CHAPTER 16   OUTLINING   186

    Typing Text in Outline View   187
    Numbering an Outline   189
    Adding Text to an Outline   189
    Collapsing and Expanding Outline Subheadings and Text   191
    Using Organize Outline   192
    Printing an Outline Without the Text   193
    Attaching a Style Sheet   193

CHAPTER 17   CREATING AN INDEX   194

    Designating Text for the Index   194
    Compiling an Index   197
    Editing the Index   197
    Using the Supplied Macro "Index_entry.mac" to
        Designate Text for an Index Entry   198

CHAPTER 18   CREATING A TABLE OF CONTENTS   200

    Designating Text for the Table of Contents   200
    Compiling the Table of Contents   203
    Adding Page Numbering to the Document   204

REINFORCEMENT EXERCISES   205

CHAPTER 16
OUTLINING

PREVIEW

The outline feature of Word is unique because it not only provides the user with a way to list ideas and automatically assign them to various levels--which is what most word processing outline features will do; but it also allows the user to write the corresponding text under each of the heading levels.

Because paragraph text can be included in the outline, the program provides a feature called "outline view" enabling the user to see the document outline without the text being displayed. Also included in the outline feature is an "organize" function allowing the writer to easily rearrange text by moving, copying, or deleting headings and accompanying text.

Another advantage of using the outline feature, is that a style sheet containing styles for each of the heading levels can be attached to the document, and the various corresponding heading levels in the document will be formatted automatically.

When using the outline feature, keep in mind the two different "views" in which you can work.

* **Outline view**

    Press Shift F2 to go from Document view to Outline view. There are two different modes in "outline view."
    1. Outline Edit
       Outline edit is where you type your various headings and where the corresponding level numbers are displayed. You also may type the text for each level in this mode. In order to easily view the portions of the document, you may "collapse" certain sections so that subheadings and text are not displayed. The section may then be "expanded" when you want to view or edit it.

    2. Outline Organize
       Press Shift F5 to go to outline organize mode. This mode allows you to view only the headings and to move, copy, delete or sort them. You cannot edit text in this mode; however when a heading is moved, all of the accompanying subheadings and text under that heading are also moved. This feature allows you to easily rearrange large portions of text in a document while viewing essentially the entire document, represented by the main headings, in one screen.

* **Document view**

    Press Shift F2 to switch between Outline view and Document view. Document view is the mode you use to enter text in any document; however, you may enter text in either Document view or Outline view.

In this chapter, exercises will include the following:
* Create an outline in Outline view.
* Enter text under each of the heading levels in Document view.
* Use Outline view to expand and collapse headings and corresponding text.
* Use Outline Organize to rearrange sections of text under main headings.
* Attach the style sheet created in the previous chapter to format the text in the various outline levels.

The following screen images show examples of text in Document view and in Outline view.

Outline view

```
╔═[········1·········2·········3·········4·········5·········]·········7····╗
║T                      EMPLOYEE PERSONNEL POLICIES¶
║T                                    ¶
║T                                    ¶
║t    I. Purpose¶
║t   II. Applicability¶
║t  III. Objectives¶
║t        A. Provide for administration¶
║t              1. Corporation¶
║t              2. Employee¶
║t        B. Reference¶
║t              1. Policies¶
║t              2. Procedures¶
║t   IV. Responsibility¶
║t        A. Administrator¶
║t        B. Employee ¶
║     ♦
║
║
║
║
║                                                                ═OUTLINE.DOC═
║ Level 1      {¶                                                 Microsoft Word
```

Document view

```
╔═[········1·········2·········3·········4·········5·········]·········7····╗
║                       EMPLOYEE PERSONNEL POLICIES¶
║                                     ¶
║                                     ¶
║    I. Purpose¶
║ The primary purpose of our personnel Policies is to
║ establish a basis for impartial personnel Administration.¶
║   II. Applicability¶
║ We are an equal employment organization and our personnel
║ policies and procedures shall apply equally to all
║ personnel.¶
║  III. Objectives¶
║ The primary objectives of our personnel policies and
║ procedures are to:¶
║ A. Provide for administration¶
║ Administration of the personnel policies shall be based upon
║ impartiality for:¶
║ 1. Corporation¶
║ 2. Employee¶
║ B. Reference¶
║ We will provide a ready reference for the following:¶
║ 1. Policies¶
║ Established policies which assures providing quality care to
║                                                                ═OUTLINE.DOC═
║ Pg1 Li4 Co2     {¶                                              Microsoft Word
```

TYPING TEXT IN OUTLINE VIEW

The outline for the document is shown on page 188. After typing the outline, text will be entered under each of the headings as shown on page 190.

<u>If the style bar is not displayed:</u>
1.   Go to the Options menu, set "show style bar" at "Yes," and press **Enter**.

To type the title:

1.   Type the title, centered and in all caps.
2.   After typing the title, press **Enter** three times.
3.   Turn off Caps lock.
4.   Press **Alt P** to return to normal paragraph.

```
              EMPLOYEE PERSONNEL POLICIES

Purpose
Applicability
Objectives
     Provide for Administration
          Corporation
          Employee
     Reference
          Policies
          Procedures
Responsibility
     Administrator
     Employee
```

To type the outline:

1.	Press:	**Shift F2** to change to Outline view. T's are displayed in the style bar at the left margin to indicate "Text" level, and "Text" is displayed in the status line at the bottom of the screen.
2.	Press:	**Alt 9** to change from Text level to level 1. An asterisk will be displayed in the style bar, and "Level 1" will be displayed in the status line.

Note: *In Outline mode, you will press Alt 0 to indent one level and Alt 9 to go back one level.*

3.	Type:	the first entry **Purpose**.
4.	Press:	**Enter**.

Note: *The outline level is repeated when Enter is pressed.*

5.	Type:	**Applicability** and **Objectives**.

To go to Level 2:

6.	Press:	**Alt 0** to move the highlight to the next lower outline level. The new level number will be displayed in the status line.
7.	Type:	**Provide for Administration** and press **Enter**.

To go to Level 3:

8.	Press:	**Alt 0** again to move to level 3.
9.	Type:	**Corporation** and press **Enter**.
10.	Type:	**Employee** and press **Enter**.

To return to Level 2:

11.	Press:	**Alt 9** to move back one outline level.
12.	Type:	**Reference** and press **Enter**.
13.	Type the remainder of the outline. Press **Alt 0** and **Alt 9** to move to appropriate levels.

14. Save the document. Name it **outline.**

Note: *You may save a document in Outline view as well as in Document view.*

Using Microsoft Word Advanced Functions, Part 9   189

NUMBERING AN OUTLINE

You must be in Outline view in order to add numbering to the outline levels. The numbering will be in roman numerals; however, as noted below, you may change to legal style numbering.

To add numbering to outline levels:

1.	Move:	the **highlight** to any position in the outline.
2.	Press:	**Esc.**
3.	Choose:	**Library, Number.**

In the Library Number menu:
4.	Move:	the **highlight** to "Update." (It should already be there.)
5.	Move:	the **highlight** to "restart sequence" field.
6.	Press:	**Y** or the **space bar** to set "Yes."
7.	Press:	**Enter** to number the outline entries.

Note: *You may use legal numbers (For example: 1, 1.1, 1.2, 2, 2.1, 2.2) instead of roman numerals when numbering items in the outline. To do this (not in this exercise):*
   a.   Type a `1.` *at the first heading in the outline.*
   b.   "Select" the number and the period.
   c.   Choose Library Number Update.
   d.   Go to "restart sequence" field and set "Yes."
   e.   Press **Enter** *to number the outline levels.*

To remove the numbering:

1.	Move:	the **highlight** to the first entry "Purpose." Notice, the **highlight** had moved to the top of the document.
2.	Press:	**Esc.**
3.	Choose:	**Library, Number.**
4.	Press:	**R** or the **space bar** to choose Remove.
5.	Press:	**Enter.**
6.		Add the paragraph numbers again to the outline.

Note: *As the highlight is moved down through the text, the level numbers are displayed at the bottom of the screen.*

ADDING TEXT TO AN OUTLINE

Text is in the box on page 190.

You may type text in either the Document view or in the Outline view; however text is usually added in Document view.

1.	Press:	**Shift F2** to move from outline to document view. The outline indents are not displayed in this mode.
2.	Move:	the **highlight** to the paragraph mark following "Purpose."
3.	Press:	**Enter** to go to the next line.
4.	Press:	**Alt P** to return the format to standard paragraph rather than the outline level number. An SP appears in the style bar.

5. Type: the text for "Purpose." <u>Do not</u> press **Enter** at the ends of the paragraphs. Spacing between levels will be entered automatically when the style sheet is attached. The spacing is displayed in this text to make typing the document easier.

6. Repeat steps 2 through 5 for the rest of the document.

```
                    EMPLOYEE PERSONNEL POLICIES

I.   Purpose
The primary purpose of our Personnel Policies is to
establish a basis for impartial personnel administration.

II.  Applicability
We are an equal employment organization and our personnel
policies and procedures shall apply equally to all
personnel.

III. Objectives
The primary objectives of our personnel policies and
procedures are to:

A.   Provide for Administration
Administration of the personnel policies shall be based
upon impartiality for:

1.   Corporation
2.   Employee

B.   Reference
We will provide a ready reference for the following:

1.   Policies
Established policies which assures providing quality care
to our residents and patients.

2.   Procedures
Procedures which will insure that our policies are carried
out without interruption.

IV.  Responsibility

A.   Administrator
It shall be the responsibility of the administrator,
through a duly appointed designee to inform all personnel
of our policies and procedures.

B.   Employee
It shall be the responsibility of the employee to become
familiar with the contents of the personnel policy.
```

---

7. Save the edited document.

COLLAPSING AND EXPANDING OUTLINE SUBHEADINGS AND TEXT

It is easier to work with an outline if some text and subheadings are collapsed. You must be in Outline view to do this. The **highlight** must always be at any position in the heading level <u>above</u> text or subheadings that are to be collapsed or expanded.

To collapse text directly below a heading, press Shift Keypad minus:

1. Press: **Shift F2** to go to Outline view. The status line will display the various level numbers. Look at this to confirm you are in Outline view.
2. Move: the **highlight** to the heading "Purpose."
3. Press: **Shift Keypad minus**.

Note: *A "t" appears to the left to indicate there is collapsed text entered at this level.*

4. Repeat for "Applicability."

To collapse all subheadings and text under a heading, press the Keypad minus:

1. Move: the **highlight** to "Objectives."
2. Press: the **Keypad minus**.

Note: *A + sign is displayed at the left margin to indicate both heading and text have been collapsed.*

3. Repeat for "Responsibility." At this point, only the level 1 headings are displayed.

Note: *If some of the subheadings and text do not "collapse," look for extra paragraph marks separating them from the headings, and delete those marks.*

To expand text below a heading, press Shift Keypad plus:

1. Move: the **highlight** to the first heading "Purpose."
2. Press: **Shift Keypad plus**.
3. Repeat for "Applicability."

To expand all heading levels (not text) below a heading, press Keypad asterisk:

1. Move: the **highlight** to the heading "Objectives."
2. Press: **Keypad asterisk ***. This procedure does not expand text.

Note: *If you wish to <u>expand just one level below a heading</u>, press the <u>Keypad plus</u> sign. A plus sign displayed in the style bar will indicate headings having subheadings below them.*

To expand all headings and all body text:

1. Press: **Shift F10** to "select" the entire document.
2. Press: **Keypad asterisk** to expand all headings
3. Press: **Shift Keypad plus** to expand all text. This moves you to "Organize" view--the mode is displayed in the status line.
4. Press: **Shift F5** to return to outline view.

Note: *Always check the status line to confirm the mode in which you are working.*

To collapse all subheadings and text:

1. Move: the **highlight** any point within the outline.
2. Press: **Shift F10** to "select" the entire document.
3. Press: **Keypad minus** to collapse all subheadings and text, and to move to Organize mode.

USING ORGANIZE OUTLINE

Look at the status line to confirm that you are in Organize mode--the word **ORGANIZE** will be displayed. If you are not in the correct mode, press Shift F5 to go to Organize mode.

To move a heading:

To move the section "Responsibility" between "Applicability" and "Objectives":
1. Move: the **highlight** to "Responsibility."

Note: *The entire heading will be highlighted in Outline Organize mode.*

2. Press: **delete** to move the section into scrap.
3. Move: the **highlight** to "Objectives."
4. Press: **Insert** key to move the section.

Note: *All subheadings and text in "Responsibility" section will be moved. If there were several pages of text under one heading, this would be a very efficient way of moving that text.*

To copy a heading:

1. Move: the **highlight** to "Applicability."
2. Press: **Alt F3** to copy text into scrap.
3. Move: the **highlight** to the end of the document.
4. Press: **Insert** key to copy from scrap.

To delete a heading:

1. Move: the **highlight** up to the first "Applicability" section.
2. Press: **Delete** or **Shift delete.**

The "Applicability" section is now located only at the end of the document, and as you will notice, the numbering is incorrect.

To renumber the levels:

You may remain in Organize mode. Numbers may be added or updated in either Outline Organize or Outline Edit mode.

1. Press: **Esc.**
2. Choose: **Library Number.** "Update" is highlighted.
3. Press: **Enter** to renumber.

Practice expanding and collapsing subheadings and text.

Using Microsoft Word Advanced Functions, Part 9   193

PRINTING AN OUTLINE WITHOUT THE TEXT

1. Press: **Shift F2** to move to outline view. (You may already be there--check the status line to confirm.)

2. Collapse all text to show just the headings and subheadings. Your screen should look like the outline on page 188.

3. Press: **Esc.**
4. Choose: **Print, Printer** to print the displayed outline.

ATTACHING A STYLE SHEET

<u>To attach the style sheet "Heading.sty" created in the previous exercise.</u>
1. Press: **Shift F2** to go to document view.
2. Press: **Esc.**
3. Choose: **Format, Stylesheet, Attach.**
4. Press: **F1** to display the list of available style sheets.
5. Move: the **highlight** to **Heading.sty** and press **Enter**.

Note: *All outline levels are reformatted to correspond to the style sheet. Notice that there are no blank lines above the level 1 headings--each main heading will be positioned at the beginning of a new page when new page marks are inserted in the following section.*

After printing the outline, enter hard page ends before each level 1 heading to prepare the document to be used in the "Index" and "Table of Contents" chapters. Follow the instructions below to remove the library numbers and to enter the new page marks.

To remove the library numbers:

1. Press: **Shift F2** to return to Outline view.
2. Press: **Esc** and choose **Library, Numbers, Remove**.

Note: *The numbers could also be removed in Document view.*

To enter new page marks before each level 1 heading:

1. Move: the **highlight** to the "P" in "PURPOSE." (The title will be on the first page by itself.)
2. Press: **Shift Ctrl Enter** to enter a new page mark.
3. Repeat for "RESPONSIBILITY," "OBJECTIVE," and "APPLICABILITY."
4. Press: **Shift F2** to return to Document view and check the page numbers in the status line.

To add page numbers to the document:

With the **highlight** at any position in the document:
1. Go to Format, Division, Page-number menu and set page numbers at "Yes."
2. Save the edited document.
3 Print the final document.
4. Clear the screen.

CHAPTER 17

CREATING AN INDEX

PREVIEW

Indexing can be a tedious process; however, Microsoft Word provides the user with help by including a program in which words or terms that you want to list in the index may be marked in the text. The Library Index menu is then used to "compile" (copy) the words with corresponding page numbers to an index at the end of the document.

Even with the help of the index program, creating an index requires some planning before marking the text. Determine the text to be included in the index and whether it is to be a main entry or a subentry. It is a good idea to first mark index items with a colored pen, in a rough draft, to use as a guide when you designate entries for the index in a final document.

Word also includes a macro in its file of supplied macros, that will mark "selected" text for index entries. You will learn how to use the macro in this chapter, as well as how to mark your own index entries.

The steps in creating an index are:

*   Designate (mark) the text for the index. This mark, .i., must be formatted as hidden text so that it won't be printed with the document.

*   Compile the index using the Library Index menu.

*   Edit and format the index to appear the way you want it. Perhaps, add a title, or format for two columns.

DESIGNATING TEXT FOR THE INDEX

The steps for designating text are:

*   Set "show hidden text" field in the Options menu at "Yes." This will enable you to see the marks you are entering; however, this field must be set at "No" before the index is compiled. If the marks are displayed, it will affect repagination.

*   Press **Alt E** to begin hidden text formatting: or press **Alt XE** to begin hidden text formatting if a style sheet is attached to the document.

*   Type **.i.** (formatted as hidden text) to designate the text for the index.

The designated text must be followed by a paragraph mark, a division mark or a semicolon formatted as hidden text to indicate the end of the text to be designated.

To designate text to be a main entry in the index:

1.   Retrieve the document named **outline** created in chapter 17.

To display hidden text:
2.   Press: **Esc.**
3.   Choose: **Options**, set "show hidden text" field at "Yes," and press **Enter**.

To format as hidden text:
4. Move: the **highlight** to the **P** in **PURPOSE** on page 2.
5. Press: **Alt XE** to begin hidden text format. A style sheet is attached; therefore, enter an **X** when using direct formatting.

To designate text:
6. Type: **.i.** to designate the text for a main entry.

Note: *The text to be designated must end with a paragraph mark. If it doesn't have the paragraph mark, enter a semicolon formatted as hidden text following the designated text.*

To use the F4 key to repeat the index designation:
7. Move: the **highlight** to the R in RESPONSIBILITY.
8. Press: **F4** to repeat the edit.
9. Repeat: for OBJECTIVE, APPLICABILITY, and for the other text to be designated as a main entry--all on page 4 of your document, and listed below.

        Provide for Administration
        Corporation
        Employee
        Reference
        Policies
        Procedures

To designate text for an index subentry:

Up to five levels of subentries may be used in the index. Each subentry is indented one level from the previous entry.

1. Move: the **highlight** to the **A** in **ADMINISTRATOR** on page 3.
2. Press: **Alt XE** to begin hidden text format.
3. Type: **.i.RESPONSIBILITY:.**
4. Repeat: for **EMPLOYEE** on the same page. Use **F4** to repeat the edit.

To use a ";" to end designated text:

A semi-colon (;) will have to be used to mark the end of the text, "**personnel policies**," on pages 2 and 5 since there is no paragraph mark following it.

1. Move: the **highlight** to **p** in **personnel** on page 2.
2. Press: **Alt XE** to begin hidden formatting and type **.i.** [period (.) i period (.)].
3. Move: the **highlight** to space following **policies**.
4. Press: **Alt XE** to begin hidden formatting.
5. Type: ; to indicate an end to the index entry.
6. Repeat: for **personnel policies** on page 5.

Your text should resemble the text in the box below.

```
                    EMPLOYEE PERSONNEL POLICIES
..............................................................
                           .i.PURPOSE

The primary purpose of our .i.personnel policies; is to
establish a basis for impartial personnel administration.
..............................................................
                         .i.RESPONSIBILITY

.i.RESPONSIBILITY:ADMINISTRATOR
It shall be the responsibility of the administrator,
through a duly appointed designee to inform all personnel
of our policies and procedures.

.i.RESPONSIBILITY:EMPLOYEE
It shall be the responsibility of the employee to become
familiar with the contents of the personnel policy.
..............................................................
                          .i.OBJECTIVES

The primary objectives of our personnel policies and
procedures are to:

.i.PROVIDE FOR ADMINISTRATION
Administration of the personnel policies shall be based
upon impartiality for:
.i.Corporation
.i.Employee

.i.REFERENCE
We will provide a ready reference for the following:
.i.Policies
Established policies which assures providing quality care
to our residents and patients.
.i.Procedures
Procedures which will insure that our policies are carried
out without interruption.
..............................................................
                         .i.APPLICABILITY

We are an equal employment organization and our
.i.personnel policies; and procedures shall apply to all
personnel.
```

COMPILING AN INDEX:

To set "show hidden text" at "No":
1. Press: **Esc,** choose **Options**, and set "show hidden text" at "No."

Reminder: If hidden text is displayed on the screen, it will affect the repagination of the document.

2. Press: **Esc.**
3. Choose: **Library, Index.**
4. Set: "cap main entries" at "No." (The first letter will be capitalized.)
5. Press: **Enter** to compile and display the index at the end of the document.

Note: The fields in the Library Index menu may be changed. The default for displaying the numbers in the index is to separate the entry and the numbers with two spaces. You may change that to a comma or some other character. The default for the subentry indent is 0.2", and that, of course, could also be changed.

The index displayed at the end of the document should resemble the text in the box below. You will notice that the index is on a new page--6--and is also in a new division. Check the status line to see the division number.

EDITING THE INDEX

To add the title "Index" at the top of the page:

1. Move: the **highlight** to the "A" in "**Applicability**."
2. Press: **Enter** three times.
3. Move: the **highlight** up to the first paragraph mark. Do not leave the highlight on the hidden text code.

Note: If your highlight is on the hidden text code, you will not be able to format and type the title.

4. Type: the title, centered and in all caps.

```
                          INDEX


Applicability   5
Corporation   4
Employee   4
Objectives   4
Personnel policies   2, 5
Policies   4
Procedures   4
Provide for administration   4
Purpose   2
Reference   4
Responsibility   3
   Administrator   3
   Employee   3
```

5. Display the hidden text again to see the "Begin Index" and "End Index" codes on the Index page. If the index were compiled again, all of the text within these codes would be replaced with a new index--including the title, since it is positioned within the codes.

To prevent the title from being deleted if the index were compiled a second time:

1. Move: the **highlight** to the "Begin Index" code and "select" it.
2. Delete the code and insert it in front of "Applicability."
3. Save the edited document

When editing the index, you may want to format it in two columns. Also, the formatting for the various index levels may be included in a style sheet. There are variants in paragraph usage which may be formatted and used with your index the same way you used heading levels to format headings in the **outline** document.

USING THE SUPPLIED MACRO "INDEX_ENTRY.MAC" TO DESIGNATE TEXT FOR AN INDEX ENTRY

Word's supplied macro file includes a macro which may be used to designate text for the index, and it will be used in this exercise to designate three additional words. The index will then be compiled again, to demonstrate how the index will be replaced.

The new words to be marked are:
    designee on page 3
    residents on page 4
    patients on page 4

1. Set "show hidden text" at "Yes."

To "select" the index entry:

1. Move: the **highlight** to the word "designee" on page 3. Use **Alt F5** to go quickly to page 3.
2. Press: **F8** to "select" the word

To use the macro to designate the text for the entry:

1. Press: **Ctrl IE** to run the macro.

Note: *The macro adds the marks formatted as hidden text, the same way you marked text in the previous exercises in this chapter. The entry must be "selected" so the beginning and end marks will be entered in the correct positions.*

2. Repeat: for "residents" and "patients" on page 4.

To compile the index a second time:

1. Set: "show hidden text" field at "No."
2. Press: **Esc** and choose **Library, Index**.
3. Press: **Enter** to display the message, "Index already exists. Enter Y to replace or Esc to cancel."
4. Press: **Y** to replace.

Your old index has been replaced with the new index shown below and now contains the three additional words.

```
Applicability  5
Corporation  4
Designee  3
Employee  4
Objectives  4
Patients  4
Personnel policies  2, 5
Policies  4
Procedures  4
Provide for administration  4
Purpose  2
Reference  4
Residents  4
Responsibility  3
   Administrator  3
   Employee  3
```

5. Save the document.
6. Print it.
7. Clear the screen.

CHAPTER 18

CREATING A TABLE OF CONTENTS

PREVIEW

The table of contents feature is similar to the index program. Text will be designated to appear in a table of contents; then, using the Library, Table menu, the program will automatically copy (compile) this designated text to a table of contents area at the end of the document, and display it with the corresponding page numbers. As with the index, the text in the table of contents may require some editing and formatting in order for it to appear the way you want it.

If you plan to have both an index and a table of contents in your document, compile the index first, in order to include the page number of the index in the table of contents.

DESIGNATING TEXT FOR THE TABLE OF CONTENTS

The steps for designating text for the Table of Contents are similar to those involved in designating text for the Index.

* Set "show hidden text" field in Window Options at "Yes."
* Press **Alt E** or **Alt XE** to begin hidden text format.
* Type **.c.** to designate for the Table of Contents.

To designate text for the main headings:

1. Retrieve the document named **outline**.

<u>To display hidden text:</u>
2. Press: **Esc,** choose **Options**, and set "show hidden text" field at "Yes."

<u>To format for hidden text:</u>
3. Move: the **highlight** to the first heading (the P in PURPOSE). Do not include the **.i.** It would be copied into the table of contents if it were part of the designated entry.
4. Press: **Alt XE** to begin "hidden text" formatting.

<u>To mark the text:</u>
5. Type: **.c.** to designate the text for the table of contents.

Note: *The text must be followed by a paragraph mark. If there is not a paragraph mark at the end, insert a semicolon, formatted as hidden text, at the end of the text to be included in the table of contents.*

6. Repeat: for each of the remaining headings--RESPONSIBILITY, OBJECTIVES, APPLICABILITY, and INDEX. Use **F4** key to repeat entering **.c.**

To designate text for the subheadings:

Designate the subheadings under "RESPONSIBILITY" and indicate that they should be indented one level.

1. Move: the **highlight** to **A** in "**ADMINISTRATOR**" on page 3. Use the **Alt F5** key to go quickly to page 3.
2. Press: **Alt XE** to turn on "hidden text" format.
3. Type: **.c.:** (one colon indicates a one-level indent).

Note: *Typing a colon (:) after the .c. designates the level. To indicate level three, type "::".*

4. Repeat: for "**EMPLOYEE**," indicating level 2 (use F4 to repeat).

5. Also designate the following for level 2 (.c.:) in the "Objectives" section on page 4.

        PROVIDE FOR ADMINISTRATION
        REFERENCE

6. Designate the following for level 3 (.c.::)

        <u>Corporation</u>--on page 4
        <u>Employee</u>   "
        <u>Policies</u>   "
        <u>Procedures</u> "

Note: *Up to five levels may be designated for the index.*

The designated text should resemble the text in the box below.

```
                   EMPLOYEE PERSONNEL POLICIES
..........................................................
                         .i..c.PURPOSE

The primary purpose of our .i.personnel policies; is to
establish a basis for impartial personnel administration.
..........................................................
                      .i..c.RESPONSIBILITY

.i.RESPONSIBILITY:.c.:ADMINISTRATOR
It shall be the responsibility of the administrator,
through a duly appointed designee to inform all personnel
of our policies and procedures.

.i.RESPONSIBILITY:.c.:EMPLOYEE
It shall be the responsibility of the employee to become
familiar with the contents of the personnel policy.
..........................................................
                        .i..c.OBJECTIVES

The primary objectives of our personnel policies and
procedures are to:

.i..c.:PROVIDE FOR ADMINISTRATION
Administration of the personnel policies shall be based
upon impartiality for:
.i..c.::Corporation
.i..c.::Employee

.i..c.:REFERENCE
We will provide a ready reference for the following:
.i..c::Policies
Established policies which assures providing quality care
to our residents and patients.
.i..c.::Procedures
Procedures which will insure that our policies are carried
out without interruption.
..........................................................
                       .i..c.APPLICABILITY

We are an equal employment organization and our
.i.personnel policies; and procedures shall apply to all
personnel.
```

COMPILING THE TABLE OF CONTENTS:

To set "show hidden text" at "No":
1. Press: **Esc** and choose **Options**.
2. Move: the **highlight** to "show hidden text" field, set it at "No," and press **Enter**.

Reminder: *If hidden text is displayed, it will affect the repagination of the document.*

3. Press: **Esc**.
4. Choose: **Library, Table**.

In the "from" field:
5. Move: the **highlight** to "Codes."
6. Press: **Enter** to compile. When finished, the system will display the text for the table of contents at the end of the document on a new page and in a new division.

The table of contents will resemble the text in the box below.

```
Purpose                                         2
Responsibility                                  3
     Administrator                              3
     Employee                                   3
Objectives                                      4
     Provide for administration                 4
          Corporation                           4
          Employee                              4
     Reference                                  4
          Policies                              4
          Procedures                            4
Applicability                                   5
INDEX                                           6
```

7. Add a title, TABLE OF CONTENTS, at the top of the page.

Other options in the Library Table menu:

The Library Table menu is shown in the screen print below.

```
LIBRARY TABLE from: Outline Codes      index code: C
          page numbers:(Yes)No         entry/page number separated by: ^t
          indent each level: 0.4"      use style sheet: Yes(No)
Select option
P8 D4 L1 C1         {¶}                                  Microsoft Word
```

Outline

The "Outline" option allows the user to compile the table of contents from the text displayed in the Outline view screen, rather than from "designated" text in the document. If you have used outline view to create your document, this would be a very easy way to compile the table of contents, as it would eliminate the need to mark your text.

index code
> The code used to denote the table of contents entry is "C." If you wish to mark text for other kinds of tables, enter a new letter in this field. Then mark the text for that table, using this letter formatted as hidden text. For example, if you wished to list all "figures" displayed in a document, you might use the letter "f" the same way you used .c. to designate text for the table of contents. Then when you compiled the list, all figures marked with the .f. would be listed with corresponding page numbers at the end of the document. You may not use the letters i, l, d, or g, in this field. Those letters are reserved for other Word 5 features.

page number (Yes)No
> If you do not want page numbers to be displayed with the entry in the table of contents, set this field at "No."

entry/page number separated by: ^t
> This option means that the entry is separated from the page number by a Tab. This could be change to a comma, for example.

indent each level: 0.4"
> If you want the subentries to be indented differently, enter a new measurement in this field.

use style sheet: Yes(No)
> If you are using a style sheet with a "Table" variant formatted for your table of contents, choose "Yes" in this field. Then that formatting will be applied automatically to the entries when they are listed in the table of contents.

ADDING PAGE NUMBERING TO THE DOCUMENT

To add page numbers in both Division 1 and Division 2:

1. Move: the **highlight** to Division 1.
2. Press: **Esc** and choose **Format, Division, Page-numbers**.
3. Set: page numbers at "Yes" and change the position where the page numbers are to be printed.
4. Press: **Enter.**
5. Repeat: for Division 2.

To add page numbers in Division 3 in a different format:

1. Move: the **highlight** to Division 3.
2. Press: **Esc** and choose **Format, Division, Page-numbers**.
3. Press: the **Tab** key to move to "number format" field and choose i.
4. Press: **Enter** to return to the document.
5. Save the edited document.
6. Print the document.
7. Clear the screen.

Note: *Word 5 includes a supplied macro for marking table of contents entries. The macro name is TOC_ENTRY.MAC^<CTRL T>E. It is used the same way the macro for marking index entries is used.*

REINFORCEMENT EXERCISES

FUNCTIONS REVIEWED

Chapter 16:
: Typing in Outline view
Numbering an outline
Collapsing and Expanding subheadings and text in Outline view
Using Organize view

Chapter 17:
: Designating text for the index
Compiling the index
Editing the index
Using the supplied macro "index_entry.mac"

Chapter 18:
: Designating text for the table of contents
Compiling the table of contents

RECALL QUESTIONS

Answers to recall questions are on page 212.

1. How do you move from Document view to Outline view?

2. How do you move from Outline Edit mode to Outline Organize mode?

3. Name the menu used to add outline numbers to text.

4. How do you collapse all subheadings and text in an outline?

5. How do you know that text has been collapsed under a heading or subheading?

6. List the steps in designating text for the index.

7. Name the menu used to compile the index.

8. What are the control codes for running the supplied macro "Index_entry.mac"?

9. How do you designate text for a subheading at the second level in the table of contents?

10. Name the menu used to compile the table of contents.

11. How can the outline be used to compile a table of contents?

12. Where are the index and table of contents displayed in your text?

DOCUMENT 13: OUTLINING

1. Type the document shown on the following page using Outline view; however in order to use Outline Organize in step 4, omit the blank lines as you are entering the text. You will insert them later.

KTech Training Proposal

Introduction
    KTech History
    KTech was founded in 1970. It began as a small company of fewer than 70 employees. KTech has always been a computer training organization. It supplies training services to organizations of all sizes. Services are provided at the site of the customer for convenience and quick access to the unique needs of the individuals within a corporation.
    KTech has grown to a large organization of well over 1000 employees. This is due largely in part to the demand for the personalized service it offers its customers.
    KTech is located in Kirkland Washington, a growing suburb of Seattle.

    Training Seminars
    Training Seminars are conducted usually at the site of the customer. Seminars can range in length from a half day to several weeks depending upon the needs of the individual customer. Information on the seminars provided is available from KTech.

    Training Manuals
    Manuals are available for purchase. They are used to conduct the training seminars and are included in the cost of the seminars. Manuals may also be purchased separately.

Documentation
    Documentation accompanies all training seminars and is included as part of the cost. Manuals and diagrams may be purchased separately and are available in the following areas:
    Word Processing
        Beginning
        Intermediate
        Advanced
        Extending the Advanced Capabilities
    Database
        Beginning
        Intermediate
        Advanced
        Programming with Your Database
        Advanced Programming
    Spreadsheet
        Introduction
        Intermediate
        Advanced
        Programming with Your Spreadsheet
        Advanced Programming

```
    MIS Structure
        Systems Analysis
            Dataflow diagrams
        Management structure
        Programming Teams
        Networking and MIS
    Networking
        Coordinating the Efforts of Team Members
        Successful Networking
        Advancements in Networking
    Communications
        Benefits
        Advanced Uses of Communications


Training
    Half and One day Seminars
    These seminars are held only as a quick introduction
to a particular topic in information systems.  They are
not intended as comprehensive instruction in a software
program.  The include the following topics:
                Word Processing Possibilities
                Advancements in Word Processing
                Spreadsheet Potentials
                An Intro to MIS Structure
                An Intro to Networking
                Expanding Your Communications Capabilities
                How to Utilize Programming with Your
                    Database

    One Week Training Seminars
    The one week training seminars are much more extensive
and include a strong introduction or followup in any one
of our topic areas.  Usually only one topic is covered in
a week.

    Two Weeks and Longer
    Training seminars lasting two weeks or longer can
cover two or more topics or may cover one topic very
extensively.  Personnel completing the two week seminars
leave with a very thorough understanding of the topic.


Followup
    KTech provides a followup as part of the cost built in
to all seminars.  The time of the followup depends on the
extent of the training received.  Questions and answer
time is provided and all seminar participants are
encouraged to participate in the followup.
```

2. Save the document. Name it **proposal**.
3. Collapse all text and subheadings, leaving only the main headings displayed.

4. Go to Organize edit mode and move Training so that it precedes Documentation.
5. Return to Outline view.
6. Expand all subheadings.
7. Add numbering to the outline.
8. Print a copy of the outline.
9. Expand all text.
10. Save the document. Name it **proposal**.

To designate text for and compile the index:
1. Designate all level 1 and level 2 headings as main entries for the index.
2. Designate level 3 headings as subentries under their corresponding level 2 headings.
3. Use the macro to mark the index headings, if it is available.
4. At this point, you should insert the blank lines between the headings levels; however, do not add blank lines following the items in part III.
5. Compile the index. Add a title "Index." It should be entered as heading "level 1" in the Outline View.

To compile the table of contents:
1. Go to Outline view and collapse all text and subheadings so that "level 1" and "level 2" headings are displayed.
2. Update the outline numbering to include the index.
3. Use the Library Table menu to compile the table of contents from the outline rather than to designate the entries.
4. Add a title to the table of contents, and add page numbers to the document. Don't forget to add page numbering in the division where the index is displayed.
5. Save the document again and then print it.
6. Clear the screen.

DOCUMENT 14: MORE ON OUTLINING, INDEX, AND TABLE OF CONTENTS

1. Create a style sheet to be used with the document shown on the following page. Enter styles for the title, the side headings, subheadings, standard paragraph, and indented paragraphs. Use at least two different font sizes if they are available to you. Double space the document-- you may add that to the paragraph styles, or use direct formatting.

2. Print a copy of the style sheet.

3. Type the document on the following page, using the style sheet to format the text. You may choose whether or not you want to use Outline view.

```
                    KTECH CORPORATION
                     Employee Handbook


Welcome to KTech

KTech managers and employees extend a warm welcome to all
of you who are joining KTech.  We look forward to
benefitting from your expertise, and know that you will be
an invaluable asset to KTech.
     Please read through this employee manual carefully.
If you have any questions, it may become your source to
finding answers.  Any questions that cannot be solved
through this manual should be given to your department
manager.  He or she will be sure that you are assisted in
any way possible.

  Floor Plan

  Appendix A contains a detailed floor plan of KTech
  headquarters.  The managers hope that you will find
  KTech a pleasant place in which to work.  A garden
  area is located in the center of the complex.  You are
  welcome to enjoy this area during any lunch and break
  times.

  Dining Facilities

  KTech Corporation houses two dining areas:

     The cafeteria:

     The cafeteria is located in the 400 section of
     the building on the east side.  It serves coffee,
     tea, juice, rolls, and pastries in the mornings
     prior to work hours; light snacks mid-morning and
     afternoon; and full course meals in cafeteria
     style during the noon hour.  Prices are extremely
     reasonable, and most KTech employees utilize this
     service for their meals.

     The dining room:

     A formal dining room is located at the center of
     the building north of the garden.  The dining
     room is open to all employees on Fridays and on
     other special company occasions.  On other days,
     the facility is used to hold sales meetings for
     clients; conduct board meetings; and other
     functions requiring reservations.
```

Where to Go for Assistance

Departmental Concerns

With any department concerns, it is strongly advised you consult your immediate supervisor first, the department supervisor second, and only after trying all avenues, the division supervisor. It is the feeling of all KTech management that concerns should be resolved within the department. KTech management supports individual department supervisors and is confident of their capabilities and expertise in handling any concerns.

General Concerns

Concerns not affecting the department and its personnel should be directed to management in writing.

Operating Procedures

Discuss all operating procedure concerns with your department manager. He/She will then refer the concern to upper-level management in written format.

Hours

Operating Hours

Normal Operating hours are 7:30 a.m. to 5:30 p.m. Monday through Friday.

Flex Time

All personnel work a 37.5 hour week. KTech is very open to arranging flexible working schedules with its employees. Some departments are more accommodating to flexible time than others. Sales, for instance, has less flexibility due to the time it needs to contact prospective clients.

Most departments, however, have some designated times they can allow their staff flexible schedules. Talk to your department supervisor for further details on making arrangements for flex time.

Overtime Policy

Overtime is occasionally required. All overtime is compensated at time and a half.

```
Leaves

    Personal

    Personal leave is allowed after one year in service at
    KTech.  A two week notice is needed for extended
    personal leave.  Only one personal leave is allowed
    with pay per year.

    Emergency

    Emergency leave is allowed two times a year.  Short
    notice is the only requirement for emergency leave.

    Maternity

    Maternity leave is given with full pay.  See personnel
    for complete details on the requirements for full
    coverage during maternity leave.

    Other

    Personnel has a separate pamphlet available to all
    employees concerning vacation leave.
```

4. Add page numbers in a header:
   "KTech Corporation Handbook_____Page #"

5. Designate main entries and subheadings for the table of contents, or use Outline View and the "from Outline" option in the Library Table menu if you used Outline View to create the document.

6. Before compiling the table of contents, repaginate and confirm page breaks so that no paragraph is divided and printed on two different pages.

7. Compile the table of contents and edit it, if you think changes need to be made.

8. Save the document. Name it **handbook**.

9. Print the document.

ANSWERS TO RECALL QUESTIONS

1. Press Shift F2.

2. Press Shift F5.

3. Library Number.

4.
    a. Press Shift F10 to "select" the entire document.
    b. Press the grey minus sign to collapse.

5. A "t" is displayed in the left margin in Outline view.

6.
    a. Move the highlight to the beginning of the text to be designated.
    b. Press Alt E or Alt XE to begin hidden text formatting.
    c. Type .i. or .i.(main entry):.
    d. Enter a ";" formatted as hidden text at the end of the block of text to be in the index, if the text doesn't end with a paragraph code or a division mark.

7. Library Index menu.

8. Control IE.

9.
    a. Move the highlight to the beginning of the text to be designated.
    b. Press Alt E or Alt XE to begin formatting as hidden text.
    c. Type .c.: to indicate a second level subheading.
    d. Type a ";" formatted as hidden text at the end of the block of text to be designated, if it doesn't end with a paragraph mark or a division mark.

10. Library Table menu.

11.
    a. Go to Outline view.
    b. Collapse all text and subheadings except the ones which you want to be included in the table of contents.
    c. Use Library Table menu and set "from" field at "Outline."
    d. Press Enter to compile the table of contents, which will include the headings which were displayed in Outline view.

12. At the end of the document.

APPENDIX I

QUICK REFERENCE GUIDE

TO

MICROSOFT WORD BASIC FUNCTIONS

The Quick Reference Guide provides summaries of the various procedures learned in this text. It is arranged in alphabetical order according to functions.

It is intended to further reinforce your learning Microsoft Word. As you use Word, you will find that some functions become so familiar that you never need any help; however, other functions that are used only occasionally, may necessitate using a "Quick Reference" to prompt you with keystrokes and procedures.

BLOCK FUNCTIONS

(Also refer to SELECTING TEXT for instructions for marking blocks of text.)

To move a block of text:

1. Move: the **highlight** to the beginning of the block.
2. Press: **F6** to turn on "Extend selection."

Note: Use any of the other modes of "selecting" text.

F7	= previous word.
F8	= next word.
Shift F7	= previous sentence.
Shift F8	= next sentence.
F9	= previous paragraph.
F10	= next paragraph.
Shift F9	= line.
Shift F10	= whole document.

3. Move: the **highlight** to the end of the block to "select" the text to be deleted.
4. Press: **Delete** to delete the block to "scrap."
5. Move: the **highlight** to the new position where you want to move the text.
6. Press: **Insert** to insert the text from "scrap."

To copy a block of text:

1. Move: the **highlight** to the beginning of the block to be copied.
2. Press: **F6** to turn on "Extend selection."

Note: Use any of the other modes of "selecting" text as listed above.

3. Move: the **highlight** to the end of the block.
4. Press: **Alt F3** to copy the block to "scrap."
5. Move: the **highlight** to the position where the block is to be copied.
6. Press: **Insert** to insert the text from "scrap."

To delete a block of text:

1. Move: the **highlight** to the beginning of the block to be deleted.
2. Press: **F6** to turn on "Extend selection."
3. Move: the **highlight** to the end of the block to be deleted.

Note: Use any of the other modes of "selecting" text as listed at the beginning of this section.

4. Press: **Delete** to delete the block to "scrap."
   or
5. Press: **Shift Delete** to delete the block permanently.

BOLD

Entering text in bold is a type of character formatting.

To add bold formatting to text as you type:

1. Press: **Alt B** (or **Alt XB** if you are using a style sheet).
2. Type: the text to be printed in bold.
3. Press: **Alt space bar** (or **Alt X space bar** if using a style sheet) to end bold.

To add bold formatting to text after it has been typed:

1. "Select" the block of text. (Refer to the section on SELECTING TEXT.)
2. Press: **Alt B** (or **Alt XB** if you are using a style sheet).

CENTERING

Centering a line is paragraph formatting.

To center text as it is typed:

1. Press: **Alt C** (or **Alt XC** if you are using a style sheet).
2. Type: the text to be centered and press **Enter**.
3. Press: **Alt P** (or **Alt XP** if you are using a style sheet) to return to normal paragraph formatting.

To center text after it is typed:

1. "Select" the block of text to be centered.
2. Press: **Alt C** (or **Alt XC** if you are using a style sheet) to center the block.

CHARACTER FORMATTING

Characteristics that are included in character formatting and the speed formatting keys used to apply that formatting are:

Characteristic	Use the speed formatting key:
Bold	= **Alt B**.
Double-underline	= **Alt D**.
Italic	= **Alt I**.
Underline	= **Alt U**.

Strikethrough	= **Alt S**. (A horizontal line will strike through text.)
Uppercase/lowercase	= "select" text and press **Ctrl F4**. The system cycles through three formats--all uppercase, all lowercase, and first letter of each word in uppercase.
Small caps	= **Alt K** (Lowercase letters are formatted in small uppercase type letters.)
Superscript	= **Alt +** or **Alt =**.
Subscript	= **Alt -**.
Font name	= **Alt F8**. (This doesn't apply the formatting, but displays the character formatting menu and highlights the "font name" field. Press F1 to display a list of available fonts.)
Font size	= **Alt F8** to go to the "font name" field, move the right arrow to the "font size" field, press F1 to display the list of available font sizes.
Hidden text	= **Alt E**.
Normal character	= **Alt space bar**.

WAYS TO ADD CHARACTER FORMATTING TO TEXT

1. Enter the formatting command, type the text, and press **Alt space bar** to end the formatting command by returning to normal character formatting.

or

2. After the text has been typed, "select" the block of text and use the appropriate speed key or use the Format Character menu to apply the character formatting commands.

To use the speed formatting keys to apply character formatting commands as text is typed:

1. Press: **Alt** and the **speed formatting key** corresponding to the type of formatting desired (or **Alt X** and the **speed key** if you are using a style sheet).
2. Type: the text.
3. Press: **Alt space bar** (or **Alt X space bar** if you are using a style sheet) to return to normal character formatting.

To use the "Format, Character" menu to apply formatting as text is typed:

1. Press: **Esc.**
2. Choose: **Format, Character** to go to the Format Character menu.
3. Press: the **arrow** keys or the **Tab** key to move the **highlight** to the desired formatting field.
4. Press: the **space bar** to set the field at "Yes."
5. Press: **Enter.**
6. Type: the text.
7. Press: **Alt space bar** (or **Alt X space bar** if you are using a style sheet) to return to normal character formatting.

CHANGING FONT NAMES AND SIZES

To change a font name after text has been typed:

1. "Select" the text to be changed.

2.	Press:	**Alt F8** to go to the "font name" field in the Format Character menu.
3.	Press:	**F1** to display the list of available font names.
4.	Move:	the **highlight** to the desired font name. (The font name will be displayed in the "font name" field.)
5.	Press:	**Enter** to use the selected font.

To change a font size after text has been typed:

1. "Select" the text to be formatted.
2. Press: **Alt F8** to go to the "font name" field.
3. Press: the **right arrow** key or the **Tab** key to move to the "font size" field.
4. Press: **F1** to display the various sizes available.
5. Move: the **highlight** to the desired size to display it in the "font size" field.
6. Press: **Enter** to add the formatting.

To change the font name before typing text:

1. Press: **Alt F8** to go to the "font name" field in the Format Character menu.
2. Press: **F1** to display the list of fonts.
3. Move: the **highlight** to the desired font to display it in the "font name" field.
4. Press: **Enter** to choose the font.
5. Type: the text.
6. Press: **Alt space bar** or **Alt X space bar** to end formatting.

To change the font size before typing text:

1. Press: **Alt F8** to go to the "font name" field.
2. Press: the **right arrow** or the **Tab** key to move to the "font size" field.
3. Press: **F1** to display the list of available font sizes.
4. Move: the **highlight** to the desired font size.
5. Press: **Enter** to begin formatting.
6. Type: the text.

At the end of the text to be formatted:

7. Press: **Alt space bar** (or **Alt X space bar** if a style sheet is being used) to end the formatting.

FORMATTING IN "UPPERCASE"

To add the formatting to text which is already entered:

1. "Select" the text to be formatted.
2. Press: **Ctrl F4** to change to uppercase.

Note: *The system cycles through three formats--all letters in uppercase, all letters in lowercase, and first letter of each word in uppercase.*

To use the Format Character menu to format in uppercase as text is entered:

1. Press: **Esc.**
2. Choose: **Format, Character** to go to the Format Character menu.
3. Press: the **arrow** keys or the **Tab** key to highlight "uppercase" field.

4. Press: **space bar** to set "Yes."
5. Press: **Enter** to begin formatting.
6. Type: text to be formatted.
7. Press: **Alt space bar** (or **Alt X space bar** if you are using a style sheet).

CHOOSE A COMMAND

1. Press: **Esc** key to move the **highlight** into the "Command" menu at the bottom of the screen.
2. Type: the capital letter displayed in the option to be selected. (Usually it is the first letter of the option; however, in some instances it is the second or third letter, so view the menu to determine which letter to type.) The menu pertaining to that option will be displayed. To choose an option in a submenu, follow the same procedure.

or

3. Press: the **arrow** keys or the **Tab** key to move the **highlight** to a selected option.
4. Press: **Enter** to display a submenu.
5. Repeat the steps above to choose an option in the submenu.

To set a response to an "Option field":

Once the **highlight** is in the "field," several responses may be displayed.
1. Press: the capital letter of the response or press the **space bar** to move the **highlight** to the desired response.
2. Press: **Enter** to return to the edit screen. (The option response will have been selected.)

CLEAR THE SCREEN

You must name the document before clearing the screen if the document is to be saved. If it has been named previously, and revisions have been made, these revisions may be saved as part of the procedure to clear the screen.

1. Press: **Esc.**
2. Choose: **Transfer, Clear, All.** (The screen will be cleared unless the document has been changed.)

If the edits have not been saved, a message will be displayed: "Press Y to save, N to lose edits, Esc to cancel."

3. Press: **Y** to save the edits and clear the screen, or **N** if you wish to cancel the edits and not save them.

COPY A BLOCK OF TEXT

Refer to BLOCK FUNCTIONS.

CREATE A DOCUMENT

1. Type: the text using wordwrap. Wordwrap means <u>do not</u> press **Enter** at the ends of paragraph lines. Press **Enter** or **Shift Enter** at the ends of short lines (inside addresses, salutations, etc.), at the ends of paragraphs, or to insert blank lines.
2. Press: **Esc.**

3. Choose: **Transfer, Save** to display the message "Transfer Save Filename:".
4. Type: a filename.

Note: *The filename must consist of one to eight characters and no spaces. If you wish to save the document on a floppy disk in Drive A or B, type A: or B: preceding the filename. If you wish to add an extension, type a period (.) and one to three characters.*

5. Press: **Enter** to save to the disk.

If the Summary Information menu is displayed:
6. Either fill in the fields, or press **Enter** to bypass.

DELETE

The **Delete** key deletes "selected" text into scrap. Pressing **Shift Delete** removes the block of text from the screen permanently, and it can only be restored by pressing the "Undo" key (**Shift F1**) before making any other editing changes.

To delete a character:

1. Move: the **highlight** to the character and press **Delete** key.
   or
2. Move: the **highlight** to the space following the character and press **Backspace** key. The Backspace key will delete text permanently.

To delete a word:

1. Move: the **highlight** to the word and press **F7** or **F8**.

Note: *If the highlight is in front of the word, press F8 to "select" it. If the highlight is following the word, press F7 to "select" it.*

2. Press: **Delete** to delete to "scrap."
   or
3. Press: **Shift Delete** to delete permanently.

To delete a line:

1. Move: the **highlight** to the line and press **Shift F9** to "select" it.
2. Press: **Delete** or **Shift Delete.**

To delete a paragraph:

1. Move: the **highlight** to the paragraph and press **F9** or **F10** to "select" the paragraph.

Note: *If the highlight is in front of the paragraph, press F10 to "select" the following paragraph, or press F9 to "select" the previous paragraph.*

2. Press: **Delete** or **Shift Delete** to delete the paragraph.

To delete a block:

1. "Select" the block of text using one of the "select" procedures.
2. Press: **Delete** or **Shift Delete.**

To delete all of the text in the document:

1. Press: **Shift F10** to "select" the entire document.
2. Press: **Delete** or **Shift Delete**.

DICTIONARY, SUPPLEMENTAL

In addition to the main English dictionary which is used in the spell check, words may be added to one of three supplemental dictionaries.

During a spell check, when the spelling menu stops at a word which isn't found in the dictionary, choose **Add**, and then choose the type of dictionary (**Standard, Document,** or **User**) to which the word will be added.

The **Standard** dictionary is located on the spelling disk or in the Word 5 directory. If you use words frequently that are not in main dictionary, you may add those words to the standard dictionary for use in spelling checks. Words that have been added to the Standard dictionary are listed in a file named UPDAT-AM.CMP. This file may be retrieved and edited in the same way any document file is edited.

The **Document** dictionary is a file attached to a specific document and contains words only in that document. It has the same name as the document file but has an extension .CMP. The dictionary can be created only after a document file has been created.

The **User** dictionary contains words which are used with specific types of documents. This dictionary is meant to contain technical words that are used only with some kinds of document files, but are not used in all your files. It is located in the default directory rather than in the Word 5 directory which contains the program files.

To add words to the Standard dictionary "updat-am.cmp" during a spell check:

1. Load a document to be checked on the screen.
2. Press: **Alt F6** or **Esc** and choose **Library spell.**

At each word to be added to the dictionary:
3. Choose: **Add** option to display the Dictionary menu.
4. Choose: **Standard** to add the word to the Standard dictionary.
5. Repeat for each word to be added to the Standard dictionary.

To retrieve the Standard dictionary if you wish to add or delete words:

1. Press: **Esc.**
2. Choose: **Transfer, Load.**

If you have a hard disk drive:
3. Type: **c:\word5\updat-am.cmp** and press **Enter**.

If you have a dual disk drive:
4. Type: **a:updat-am.cmp** and press **Enter**.
5. Edit the file as you would any document file, save, and clear the screen.

To create a list and add to the dictionary program:

Clear the screen:
1. Type: all the words you wish to add to the dictionary, in any order. (You do not have to press **Enter** between words.)
2. Save the document.
3. Press: **Alt F6** or choose **Library Spell**.

At each word where the spell check stops:
4. Choose: **Add**.

In the Add menu:
5. Choose: **Standard, User,** or **Document**.

To edit or to delete a word from a dictionary:

1. Press: **Esc** and choose **Transfer, Load**.
2. Type: the dictionary name including the .CMP extension. (If you use a hard disk, you may have to look in the directory containing the Word program for the dictionary name.) The dictionary files will not be listed with the rest of the document filenames.

When the file is displayed on screen:
3. Delete any words, or edit them as you would edit any text.
4. Save the file and clear the screen.

DIVISION FORMATTING

When a change in division formatting is made, the system automatically begins a new page unless the Format, Division, Layout menu is accessed and the "division break" field is set at "Continuous."

Division formatting includes the following:

Margins	Top/bottom
	Right/left
	Page length/width
	Gutter margins
	Running-head position
	Mirror margins
Page Numbers	Starting page numbering
	New page number
	Position -- from top, from left
	Format ((1) I i A a)
Layout	Number of columns
	Space between columns
	Division break
	Footnote position
Line numbers	On/off
	Restart
	Position
	Increments

Using Microsoft Word Advanced Functions, Appendix I

To change division formatting:

The **highlight** may be at any position within the division.
1. Press: **Esc.**
2. Choose: **Format, Division.**
3. Move: the **highlight** to the desired option in the Division menu, or type the capital letter corresponding to the desired option.
4. Set the response to the "fields" as desired.
5. Press: **Enter** to return to the document.

Refer to MARGINS, LEFT/RIGHT; MARGINS, TOP/BOTTOM; and PAGE NUMBERS for further information.

DOUBLE SPACING

Line spacing is paragraph formatting.

To double space text as it is typed:

1. Press: **Alt 2** (or **Alt X2** if you are using a style sheet).
2. Type: the text--as many paragraphs as you desire. Each time you press **Enter** the formatting for the paragraph will be repeated.
3. Press: **Enter** after the last paragraph to be double-spaced.
4. Press: **Alt P** (or **Alt XP** if you are using a style sheet) to return to normal paragraph.

To double space text after it has been entered:

1. "Select" the text to be double spaced.
2. Press: **Alt 2** (or **Alt X2** if you are using a style sheet) to double space.

FIRST LINE INDENT

The first line indent command is paragraph formatting.

To indent the first line of every paragraph as it is typed:

1. Press: **Alt F** (or **Alt XF** if you are using a style sheet).

Note: If Alt F is pressed three times, you will indent to the third tab stop.

2. Type: the text and press **Enter**.
3. Press: **Alt P** (or **Alt XP** if you are using a style sheet) to return to normal paragraph formatting.

GLOSSARY

The glossary feature is used to store frequently used text or features. There are seven user-supplied glossary entries:

Date	=	Inserts the current date.
Dateprint	=	Inserts the word (dateprint) in a document and whenever that document is printed, the current date will be inserted.
Time	=	Inserts the current time in the document.

Timeprint	=	Similar to dateprint, except it inserts the word (timeprint) and the current time will be inserted when the document is printed.
Page	=	Inserts the word (page) in text, but prints out the page number. Use this entry to enter a page number in a running-head.
Footnote	=	Inserts a footnote number.
Nextpage	=	Inserts a reference page number for the following page.

To use the user-supplied glossary entries:

1. Move: the **highlight** to the point where the entry is to be used.
2. Type: the name of the entry to be used.
3. Press: **F3** to expand, (enter) the item in the text.

or if you aren't certain of the entry name:
4. Press: **Esc.**
5. Choose: **Insert**--do not press the Insert key.
6. Press: **F1** to display the list of glossary entries.
7. Move: the **highlight** to the entry to be selected.
8. Press: **Enter** to display on the screen.

To create a glossary entry:

1. Type: the text to be included in the entry.
2. "Select" (highlight) the block of text.
3. Press: **Esc.**
4. Choose: **Copy** (do not use the **Alt F3** key to copy) or **Delete.**

The menu "Copy to: {}" or "Delete to: {}" will be displayed.
5. Type: an appropriate short name which will identify the entry.
6. Press: **Enter** to save.

To use the glossary entry:

1. Follow the steps outlined above for using the user-supplied glossary entries.

HANGING INDENT

A hanging indent is a type of paragraph formatting.

A hanging indent aligns the first line of a paragraph at the left margin, but indents the remaining lines of the paragraph at the tab stops.

To format a hanging indent as text is being typed:

1. Press: **Alt T** (or **Alt XT** if a style sheet is being used).
2. Type: the text--type as many paragraphs as desired. The formatting is repeated each time **Enter** is pressed.
3. Press: **Enter** after the last paragraph to be formatted with a hanging indent.
4. Press: **Alt P** (or **Alt XP** if a style sheet is being used) to end the formatting.

To format text after it has been typed:

1. Move: the **highlight** to the beginning of the text to be formatted.
2. "Select" the text.

Using Microsoft Word Advanced Functions, Appendix I

3. Press: **Alt T** (or **Alt XT** if a style sheet is being used).

Note: **Alt M** *will move (reduce) the indent to the previous tab stop.*

HELP MENU

The Help menu may be accessed from any point in the document or from any menu. Depending on your **highlight** position, different information will be displayed on the screen. For example, if you are in the Tab Set menu when you press Alt H, the screen will display information about that menu.

1. Press: **Alt H** to display the menu.

Respond to the menu at the bottom of the screen to:
    N for Next to see the next page of the menu.
    P for Previous to see the previous page of the menu.
    B for Basics, to see information about how to use the Help menu.
    I for Index to see an index of the various Microsoft Word functions.
    T for Tutorial to do some practice exercises.
    R for Resume to return to the edit screen.

HYPHENATION

The hyphenation program is located in the Library menu. Hyphenation allows you to insert hyphens in text which is positioned at the ends of lines. If the hyphenation is to be automatic, choose "No" in the "confirm" field. The system will automatically enter hyphens at the appropriate positions in words. If the "confirm" field is set at "Yes", the system will stop at each hyphenated word, and the user will have to confirm the hyphenation or cancel it.

To hyphenate text without confirming:

1. Move: the **highlight** to the beginning of the text to be hyphenated.
2. "Select" the text if you want to hyphenate a block of text rather than the entire document.
3. Press: **Esc.**
4. Choose: **Library, Hyphenate.**
5. Press: **Enter** to hyphenate without confirming.

To hyphenate text and confirm each hyphenation:

1. "Select" the text to be hyphenated.
2. Press: **Esc.**
3. Choose: **Library, Hyphenate.**
4. Press: **space bar** to set "confirm" field at "Yes."
5. Press: **Enter.**

To respond when the system stops at a word to be hyphenated:
6. Press: **Y** to accept the system hyphenation position.
    or
7. Press: **N** if you do not want to hyphenate the word. It will be automatically wrapped to the following line.
    or
8. Press: the **arrow** keys to move the hyphen to a new position, and press **Y** to confirm the hyphen point.

HYPHENATION, MANUAL

Manual hyphenation refers to the hyphens the user enters as text is being typed. Word 5 has four types of hyphens. The Long hyphen is new in Word 5.

Normal hyphen
1. Press: **- (hyphen key)** to enter a hyphen in a word such as mother-in-law. The normal hyphen will allow the word to break at the end of a line.

Optional hyphen
1. Press: **Ctrl -**.
   The optional hyphen will not be printed and is invisible if the "show non-printing symbols" field is set at "none," unless the word is located at the end of a line. Then the word will be divided at the hyphen point.

Nonbreaking hyphen
1. Press: **Ctrl Shift -**.
   The nonbreaking hyphen will keep the hyphenated word together on one line. For example, use this type of hyphen to keep a hyphenated name (Smith-Brown, for example) together on the same line.

Long hyphen
1. Press: **Ctrl Alt -**.
   The long hyphen is longer than the usual hyphen. Not all printers will be able to print a long hyphen. You should experiment with this before using it extensively.

INDENT FROM LEFT MARGIN

See LEFT INDENT.

INDENT FROM LEFT AND RIGHT MARGINS

Text is indented one tab stop from both margins each time the indent command is entered.

To format with indents from both margins as text is typed:

1. Press: **Alt Q** (or **Alt XQ** if a style sheet is being used).
2. Type: the text and press **Enter** after the last paragraph to be indented.
3. Press: **Alt P** (or **Alt XP** if a style sheet is being used) to end the formatting.

To format text after it has been typed:

1. Move: the **highlight** to the beginning of the text to be formatted.
2. "Select" the text.
3. Press: **Alt Q** (or **Alt XQ** if a style sheet is being used).

Note: **Alt M** *will move (reduce) the indents to the previous tab stop.*

Using Microsoft Word Advanced Functions, Appendix I

ITALIC FORMATTING

Formatting text in italic is character formatting.

To format text in italic as it is typed:

1. Press: **Alt I** (or **Alt XI** if a style sheet is being used).
2. Type: the text to be formatted in italic.
3. Press: **Alt space bar** (or **Alt X space bar** if a style sheet is being used) to end the formatting.

To format text in italic after it has been entered.

1. "Select" the text to be formatted in italic.
2. Press: **Alt I** (or **Alt XI** if a style sheet is being used) to apply the formatting.

JUSTIFIED RIGHT MARGIN

Justified text is a type of paragraph formatting.

To format text as it is typed:

1. Press: **Alt J** (or **Alt XJ** if a style sheet is being used).
2. Type: text to be justified and press **Enter** after the last paragraph to be formatted.
3. Press: **Alt P** (or **Alt XP** if a style sheet is being used) to end the formatting.

To justify text after it has been typed:

1. "Select" the text to be justified.
2. Press: **Alt J** (or **Alt XJ** if a style sheet is being used).

LANDSCAPE MODE

Landscape mode is used to print text lengthwise on the page rather than across the page. The paper size is 11" wide by 8.5" long, rather than 8.5" wide by 11" long which is portrait mode.

To change the paper size:

If you have a printer that will accept paper 11" wide and doesn't require font changes for landscape mode, all you need to do to print in landscape mode is to change the paper size.

1. Press: **Esc.**
2. Choose: **Format, Division, Margins.**
3. Move: the **highlight** to "paper length" field.
4. Type: **8.5.**
5. Move: the **highlight** to "width" field.
6. Type: **11.**
7. Press: **Enter** to return to edit screen.
8. Type: text and print. Be sure to adjust printer. Perhaps you will have to insert the paper manually.

To choose a printer file:

(If you have a laser printer which requires a printer file change):

1. Press: **Esc.**
2. Choose: **Print, Options.**
3. Move: the **highlight** to the "printer" field.
4. Press: **F1** to display the list of available printers. You should see a printer file for landscape mode and one for portrait mode. (For example: the printer files for a Hewlett-Packard Laserjet+ are "HPDWNFSP" for portrait, and "HPDWNFSL" for landscape.)
5. Press: **Enter.**
6. Then make the Division formatting changes outlined above to change the page length to 8.5," and the width to 11."

LEFT FLUSH PARAGRAPH

A left flush paragraph aligns all lines of the paragraph at the left margin.

To left-align text as it is typed:

1. Press: **Alt L** (or **Alt XL** if you are using a style sheet).
2. Type: the text of the paragraph and press **Enter.**
3. Press: **Alt P** (or **Alt XP** if you are using a style sheet) to return to normal paragraph formatting.

To left-align text after it has been typed:

1. "Select" the text.
2. Press: **Alt L** (or **Alt XL** if you are using a style sheet).

LEFT INDENT

All lines of a paragraph may be indented to the next tab stop by pressing **Alt N**. If **Alt N** is pressed twice, all lines will be indented to the second tab stop from the left margin.

To indent all lines from the left margin to the first tab stop as text is typed:

1. Press: **Alt N** (or **Alt XN** if you are using a style sheet).
2. Type: text to be indented and press **Enter** after the last paragraph.
3. Press: **Alt P** (or **Alt XP** if you are using a style sheet) to return to normal paragraph formatting.

To indent all lines after text has been typed:

1. "Select" the text to be indented.
2. Press: **Alt N** (or **Alt XN** if you are using a style sheet).

Note: **Alt M** *will move (reduce) the indent to the previous tab stop.*

Using Microsoft Word Advanced Functions, Appendix I   227

LIBRARY DOCUMENT-RETRIEVAL

Also see SUMMARY SHEETS.

To use the Library Document-retrieval menu:

1. Press: **Esc.**
2. Choose: **Library Document-retrieval.**

The following options may be selected:

Option	Explanation
Query	allows the user to search for files on the basis of information in one or more of the fields. In the Query menu, move the **highlight** to the field, type the appropriate information, repeat for each remaining field to be used in the search, and press **Enter** to display the selected files on the screen. To restore the complete list of files, go to the Query menu, delete each entry and press **Enter** to display the list of files.
Exit	returns you to the document screen.
Load	retrieves a document and displays it in the document screen. The **highlight** must be on the document name, choose **load**, and press **Enter** to load the document.
Print	prints a document that is highlighted.
Update	allows you to enter additional information or change existing information in the summary sheet for a document. Move the **highlight** to the document, choose **update**, fill in the fields in the summary sheet, and press **Enter**.
View	allows you to sort your files on the basis of entries in the various fields in the summary sheet. It also allows you to change the way the list of files is displayed. Short view is the default choice. Long view displays the files by drive, path and filename, author, and title. Full view displays the filename and also displays the summary sheet for each as the **highlight** is moved from one document to the next.
Copy	allows you to mark one or more files and copy to another drive or directory. Files are marked by pressing the space bar at each file. The screen instructs you for this and for "unmarking" files.
Delete	allows you to mark one or more files and delete. See the screen instruction for marking and "unmarking" files.

LIBRARY RUN

The Library Run menu is used to enter DOS commands without leaving the Word 5 program.

1. Press: **Esc.**
2. Choose: **Library Run.**

3. Type: the DOS command. For example, enter a COPY, DELETE, DIR, or CHKDSK command.
4. Press: **Enter** to run the command.
5. After the DOS command is completed, the screen will display a message telling you to press a key to resume Word.

LOAD (RETRIEVE) A DOCUMENT

To use the speed key to retrieve a document in the default directory:

1. Press: **Ctrl F7** to display the list of documents with .DOC extensions.
2. Move: the **highlight** to the document to be loaded.
3. Press: **Enter** to load the document on the screen.

To use the Transfer menu to load a document:

1. Press: **Esc.**
2. Choose: **Transfer, Load** to display the Transfer Load menu.
3. Type: the name of the document.
4. Press: **Enter** to load the document onto the screen.

or

5. Press: **F1** in the Transfer, Load menu to display the list of documents with .DOC extensions.
6. Move: the **highlight** to the document to be retrieved.
7. Press: **Enter** to display on the screen.

Note: *If, when you load the document, your screen remains blank, a message: "Press Y to save, N to lose edits, Esc to cancel." will be displayed. Press N to lose edits. You will then be able to retrieve your document onto screen. This happens if text or even a paragraph mark is on the screen. Word thinks there is a document there that you might want to save.*

To use the Library Document-retrieval menu to retrieve a document:

1. Press: **Esc.**
2. Choose: **Library, Document-retrieval.**

A list of the files in the default directory is displayed.

3. Move: the **highlight** to the document to be retrieved.
4. Choose: **Load** to retrieve the document.

MARGINS, LEFT/RIGHT

To change left and right margins, you must go to the Format, Division, Margins menu.

1. Press: **Esc.**
2. Choose: **Format, Division, Margins.**
3. Move: the **highlight** to the "left" field and type a measurement for the width of the left margin.
4. Move: the **highlight** to the "right" field and type a measurement for the width of the right margin.
5. Press: **Enter** to return to the screen.

Note: *A double row of dots will appear at the end of the text which means that all text typed <u>above</u> the row of dots will be formatted with the new margin settings.*

Using Microsoft Word Advanced Functions, Appendix I

MARGINS, TOP/BOTTOM

To change the top and bottom margins, go to the Format, Division, Margins menu.

1.	Press:	**Esc.**
2.	Choose:	**Format, Division, Margins.**
3.	Move:	the **highlight** to the "Top" field and type the desired measurement for a top margin.
4.	Move:	the **highlight** to the "Bottom" field and type the desired measurement for the bottom margin.
5.	Press:	**Enter** to return to the screen. A double row of dots will appear on the screen.

Note: *All text typed <u>above</u> the double row of dots will be formatted with the new margin settings.*

NAMING A FILE

In order to save text displayed on the screen, it must be named so the system may save it (write) on a disk and be able to locate it later.

To name (save) a file:

1.	Press:	**Esc.**
2.	Choose:	**Transfer, Save.**
	or	
3.	Press:	**Ctrl F10** to display the Save menu.
4.	Type:	a filename according to the following rules:

A filename must contain one to eight characters.
A filename must not contain a space.
An extension consisting of a period and one to three characters <u>may be</u> added.

5.	Press:	**Enter** to save in the default directory.

Note: *If the document has been named, when you press Ctrl F10 a second time, you will automatically save the edited document again, but you will not have the opportunity of renaming it.*

NORMAL CHARACTER FORMATTING

Normal character formatting returns formatting to the default type style and size. It turns off special formatting such as bold, underline, italic, etc.

To end special formatting and return to normal character formatting:

1.	Press:	**Alt space bar** (or **Alt X space bar** if you are using a style sheet) at the end of the formatted text.

To return text which has been formatted to normal character formatting:

1.	"Select" the text.	
2.	Press:	**Alt space bar** (or **Alt X space bar** if you are using a style sheet).

NORMAL PARAGRAPH FORMATTING

Normal paragraph formatting returns paragraph formatting to left-aligned, single-spaced text.

To end special formatting, such as centering, and return to normal paragraph formatting:

1. Press: **Enter** at the end of the formatted paragraph.
2. Press: **Alt P** (or **Alt XP** if you are using a style sheet). The following text will be in normal paragraph formatting.

To return a section of text to normal paragraph formatting:

1. "Select" the text.
2. Press: **Alt P** (or **Alt XP** if you are using a style sheet).

OVERTYPE

The Overtype mode allows the user to type over (and thereby delete) old text with new text. Remember, pressing the space bar is the same as typing a character and will delete text in Overtype mode.

To change to Overtype mode:

1. Press: **F5** (**OT** will be displayed in the status line).

To return to "insert" mode (default mode):

1. Press: **F5** again (check the status line--**OT** should not be displayed).

PAGE NUMBERS

Page numbers may be set in the Format, Division, Page numbers menu, or they may be set in either Headers, or Footers (Running-heads).

To set page numbers in Format, Division menu:

1. Press: **Esc.**
2. Choose: **Format, Division, Page-numbers.**
3. Move: the **highlight** to "Yes" in "Page-number" field.

Note: *The default is for page numbers to appear at the top left of every page including the first page.*

To change other settings:

1. Move: the **highlight** to "from top" and type a measurement. (If you want the number to appear at the bottom of the text, type 10.5.)
2. Move: the **highlight** to "from left" field and type a measurement. (If you want the number to be centered, type 4.25.)
3. Move: the **highlight** to "numbering" and set it at "Start" to begin the numbering with a number other than "1."
4. Move: the **highlight** to "at" field and type the number to start the numbering.
5. Move: the **highlight** to "format" and choose the type of number style desired.
6. Press: **Enter** to set page numbering and return to screen.

To set page numbers in running-heads:

1.	Move:	the **highlight** to the desired position for the page number, i.e, center of line, right margin, left margin, etc.
2.	Type:	**page**.
3.	Press:	**F3** to expand the glossary entry "page." This will display parentheses around the word "page," and will insert appropriate page numbers when the document is printed.
4.	Press:	**Ctrl F2** to set the page number as a header.
	or	
5.	Press:	**Alt F2** to set the page number as a footer.

To set page numbering to begin on the <u>second</u> page of a document:

Begin a second division at the top of page 2.

1.	Move:	the **highlight** to the end of page 1.
2.	Press:	**Ctrl Enter** to insert a new division break.
3.	Move:	the **highlight** to the top of Div 2 (it probably is already there).
4.	Press:	**Esc.**
5.	Choose:	**Format, Division, Page-numbers.**
6.	Press:	**space bar** to set "Page numbers" field at "Yes."
7.	Make any other changes to the various fields.	
8.	Press:	**Enter** to set.

or

Set page numbering in a running-head using the glossary entry "Page."

Note: *The default for running-heads is to begin printing on page 2; therefore this will avoid printing the page numbers on the first page.*

1.	Move:	the **highlight** to the beginning of the document.
2.	Press:	**Enter** to insert a blank line at the top of the page.
3.	Press:	**up arrow** to move the **highlight** to the top line.

Note: *You may have to press Alt P to return to normal paragraph formatting, if the top line was a centered title, or if it contained other formatting which you don't want in the running-head.*

4.	Move:	the **highlight** to the position on the line (center, right flush, etc.) where you want the page number to be printed.
5.	Type:	**page**.
6.	Press:	**F3** to expand the glossary name "page" (the word "page" will appear in parentheses).
7.	Press:	**Ctrl F2** to set the page number as a header.
	or	
8.	Press:	**Alt F2** to set the page number as a footer.

PAPER SIZE

The paper size is located in the Format, Division, Margins menu.

To change paper size:

1.	Press:	**Esc.**
2.	Choose:	**Format, Division, Margins.**

3. Move: the **highlight** to "Page Length" field and type the desired measurement (8.5 or 14, for example).
4. Move: the **highlight** to "Width" field and type the measurement (11 for example).
5. Press: **Enter** to return to screen. A double row of dots will be displayed at the bottom of the screen. Remember, all text typed above the rows of dots will be formatted with the new measurements.

See LANDSCAPE reference for more information.

PARAGRAPH FORMATTING

Paragraph formatting includes the following:

Speed formatting for:

Centered text	**Alt C**
Indent first line	**Alt F**
Justified	**Alt J**
Left flush	**Alt L**
Reduce left indent	**Alt M**
Left indent	**Alt N** (All lines of paragraph will be indented.)
Open paragraph	**Alt O** (Inserts blank line above paragraph.)
Normal paragraph	**Alt P** (Left-aligned, single spaced.)
Indent from both left and right margins	**Alt Q** (All lines will be indented from both left and right margins.)
Right flush	**Alt R** (Aligned at right margin.)
Hanging indent	**Alt T** (First line aligned at left margins, remaining lines indented to tab stop.)
Double spacing	**Alt 2**

Use Format, Paragraph menu for:

(The menu includes the formatting just listed plus the following fields):

Space before	Inserts blank lines above each paragraph.
Space after	Inserts blank lines below each paragraph.
Keep together	Prevents a page break within paragraph.
Keep follow	Prints last two lines of paragraph on the same page with the first two lines of the following paragraph.
Side-by-side	Used to print side-by-side paragraphs.

To begin using a specific kind of paragraph formatting:

1. Press: the speed formatting key listed above which corresponds to the type of formatting desired.

   or

2. Press: **Esc.**
3. Choose: **Format Paragraph** to display the menu and set the desired formatting at "Yes."
4. Type: the text to be formatted and press **Enter** to go to the next paragraph.
5. Press: **Alt P** (or **Alt XP** if you are using a style sheet) to end the formatting and return to normal paragraph formatting.

Using Microsoft Word Advanced Functions, Appendix I   233

To add paragraph formatting to a section of text:

1. "Select" the text to be formatted.
2. Press: the speed formatting key which will apply a particular formatting command to the text.

    or

3. Press: **Esc.**
4. Choose: **Format, Paragraph** to go to the Paragraph Formatting menu.
5. Move: the **highlight** to the field pertaining to the type of formatting to be set.
6. Press: **space bar** to set the field at "Yes" or type in a dimension, if that is needed.
7. Press: **Enter** to apply the formatting to the selected text.

Note: *Refer to SELECT TEXT for instructions to "select" a block of text.*

PORTRAIT MODE

Portrait mode is the default mode for using Microsoft Word. Portrait mode means the text is printed across the page, rather than lengthwise of the page as in landscape mode.

If you have changed to landscape mode and need to return to portrait:
1. Press: **Esc.**
2. Choose: **Format, Division, Margins** to display the menu.
3. Set "page length" field at 11, and "width" field at 8.5.
4. Press: **Enter** to return to the screen.

Note: *If you have a laser printer, you may have to go to the Print Options menu and choose the printer file which prints in portrait mode.*

PRINT A DOCUMENT

To use the speed key to print:

1. Press: **Ctrl F8.** (This sends the document on screen to the printer using the printer defaults and prints the entire document.)

To use the Print menu to print:

1. Press: **Esc.**
2. Choose: **Print, Printer** to print the entire document.

Use the Print Options menu to change the default printing commands:

Option	Used to:
printer	Choose a different printer file (portrait/landscape, for example)--press **F1** to display list of files.
setup	Choose the printer port to be used. Press **F1** to see a list.
model	Press **F1** to see a list of the possible printers you could use.
graphic resolution	Specify the number of dots per inch (DPI). Press **F1** to see a list of available options.
copies	Specify the number of copies to be printed.
draft	Specify whether to print in draft mode or not.

hidden text	Specify whether or not to print hidden text (index, table of contents marks, etc.).
summary sheet	Specify whether or not to print the summary sheet.
range	Specify whether to print all of the text, or text which has been "selected," or specific pages.
page number	Type in the page numbers to be printed ("Pages" must be selected in the "range" field).
widow/orphan control	Prevent printing single lines of paragraphs on pages by themselves.
queued	Enable you to work on a document while printing; however, it does slow down your work. If you choose "Yes," you may then pause, continue, restart, or stop printing.
paper feed	Specify type of paper feed. **Continuous** is the default and used with most printers. Press **F1** to see other options available to you depending upon the type of printer you are using.
duplex	Print on both sides of the paper, if your printer supports this feature.

PRINT PREVIEW

The Print preView feature allows you to view entire pages of your document as they will look when printed. Page numbers, headers, footers, footnotes, graphics and columns will be displayed, as well as all formatting. You may view one page, two pages, or facing pages.

To view your document in Print preView:

The page you wish to view should be displayed in the document screen.
1. Press: **Esc.**
2. Choose: **Print PreView.**
   or
3. Press: **Ctrl F9** to move between the document and the preView screen.

The following options are displayed in the Print preView menu:

Option	Explanation
Jump	Allows you to display a different page. Choose Page, type the page number, and press **Enter**.
Options	Allows you to view two pages or to view facing pages.
Print	Allows you to go to the Print menu directly from this screen.
Exit	Returns to the normal document screen.

QUIT MICROSOFT WORD

At the end of a word processing session, before turning off the power, you need to "Quit" the program.

1. Press: **Esc.**
2. Choose: **Quit.**

Note: *If you have named and saved the document and the most recent edits, you will return to the DOS prompt.*

If you haven't named and saved the document, you must first do that, then you may "Quit." The Transfer Save menu will be displayed which will allow you to name the document.

If you haven't saved the latest edits, but have previously named the file, you will be prompted to save the last edits when you "Quit." Press Y to save the edits.

REPAGINATE

Repagination divides a document into pages. If you have set the "paginate" field at "Auto" in the OPTIONS menu, the page breaks will be displayed as you type. However, this may slow down your work. If you choose not to paginate as you work, the system will automatically paginate the document before printing, but if you wish to see the page breaks before printing, you may choose Print Repaginate. This feature will allow you to control the page breaks if you choose to confirm each page break. If you do not confirm the page breaks, the system will insert them automatically--then you may view the pages before printing.

To repaginate a document without confirming page breaks:
1. Press: **Esc.**
2. Choose: **Print, Repaginate** to display the menu.
3. Press: **Enter** to repaginate the document.

To confirm the page endings during repagination:
1. Press: **Esc.**
2. Choose: **Print, Repaginate.**
3. Press: **Y** or press the **space bar** to set "confirm page breaks" at "Yes."
4. Press: **Enter** to begin the pagination.

Note: *The screen will display each page ending and a message asking you to press Y to confirm the page break, or move the highlight to a new position (usually you can press only the up arrow) and press Y to confirm the new page break. If you have entered a required page break by pressing Ctrl Shift Enter when you entered text, you will have the opportunity to remove it or confirm it during pagination.*

REPEAT EDITS

A "last edit" refers to all keystrokes entered since you last moved the **highlight** or since the last command was entered.

To repeat your last edit:

1. Press: **F4** key.

REPLACE

To replace text with new text:

1. Press: **Esc.**
2. Choose: **Replace.**
3. Type: text to search for.
4. Move: the **highlight** to "with text" field.
5. Type: text to replace with.

6. Set the other fields, if desired.

Field	Explanation
Confirm	Default is "Yes"--no replacement will take place until the user presses Y to confirm the replacement. Set at "No" for automatic replacement.
Case	Default is "No" which means the word will be found regardless of case. If case is set at "Yes" then the word will be found only if the case is a match.
Whole word	Default is "No" which means that the word will be located even if it is part of another word. If this field is set at "Yes," then the word to be located will be found only if it is preceded and followed by a space.

7. Press: **Enter** to begin the procedure.

RETRIEVE A DOCUMENT

Refer to LOAD DOCUMENT.
Refer to SUMMARY SHEETS.

REVISE TEXT

Text revisions include:

overtype mode	Press **F5** to go to overtype mode. Type new text over existing text. The old text will be deleted permanently.
insert mode	Insert mode is the default mode. When new text is added to a document in insert mode, the original text will move ahead of it.
delete	"Select" the text to be deleted and press **Delete** key to delete text to "scrap."
shift delete	"Select" the text to be deleted and press **Shift Delete** to delete the text permanently--it will not be deleted into "scrap," and therefore may not be retrieved or reinserted. You can use Undo **Shift F1** to reverse the last edit, which will restore the deleted text.
backspace	Deletes characters to the left of the **highlight**. Text is deleted permanently.

RIGHT FLUSH PARAGRAPH

The text in a right flush paragraph is aligned at the right margin rather that the left margin. This is used for dates, report numbers, contract numbers, for example.

To align a paragraph before text is entered:

1. Press: **Alt R** (or **Alt XR** if you are using a style sheet).
2. Type: the text to be right-aligned and press **Enter**.

Using Microsoft Word Advanced Functions, Appendix I   237

3. Press: **Alt P** (or **Alt XP** if you are using a style sheet) to return to normal paragraph formatting.

To right-align text already entered:
4. "Select" the block of text.
5. Press: **Alt R** (or **Alt XR** if you are using a style sheet).

RUNNING-HEADS

Running-heads are blocks of text printed at the top (headers) or bottom (footers) of every page. The default is for running-heads to <u>not</u> be printed on the first page.

1. Type: the text to be in the running-head including character and paragraph formatting.

Be sure the **highlight** is in the paragraph (or line) to be set as a running-head.
2. Press: **Ctrl F2** to set a header on every page.
   or
3. Press: **Alt F2** to set a footer on every page.

To make changes to the Running-head menu:

1. Press: **Esc.**
2. Choose: **Format, Running-head** to display the menu.
3. Make any changes to the fields. Set running-heads to appear at the Top, Bottom, first, odd, or even pages. Use this menu to change the default so that the running-head will be printed on the first page of a document.
4. Press: **Enter** to return to the screen.

SAVE A DOCUMENT

The process of naming and saving a document writes or copies the document on a disk, either the hard disk, or a floppy disk. Naming the document provides the program with a way to locate the file when you want to retrieve it for editing. If you don't save the document that is displayed on the screen, you will lose the text when you clear the screen, or in the case of a power outage or surge, you may lose text that has not been saved.

To name and save a document:

1. Press: **Ctrl F10** or press **Esc** and choose **Transfer, Save** to display the Save menu.
2. Type: the filename (see NAMING A DOCUMENT for rules).
3. Press: **Enter** to save. A filename will be displayed in the lower right corner of the screen.

Note: *If the document has been saved once, when you press Ctrl F10 key the next time, the save will be automatic.*

SCREEN DISPLAY

To display paragraph codes, tabs, and spaces (represented by dots):

1. Press: **Esc.**
2. Choose: **Options.**

3. Set "show non-printing symbols" field at "None" to display no marks.

Set "show non-printing symbols" field at "Partial" to display only the paragraph marks and new line marks.

Set "show non-printing symbols" field at "All" to display paragraph marks, tab marks, and dots representing spaces. Also, optional hyphens will be displayed.

4. Press: **Enter** to return to the screen.

To display the ruler line:

1. Press: **Esc.**
2. Choose: **Options.**
3. Move: the **highlight** to "show ruler" field and press space bar to set "Yes."
4. Press: **Enter.**

To display line numbers in the status line at the bottom of the screen:

1. Press: **Esc.**
2. Choose: **Options.**
3. Move: the **highlight** to the "line numbers" field and set it at "Yes."
4. Press: **Enter.**

To display the text in graphics mode which will display italics, etc.:

1. Press: **Alt F9** to change from text to graphics or reverse.
   or
2. Press: **Esc.**
3. Choose: **Options.**
4. Move: the **highlight** to "display mode" field.
5. Press: **F1** to display a list of available options.
6. Press: the **highlight** to choose the type of display mode.
7. Press: **Enter** to return to the document screen.

Note: *The options in the list depend upon your computer's capabilities. The list was entered at the time you installed Word 5. Changes will remain in effect until they are changed again.*

SCROLLING

Scrolling is moving the text up and down or across the screen to view it. The **highlight** is used to move the text.

To move the highlight:	Press:
One line up	**Up arrow**
One line down	**Down arrow**
One character to right	**Right arrow**
One character to left	**Left arrow**
One word to right	**Ctrl right arrow**
One word to left	**Ctrl left arrow**
End of line	**End key**
Beginning of line	**Home key**

Using Microsoft Word Advanced Functions, Appendix I

Beginning of the document	**Ctrl Page Up**
End of the document	**Ctrl Page Down**
Down one screen length	**Page Down**
Up one screen length	**Page Up**
First character in window	**Ctrl Home** key
Last character in window	**Ctrl End** key
To move to a new page	**Alt F5** or press **Esc** and choose **Jump**, **Page**, type the page number and press **Enter**

SEARCH

To search for text:

1. Press: **Esc.**
2. Choose: **Search** to display menu.
3. Type: text to search for.
4. Specify direction, case, whole word if desired.
5. Press: **Enter** to search for the first occurrence of the word.

To repeat the search:

1. Press: **Shift F4.**

SELECTING TEXT

In order to work with blocks of text, the text must be "selected." Selected text appears as highlighted text on the screen. Text is selected before formatting commands are added, or before a block of text is moved, copied, or deleted.

To "select":	Press:
character	up, down, right, left arrow keys
previous word	**F7**
next word	**F8**
previous sentence	**Shift F7**
next sentence	**Shift F8**
previous paragraph	**F9**
next paragraph	**F10**
current line	**Shift F9**
whole document	**Shift F10**

To extend a selection:

1. Press: **F6** (EX appears in the status line).
2. Move: the **highlight** in any direction using any of the **arrow keys**, or the **Home, End, Page Up, Page Down, F7, F8, F9,** or **F10 keys**. The block appears highlighted on the screen.
3. Enter format commands, or copy, delete, move, etc.

To turn off "extend":

1. Press: **F6.**

To extend a column selection:

1. Press: **Shift F6** (a CS appears in the status line).
2. Move: the **highlight** down to "select" an entire column.

To turn off column selection:

1. Press: **Shift F6** (the CS no longer appears in the status line).

To use the Shift key to extend a selection:

1. Move: the **highlight** to any point.
2. Press: **Shift key** and **any arrow key, Home, End, Page Up,** or **Page Down key** to extend the selection from the **highlight** position.

SMALL CAPS

Small caps are letters generally the size of lowercase, but printed in uppercase format.

To format in small caps as text is being typed:

1. Press: **Alt K** (or **Alt XK** if you are using a style sheet).
2. Type: the text to be formatted.
3. Press: **Alt space bar** (or **Alt X space bar** if you are using a style sheet) to end the formatting.

To apply formatting to text which has been typed:

1. "Select" the text to be formatted.
2. Press: **Alt K** (or **Alt XK** if a style sheet is being used) to apply the formatting.

SPACES, NONBREAKING

Nonbreaking spaces are used to keep words together on one line. For example, a title may be kept on the same line with a proper name, or all words in an address may be kept together on one line.

To enter a nonbreaking space:

1. Type: the first word.
2. Press: **Ctrl space bar**.
3. Type: the following word.

SPELLING

The command for beginning a spell check is **Alt F6** or press **Esc**, and choose **Library, Spell**.

To check the spelling in a document:

1. Press: **Alt F6** or press **Esc** and choose **Library, Spell**.

The program will stop at a misspelled word and display a list of possible correct spellings of that word:

2. Move: the **highlight** to the correct word.
3. Press: **Enter**.

Using Microsoft Word Advanced Functions, Appendix I   241

Note: *If no correct spellings are displayed, choose "Correct," type the correct spelling, then press Enter. If the word is not included in the dictionary, a message will be displayed, "Not in dictionary. Enter Y to confirm or N to retype." Press Y to confirm, if the spelling is corrected.*

The other option in the Correct menu is "remember correction." If you select "Yes" in response to this option, the system will remember the misspelled word, plus the correction, and will make the appropriate correction in every document after that. For instance, if you have a habit of typing "ot" instead of "to," Word will remember the misspelled word and its correction, and will make that correction in other documents.

To add a word to the supplement:

When the spelling check stops at a word which is to be added to the supplement:
1. Choose: **Add.**
2. Choose: **Standard** to add the word to the Standard Dictionary UPDAT-AM.CMP.
   Document to add the word to the Document Dictionary (which is attached to a document file).
   User to add the word to the User Dictionary which contains words for specific purposes or by specific users.

Refer to DICTIONARIES for further information about the supplements to the dictionary.

To use the Options menu to tailor the spelling program to your needs:

1. Press: **Alt F6** or press **Esc** and choose **Library, Spell.**

At the first word which the program doesn't recognize:
2. Choose: **Options.**

The following fields will be displayed and may be changed:

Field	Choices
user dictionary	Specify the name of the user dictionary to which you want to add words, or create a new user dictionary by typing a new filename.
lookup	"Quick" option assumes that the first two letters of a word are correct. If you want the dictionary to assume no letters are correct, select "complete" which is a slower process.
ignore all caps	If you want the program to ignore text in all caps, such as acronyms, set the response at "No."
alternatives	If the response is set at "Manual" no list of correct words will be displayed. When in this mode, choose "correct" to display a list of words.
check punctuation	The response "Yes" causes the program to stop at incorrect or inappropriate punctuation.

After changing the options, continue on with your spell check. The changes will remain in effect until they are changed again.

STARTUP

To start Word 5 when using a dual disk drive system:

1. Insert DOS disk in Drive A.
2. Turn the power on.

At the DOS Date prompt:

3. Type: the current date (#/#/90) and press **Enter**, or press **Enter** to bypass the date.

At the Time prompt:

4. Type: the time (##:##:##) and press **Enter**, or press **Enter** to bypass.

At the DOS prompt A:>:

5. Remove the DOS disk and insert the Word 5 program disk in Drive A:
6. Type: **word**.
7. Press: **Enter** to load Word 5.

To start Word 5 when using a hard disk drive system:

1. Turn the power on.

At the Date prompt:

2. Type: the current date (#/#/90) and press **Enter**, or press **Enter** to bypass.

At the Time prompt:

3. Type: the time (##:##:##) and press **Enter**, or press **Enter** to bypass.

At the DOS prompt C:>:

4. Type: **word** and press **Enter**.

If you have Word in its own directory:

At the C:>:

1. Type: **cd word5** and press **Enter**. (The **cd**--change directory--command is used to change to the "Word5" directory.)

At the C:\word5:\> prompt:

2. Type: **word** and press **Enter**.

STRIKETHROUGH

The strikethrough feature is used to mark text for revisions by striking through the characters with the hyphen. It is generally used to mark text to be deleted.

To format text as it is typed:

1. Press: **Alt S** (or **Alt XS** if a style sheet is being used).
2. Type: the text.
3. Press: **Alt space bar** (or **Alt X space bar** if a style sheet is used) to end formatting.

To apply the formatting after text is typed:

1. "Select" the text to be formatted.
2. Press: **Alt S** (or **Alt XS** if a style sheet is being used) to apply the formatting.

SUMMARY SHEETS

A summary sheet may be included with your document and is actually part of a database program which contains information about the document, such as the name of the author, the operator who typed the document, the title, key words and comments, and the creation and revision dates. The summary sheet is not printed with the document unless you specify that it be printed.

The summary sheet is used in the Library Document-retrieval menu to help you organize your files by providing a means for you to sort or search for specific files, copy and/or delete files, or retrieve files. Also you may update the summary sheet in the Library Document-retrieval menu.

To include a summary sheet when saving your document:

1. Go to the Options menu and set "summary sheet" field at "Yes." Once this has been set, it will remain that way for every session.

To save the document and fill in the summary sheet:
2. Press: **Ctrl F10** to go to the Transfer Save menu.
3. Type: a filename.
4. Press: **Enter.**

The Summary Information menu will be displayed.
5. Type appropriate responses to each field. It is not necessary to fill in every field.
6. Press: **Enter** to save the summary sheet with the document.

To use the Library Document-retrieval menu:

1. Press: **Esc.**
2. Choose: **Library Document-retrieval.**

The following options may be selected:

Option	Explanation
Query	Allows the user to search for files on the basis of information in one or more of the fields.
Exit	Returns you to the document screen.
Load	Retrieves a document and displays it in the document screen.
Print	Prints a document that is highlighted.
Update	Allows you to enter additional information or change existing information in the summary sheet for a document.
View	Allows you to sort your files on the basis of entries in the various fields in the summary sheet. It also allows you to change the way the list of files is displayed. Short view is the default choice. Long view displays the files by drive, path and filename, author, and title. Full view displays the filename and also displays the summary sheet for each as the **highlight** is moved from one document to the next.

Copy	Allows you to mark one or more files and copy to another drive or directory. Files are marked by pressing the space bar at each file. The screen instructs you for this and for "unmarking" files.
Delete	Allows you to mark one or more files and delete. See the screen instruction for marking and "unmarking" files.

SUPERSCRIPT/SUBSCRIPT

To format text as it is typed:

For superscript:
1. Press: **Alt =** or **Alt +** (or **Alt X=** or **Alt X+** if you are using a style sheet).

For subscript:
   Press: **Alt -** (or **Alt X -** if you are using a style sheet).

2. Type: the text to be in super/subscript.
3. Press: **Alt space bar** (or **Alt X space bar** if you are using a style sheet) to return to normal character formatting.

To format text after it has been entered:

1. "Select" the text to be super/subscripted.

For superscript:
2. Press: **Alt =** or **Alt +** (or **Alt X=** or **Alt X+** if you are using a style sheet).

For subscript:
   Press: **Alt -** (or **Alt X -** if you are using a style sheet).

TABS

It is important to remember that the tab sets are formatting, and the new tab sets are carried in the paragraph marks. If you accidentally delete the paragraph marks which carry the tab sets, you will lose your tabs. It helps to have the ruler line displayed (go to the Options menu to set "show ruler" at "Yes") in order to see where your tabs are located.

The types of tabs are:

Left	= text is aligned at the left side of the column.
Right	= text is aligned at the right side of the column.
Center	= text is centered at the tab set position.
Decimal	= text is aligned at the decimal point.
Vertical	= a vertical line is inserted at the tab set position.

A **leader character** is the character which is automatically inserted between two columns. The leader character is added to a tab set and inserts dots or hyphens in the area preceding the tab set position. This is useful for entering dot leaders to connect text in two columns, or may also be used to draw horizontal lines.

To set new tabs:

1. Move: the **highlight** to the position where the tabs are to be set.
2. Press: **Alt F1** or press **Esc** and choose **Tab, Set** to display the Tab Set menu.
3. Type: the position number where the tab is to be set.
   or
4. Press: the **right arrow key** to move the **highlight** to the desired position in the ruler line.
5. Type: the letter corresponding to the type of tab to be set.
6. Type: the leader character, if one is to be set.

Note: The ruler line displays each tab as it is set.

7. Repeat for remaining tabs.

After all tab positions have been set:
8. Press: **Enter**.

Note: When new tabs are set, all of the default tabs to the left of that tab, are automatically deleted.

To type text in tables:

1. Press: **Tab** key to move to the tab position.
2. Type: text.
3. Repeat for each column.

At the end of the lines in the table:

4. Press: **Shift Enter** to insert a down arrow. This will format the table as one paragraph.

To restore the preset tabs:

1. Move: the **highlight** to the position where you wish to restore the default tabs.
2. Press: **Esc.**
3. Choose: **Format, Tab, Reset-all**.

To change the tab sets in a table:

1. If you have pressed **Shift Enter** at the end of each line, just move the **highlight** to any point within the table.

   Or if you have pressed **Enter** at the end of each line, then the entire table must be "selected."

2. Press: **Alt F1** or press **Esc** and choose **Format, Tab, Set**.
3. Press: the **right** or **left arrow keys** to move the **highlight** to the tab to be deleted.
4. Press: **Delete** key to remove the tab.
5. Type: the position number, the letter corresponding to the type of tab, and the leader character, if any, for each new tab.
6. Press: **Enter** when finished setting new tabs.

Note: The text in the table will be automatically realigned at the new tab stops, providing you have pressed the Tab key the correct number of times between columns.

THESAURUS

The Thesaurus function displays a list of synonyms for words in the document.

To use the Thesaurus:

1. Move: the **highlight** to any position in the word.
2. Press: **Ctrl F6** (or press **Esc** and choose **Library, thEsaurus**).

A list of synonyms will be displayed. Respond to the screen prompts to replace the word, look it up, or view more words. The screen explains what your options are.

To replace the word with a synonym displayed on screen:

1. Move: the **highlight** to the new word.
2. Press: **Enter** to replace.

To leave the Thesaurus without making a change to your text:

1. Press: **Esc**.

UNDERLINE/DOUBLE-UNDERLINE

To add underlining or double-underlining as you type text:

To underline:
1. Press: **Alt U** (or **Alt XU** if you are using a style sheet).

To double-underline:
   Press: **Alt D** (or **Alt XD** if you are using a style sheet).

2. Type: the text.
3. Press: **Alt space bar** (or **Alt X space bar** if you are using a style sheet) to end the formatting.

To add underlining or double-underlining after you have entered text:

1. "Select" the text to be formatted.

To underline:
2. Press: **Alt U** (or **Alt XU** if you are using a style sheet) to underline.

To double-underline:
   Press: **Alt D** (or **Alt XD** if you are using a style sheet) to double-underline.

UNDO

The "Undo" feature of Word reverses the last edit or revision.

Note: A "last edit" is defined as all keystrokes entered <u>since</u> you last moved an arrow key.

To undo (reverse) the last edit:

1. Press: **Shift F1** or press **Esc** and choose **Undo**.

Using Microsoft Word Advanced Functions, Appendix I

You can reverse:
  Copy
  Delete
  Format
  Insert
  All Library commands except Run and Document-retrieval
  Replace
  Transfer Merge
  Undo

You cannot reverse:
  Gallery
  Help
  Jump
  Library Run
  Options
  Print
  Quit
  Search
  Transfer (except Transfer Merge)

WINDOWS

You may divide the window into eight windows, then work in each window the same way you work in the one large window. While working in one small window, it may be expanded to fill the entire screen by using the Zoom function (**Ctrl F1**).

To split a window:

1. Press: **Esc.**
2. Choose: **Window, Split.**
3. Choose: **Horizontal, Vertical,** or **Footnote** to go to the Footnote window--(this feature will display the footnotes on the screen).
4. Type: the line number for "Horizontal."
5. Type: the column number for "Vertical" to indicate the position where you want to split the screen.
6. Move: the **highlight** to the "clear new window" field and set it at "Yes" to clear the window, or leave it as is, if you wish to display sections of the same document in both windows.
7. Press: **Enter** to split the windows. Notice there are numbers in the upper left corners of each window to designate the window.

You may load a different document into the new window and work on two documents simultaneously.

To move the highlight from one window to another:

1. Press: **F1** to move to the next window.

To zoom a window (expand it to fill the screen):

1. Move: the **highlight** into the window to be "zoomed."
2. Press: **Ctrl F1.**

Note: *A ZM will be displayed in the status line.*

To leave the "Zoom" mode:

1. Move: the **highlight** into the "zoomed" window.
2. Press: **Ctrl F1** to restore the original size.

To close one window:

1. Press: **Esc.**
2. Choose: **Window, Close.**
3. Type: the number of the window to be closed.
4. Press: **Enter** to close.

To close all windows:

Be sure you have saved any edits in each window, although you will be prompted to save any changes.

1. Press: **Esc.**
2. Choose: **Transfer, Clear.**
3. Press: **Enter.** (You may have to respond to a screen prompt to press Y to save, or N to lose edits.)

WORDWRAP

Wordwrap is the feature which allows the user to type the text of a paragraph without pressing **Enter** at the ends of lines. The system ends the lines automatically and moves following text to the beginning of the next line.

Do not press **Enter** at the ends of lines within a paragraph.

Press **Enter** at the end of a paragraph to begin a new paragraph.

Press **Shift Enter** to begin a new line (in a table or inside address).

APPENDIX II

QUICK REFERENCE GUIDE

TO

MICROSOFT WORD ADVANCED FUNCTIONS

The Quick Reference Guide provides summaries of instructions for using the various advanced Microsoft Word functions learned in this manual. These functions are in alphabetical order.

ANNOTATIONS

Annotations are actually footnotes in a different form. Annotations are generally used to insert reminders to those who work with a document. They are listed on the page with the text referred to, in the same area with footnotes. Also, the numbering is part of footnote numbering. For example, if an annotation is between two footnotes, the first footnote would be numbered 1, the annotation would be numbered 2, and the last footnote would be numbered 3.

To enter an annotation:

1. Press: **Esc** and choose **Format, Annotation**.
2. Type: a maximum of twenty-eight keystrokes to name the annotation. Usually a person's initials are entered.
3. Move: the **highlight** to the "insert date" field and set it at "yes" to include the date of the annotation. You also may set "insert time" field at "Yes."
4. Press: **Enter** to go to the area where the annotation will be typed.
5. Type: the text of the annotation.

To return to the document area:
6. Press: **Esc** and choose **Jump, Annotation**.

Note: The annotation reference characters may be formatted the same way footnote numbers are formatted. "Select" the character and apply formatting, usually superscript.

To specify the position for printing annotations:

The choices for printing annotations are the same as the choices for printing footnotes, that is they may be printed on the same page with the accompanying reference, or they may be printed in a list of references at the end of the document.

To change the options for printing annotations:
1. Press: **Esc** and choose **Format, Division, Layout**.
2. Choose: either "Same page" or "End."
3. Press: **Enter**.

BOOKMARKS

When selected text is formatted as a bookmark, that section may then be used in cross-referencing for page numbers, or you may "jump" to that section of text using the Jump Bookmark menu.

To designate text as a bookmark:

1. "Select" the block of text to be formatted as a bookmark section of text.

2.	Press:	**Esc,** and choose **Format, bookmarK** to display the menu.
3.	Type:	a name for the section of text. You may use up to thirty-one characters for the name.
4.	Press:	**Enter** to save as a bookmark.

To jump to a bookmark:

1.	Press:	**Esc** and choose **Jump bookmarK**.
2.	Type:	the name of the bookmark.
or		
3.	Press:	**F1** to display the list of bookmark names.
4.	Move:	the **highlight** to the bookmark name.
5.	Press:	**Enter** to go to that section of text.

Note: *Since the section of text is highlighted when you jump to it, this is an easy way to delete blocks of text.*

To remove a bookmark designation:

1.	"Jump" to the bookmark.	
2.	Press:	**Esc** and choose **Format, bookmarK**.
3.	Press:	**Enter** without entering any name. A message "Enter Y to confirm deletion of bookmark" will be displayed.
4.	Press:	**Y** to remove the name.

To use bookmark formatting to enter a cross-reference to a page:

1.	Format as a bookmark, the text to be referenced.	
2.	Move:	to the position where the reference is to be entered.
3.	Type:	**page:** and type the name of the bookmark. Example: page:bookmark.
4.	Press:	**F3** to expand the entry. The entry then becomes: (page:bookmark). When the document is printed, the page number of the bookmark will be entered automatically.

BORDERS

Borders are a type of paragraph formatting. You may choose to have paragraph text formatted with lines on any one side--above, below, left, or right--or you may have text formatted in a box. Each time **Enter** is pressed, the formatting for the box or the lines is repeated in the next paragraph.

To format for a box:

1.	Press:	**Esc** and choose **Format, Border**.
2.	Press:	**B** or press the **space bar** to highlight "Box."
3.	Change the "line style" field to double or bold, if desired.	
4.	Press:	**Enter.**
5.	Type:	the text to be in the box using wordwrap.

Note: *For example, if you wish to type a list of names in a box, press* Shift Enter *after each name, so the entire list is formatted as one paragraph. The box will expand to include all lines in the list.*

Using Microsoft Word Advanced Functions, Appendix II

To format for a line:

1.	Press:	**Esc** and choose **Format, Border**.
2.	Press:	**L** or press the **space bar** to move highlight to "Lines."
3.	Change the "Line style" field to double or bold, if desired.	
4.	Move:	the **highlight** into any of the line position fields--"left," "right," "above," or "below" and set "Yes" as the response.
5.	Press:	**Enter.**
6.	Type:	text using the same procedure as given for "box" formatting.

COLUMNS, NEWSPAPER

To format text for newspaper columns, use the Format, Division, Layout menu.

To format text into multiple columns:

1.	Type:	the text in normal paragraph formatting.
2.	Move:	the **highlight** to any position within the text (since this is Division Formatting).
3.	Press:	**Esc** and choose **Format, Division, Layout**.
4.	Move:	the **highlight** to "number of columns" field.
5.	Type:	the number of columns to be set.
6.	Move:	the **highlight** to "space between columns" field if you wish to change the default space 0.5" and type a new measurement.
7.	Press:	**Enter** to set column formatting and return to the screen.

Note: *The text will be formatted into columns; however, the columns will not appear side by side on the screen, but will be in one long column. If you wish to see the columns as they will be printed, press Alt F4 to go to "show layout." The columns will be displayed on the screen, side by side.*

Note: *If you prefer, you may set the column formatting <u>before</u> typing the text.*

To adjust the column endings:

If you wish to move several lines of text from the end of column 1 to the top of column 2, for example:

1.	Move:	the **highlight** to the position when you wish to enter a column break.
2.	Press:	**Ctrl Alt Enter** to enter a new column mark. The text below that mark will be moved to the next column.

To enter a title which will be printed over all columns:

This is a new feature with Word 5. The key to it, is to set "division break" field in the Format Division Layout menu at "Continuous," which allows more than one type of column formatting to be used on one page.

1.	Type:	the title in whatever format you choose.
2.	Press:	**Esc** and choose **Format, Division, Layout.**
3.	Move:	the **highlight** to "division break" field.
4.	Choose:	"Continuous."
5.	Press:	**Enter** to return to the document.

To set layout for multiple columns to appear below the title:

6.	Move:	the **highlight** below the division mark.
7.	Press:	**Esc** and choose **Format, Division, Layout.**
8.	Move:	the **highlight** to the "numbers of columns" field.
9.	Type:	the number of columns.
10.	Move:	the **highlight** to the "division break" field.
11.	Choose:	"Continuous."
12.	Press:	**Enter** to return to the document.
13.	Move:	the **highlight** above the second division mark (between the first and second division marks), and type the text of the columns.

COLUMNS: SIDE-BY-SIDE PARAGRAPHS

See SIDE-BY-SIDE PARAGRAPHS.

CROSS-REFERENCE

To enter a cross-reference to a page:

1. "Select" and format as a bookmark, a block of text on the page which is to be referenced.
2. Move: the **highlight** to the position where the reference is to be typed.
3. Type: **page:** and the name of the bookmark to be referenced.
4. Press: **F3** to expand the entry. It will look similar to this: (page:bookmark_name). When the text is printed, the page number of the bookmark will be printed automatically in this position.

To enter a cross-reference to a footnote:

1. Format a footnote number as a bookmark. (Use Format, bookmarK menu, type a name for the number formatted as a bookmark, and press **Enter**.)
2. Move: the **highlight** to the position where the reference is to be made to a footnote.
3. Type: **footnote:** and the bookmark name.
4. Press: **F3** to expand the entry. It will look something like this: (footnote:bookmark_name). When the document is printed the footnote number will be automatically entered in this position.

Note: A similar procedure may be used to enter a reference to a paragraph number; however, the paragraph must be numbered when it is formatted as a bookmark. Then in the reference position, type `para-num:` *and the bookmark name, and press F3 to expand the entry.*

FOOTNOTES

To enter a footnote:

1. Type: the text to the point where the footnote is to be entered.
2. Press: **Esc** and choose **Format, Footnote.**
3. Press: **Enter** to automatically insert a footnote number, and to go to the footnote typing area. (Notice the two "End marks" above and below the footnote text area.)
4. Type: the text of the footnote.

Using Microsoft Word Advanced Functions, Appendix II   253

5.	Press:	**Esc** and choose **Jump, Footnote**.
6.	Press:	**Enter** to return to the text.
7.	Move:	the **highlight** to the space following the footnote number and press **Enter**.
8.	Type:	the remaining text.

To edit footnote text:

1.	Move:	the **highlight** to the footnote number.
2.	Press:	**Esc** and choose **Jump, Footnote** to move to the footnote text.
3.	Make the necessary revisions to the footnote text.	
4.	Press:	**Esc** and choose **Jump, Footnote** to return to the typing area.

To use footnote window:

1.	Press:	**Esc** and choose **Window, Split, Footnote**.
2.	Press:	**F1** to move highlight to the left side of screen.
3.	Press:	**up** or **down** arrows to move highlight to the point where you want the footnote window to be displayed (probably in the lower third of the screen).
4.	Press:	**Enter**.
5.	Press:	**F1** to move the highlight into the footnote window to make edits to footnotes.
6.	Press:	**F1** to return the highlight to the text.

To close the footnote window:

1.	Press:	**F1** to move the highlight into the footnote window.
2.	Press:	**Esc** and choose **Window, Close** and **Enter**.

To delete a footnote (both number and text):

1.	Move:	the **highlight** to the footnote number in the text.
2.	Press:	**delete** or **shift delete**. The remaining footnote numbers readjust automatically.

To move a footnote:

1.	Move:	the **highlight** to the footnote number to be moved.
2.	Press:	**delete key** to delete to scrap.
3.	Move:	the **highlight** to a new position.
4.	Press:	**Insert key** to insert footnote in new position. This will not only move the number, but will also move the accompanying footnote text.

To print a footnote text at the end of the document:

The default is for footnote text to be printed at the <u>bottom</u> of the page corresponding to the footnote number.

<u>To change the default:</u>
1.	Press:	**Esc** and choose **Format, Division, Layout**.

Be sure the highlight is in the "footnotes" field:
2.	Press:	**space bar** to choose "end" and press **Enter**.

FORMAT POSITION MENU

Refer to GRAPHICS.

FORMS

Refer also to the sections on BORDERS, LINE DRAW, and VERTICAL TABS for information about producing text with lines which you would use to create forms.

To create a form:

1. Type the labels in the various positions in the form. Example is shown below.
2. Format the labels with boxes or lines. The example below is formatted with each line as a box and vertical tabs used to insert the vertical lines in the box.
3. Enter a chevron » formatted as hidden text following each label, so it can be used to quickly jump to each label when filling in a form.

Last Name»	First Name»	MI»
Company Name»		
Mailing Address»		
City»	State»	Zip»

4. Save the document.

To fill in a form:

1. Load the form as a "read only" file. An asterisk will appear in front of the file name on the screen.
2. Press: **Ctrl >** to jump quickly to each label.
3. Type: the appropriate information.
4. Print: the document as it appears on screen.

To save the filled-in form:

5. Use Transfer Save and type a new name. You will not be able to use the name of the retrieved form, since it is a "read only" file.

FORMS: FILLING IN PREPRINTED FORMS

To create a guide for filling in a preprinted form:

1. Type: each label followed by a chevron (») on a separate line.
2. "Select": each label and chevron and format them as hidden text.
3. Press: **Alt E** or **Alt XE** if you are using a style sheet to format as hidden text.

Your guide might look something like the example shown below:

```
Last name»
First Name»
MI»
Company Name»
Mailing Address»
City»
State»
Zip»
```

<u>Use the Format pOsition menu to position the labels to correspond to the form:</u>
4. Move: the **highlight** to the first label.
5. Press: **Esc** and choose **Format, pOsition** to display the menu.
6. Choose: "horizontal frame position" and type the distance from the left margin.
7. Choose: "vertical frame position" and type the distance from the top margin.
8. Repeat: for every label in the list.

Note: *You will need to determine the distance from the left margin for the horizontal frame position, and the distance from the top margin for the vertical frame position. This may take some experimenting with measurements.*

9. Save the document.

To use the guide to fill in a form:

1. Load the guide as a "read only" file.
2. Press: **Ctrl >** to jump quickly to each label.
3. Type: the appropriate information for each label.

<u>To print:</u>
4. Load the preprinted forms in the printer. Be sure you are consistent in loading them the same way each time.
5. Press: **Esc** and choose **Print, Printer.**

6. Clear the screen without saving, since the guide is a "read only" file. If you want to save the fill-in information, save the document with a different name.

GRAPHICS

Working with graphics layout in Microsoft Word can include using two different menus. Use the Format pOsition menu to manipulate paragraphs, placing them in specific positions in a page. Use the Library Link menu to import graphics from other graphics programs, to import files from spreadsheet programs, or to import bookmarked text from other Word documents.

When files are imported from other programs, you may use the Format pOsition menu and the Format Paragraph menu to position them in your document.

Note: *Also refer to the sections on Columns, Side-by-Side paragraphs, Borders, Line Draw, and Forms for further ideas for using Word to create professional looking documents.*

USING THE FORMAT POSITION MENU:

To position a paragraph:

1. Move: the **highlight** into the paragraph to be positioned.
2. Press: **Esc** and choose **Format, pOsition** to display the menu.

An example of the menu is shown below.

```
FORMAT POSITION
        horizontal frame position: Left       relative to:(Column)Margins Page
        vertical frame position: In line      relative to:(Margins)Page
        frame width: Single Column            distance from text: 0.167"
    Enter measurement or press F1 to select from list
```

The fields and how they may be used are as follows:

> **horizontal frame position:**   **relative to:(Column)Margin Page**
> These two fields allow you to position a paragraph at the left, center, right, outside, or inside, of columns, margins, or pages. (Obviously you won't be able to position a paragraph outside or inside a page.) Or you can specify you own measurement in "horizontal frame position" rather than selecting from the supplied list which you see when you press F1 in that field.
>
> **vertical frame position:**   **relative to:(Margins)Page**
> The vertical frame position sets a paragraph vertically in the page, and the choices are "in line" which means the paragraph will move up or down the page as text is entered or deleted above the paragraph; or other choices are to set the vertical position at the top, the bottom, or the center in relation to either the margins or the page.
>
> **frame width:**
> The frame width may be entered as a measurement or may be set to the width of a graphic, if that is what you are working with, or the width of a single column. If you have set Format Division Layout at multiple columns, you may then set the frame width for the number of columns you are entering on the page. This allows you to format a box to expand over two or more columns, for example.
>
> **distance from text:**
> The default, 0.167" means that there will be 0.167" of while space between the positioned paragraph and adjoining text. Any other measurement may be entered in the field to increase or decrease that white space.

<u>After entering responses in the Format pOsition menu fields:</u>
3. Press: **Enter** to return to the document.
4. Press: **Ctrl F9** to go to Print preView to see how the positioned paragraph will appear when it is printed.

Using Microsoft Word Advanced Functions, Appendix II

USING THE LIBRARY LINK GRAPHICS MENU:

To import a graphic:

1. Move: the **highlight** to the position in the document where the graphic is to be entered.
2. Press: **Esc** and choose **Library, Link, Graphics.**

An example of the menu is shown below.

```
LIBRARY LINK GRAPHICS filename: ▊
        file format:                    alignment in frame: Centered
        graphics width: 6.5"            graphics height: 6.5"
        space before: 0.167"            space after: 0.167"
    Enter filename or press F1 to select from list
```

The fields and how they may be used are as follows:

filename:
Type the path, filename, and extension of the graphic to be imported. The path must be included so Word will know where to find the file when it is printed, and the extension, which usually identifies the program used to create the graphic, must also be added.

file format:
Type the name of the program used to create the graphic which is being imported, or it may be displayed automatically when the direction arrow is pressed to move to this field.

alignment in frame:
The choices here, if you press F1, are Left, Centered, or Right. This will position the graphic within the paragraph.

graphics width/graphics height
A recommended measurement is displayed in both of these fields after the name of the graphic is entered; however, you may enter a new measurement in either or both fields which will change the size of your graphic.

space before/space after
These fields are similar to the "space before" and "space after" fields in the Format Paragraph menu. Leave them at 0 or enter a measurement.

After the responses have been set in the various fields:
3. Press: **Enter** to return to the document.

A paragraph containing the import instruction will be displayed in your document indicating the name of the graphic. An example is shown below.

.G.C:\WORD5\FORMPOS.SCR;4";0.586;Capture

The .G. identifies the message as a graphic and is automatically formatted as hidden text. This code is used by Word to find the graphic and print it. The remainder of the line consists of the path, filename, and extension, followed by the measurements for height and width, plus the name of the program used to create the graphic. In this case "Capture.COM" is the program included in the Microsoft Word package which is used to save screen images.

To change the size of the imported graphic:

After the document is printed, if you wish to change the measurements for the imported graphic, you may use the Library Link Graphic menu to do that.

1. Move: the **highlight** to the paragraph containing the graphic instruction.
2. Press: **Esc** and choose **Library, Link, Graphic**.
3. Move: the **highlight** to the height and width fields and type new measurements.
4. Press: **Enter** to return to the document.

You will notice that the paragraph will show the new measurements.

USING CAPTURE.COM

The CAPTURE.COM program may be used to save a screen image as a file, and the file may then be imported into a Word document. Capture.COM is part of Microsoft Word's program and is located in the directory where the Word program files have been installed.

To use Capture.Com the first time:

1. Go to DOS prompt or use Library Run.
2. Type: **capture/s** to load the capture program and display the setup menu.

The Capture Setup menu displays the options discussed below.

To change the setup:

1. Press: the letter that corresponds to the option you wish to choose.

Note: *When you display the screen corresponding to each option, an explanation is shown which helps you make the correct choices.*

    to select a display adapter press D
        Specifies the type of screen display your computer has.

    to enable/disable text screen as picture press T
        Capture can save in text mode; however, if you change this to save in graphics mode, you may then clip the boundaries of the screen image.

    to enable/disable saving in reverse video press V
        In reverse video, black will be saved as white, and white will be saved as black.

    to enable/disable clipping press P
        Clipping allows you to change the boundaries of the screen image. You cannot clip a Microsoft Windows screen; however, and must disable clipping if you are using Windows.

Using Microsoft Word Advanced Functions, Appendix II

    to enter the number of text lines per screen press N

    to quit and save settings press Q

To load the capture program the next time after setup:

1. Go to the DOS prompt or the Library Run menu.
2. Type: **capture** instead of **capture/s**.
3. Press; **Enter.**

To capture and save a screen image:

If you change the setup menu to enable clipping, you must be in graphics mode. Press **Alt F9** to go to graphics mode, if you normally type in text mode.

To begin to use the program:
1. Press: **Shift Print Screen** to begin the program.
2. Type: a name for the image or accept the recommended name displayed at the top of your screen.
3. Press: **Enter.**

To clip the boundaries of the image:
4. Press: the direction keys to move the boundary lines at the top and right sides of the screen.
5. Press: the **Tab** key to change so the boundary lines at the bottom and left sides of the screen may be moved by using the direction keys.
6. Press: the grey plus (+) sign (on the number key pad) to increase the increments by which the lines may be moved.

or

7. Press: the grey minus (-) sign (on the number key pad) to decrease the increments.

To save the image:
8. Press: **Enter.** When you hear a beep, the system will have completed the save. It may take several seconds to do this.

INDEX

To use the Index feature of Microsoft Word, you must mark or designate text to be included in the index. After designating the text, you will have to compile the index, which will copy the designated text to the end of the document and insert it with the appropriate page numbers.

To designate text which will be in the index as a main entry (first level):

Note: *The text to be designated must be followed by either:*
      a.   *a paragraph code.*
      b.   *a division code.*
      c.   *a semicolon formatted as hidden text.*
Any of these will indicate the end of the text to be designated.

1. Set "show hidden text" field to "yes" in the Options menu.
2. Move: the **highlight** to the text to be designated for the index.
3. Press: **Alt E** (or **Alt XE** if you are using a style sheet)to begin hidden text formatting.
4. Type: **.i.** to designate the text for the index.

5.	Move:	the **highlight** to the space following the text unless it is followed by a paragraph code or a division mark.
6.	Press:	**Alt E** (or **Alt XE** if you are using a style sheet).
7.	Type:	**;** to indicate an end of the text to be designated.

To designate text for index as a subentry (indented one level):

Note: Up to five levels may be designated.

1.	Move:	the **highlight** to the text to be designated.
2.	Press:	**Alt E** (or **Alt XE** if you are using a style sheet) to begin hidden text formatting.
3.	Type:	**.i.,** the text which will be the main entry, followed by a colon. Example: **.i.Format:**
4.	Move:	the **highlight** to the end of the text which is designated for the subentry.
5.	Press:	**Alt E** (or **Alt XE** if you are using a style sheet).
6.	Type:	**;** to indicate an end unless the text is followed by a paragraph code or a division break.

Hint: You may use the F4 (repeat edits) key to repeat entering the marks, if they are all the same.

To compile the index:

(The highlight may be in any position in the document.)

1.	Press:	**Esc,** choose **Options**, and set "show hidden text" at "No."

Note: If hidden text is displayed on screen, it will affect the repagination of the document.

2.	Press:	**Esc** and choose **Library, Index**.
3.	Press:	**Enter** to compile. The words to be included in the index will be displayed at the end of the document.

Note: The default for displaying the numbers in the index is to separate the entry and the numbers with two spaces. This may be changed in the Library Index menu to a comma or some other character.

To use the supplied macro "Index_entry.mac" to designate text:

1.		"Select" the text to be marked. The text must be "selected" in order for the beginning and end marks to be entered correctly.
2.	Press:	**Ctrl IE** to run the macro.

LINE DRAW

To use line draw:

1.	Move:	the **highlight** to the position where you wish to begin the line draw.
2.	Press:	**Ctrl F5** (an **LD** appears in the status line).
3.	Press:	the arrow keys to draw lines on the screen.
4.	Press:	**Ctrl F5** to exit the Line Draw mode.

To change the line draw character:

1. Press: **Esc** and choose **Options**.
2. Move: the **highlight** to the "line draw character" field.
3. Press: **F1** to display a list of the available characters.
4. Move: the **highlight** to the selected character.
5. Press: **Enter**.
6. Press: **Ctrl F5** to go to Line Draw mode and use the arrow keys to draw.
7. Follow steps 1 through 5 in this section to return to the default draw character.

To type text in a box created in the line draw mode:

1. Press: **F5** to go to Overtype mode.
2. Type: the text.

Note: *Do not use tabs, centering or other paragraph formatting commands, as they will distort the lines. Also, use the down arrow to move down a line, rather than Enter, to avoid distortion.*

To use a tab set with an underscore as a leader character to draw horizontal lines:

1. Press: **Alt F1** to go to the Tab Set menu.
2. Type: the position number of the tab and the letter corresponding to the type of alignment.
3. Press: **Tab** key to move the **highlight** to "leader char." field.
4. Choose: the underscore character.
5. Press: **Enter** to return to the document.
6. Press: **Tab** key to draw the line in the text.

MACROS

USING A SUPPLIED MACRO

Microsoft Word includes some user-supplied macros with the Microsoft Word package. Before any of the user-supplied macros can be run, you must merge the macro file, MACRO.GLY, with your glossary file.

To merge supplied macros:

<u>If you have a floppy disk system:</u>
1. Insert the Word Utilities disk into Drive B.
2. Press: **Esc** and choose **Transfer, Glossary, Merge**.
3. Type: **macro** and press **Enter** to merge.

<u>If you have a hard disk:</u>
(The MACRO.GLY file was copied automatically to the **word** directory when SETUP was run.)
4. Press: **Esc** and choose **Transfer, Glossary, Merge**.
5. Type: **c:\pathname\macro**.
6. Press: **Enter** to merge.

To run a supplied macro:

1. Press: **Esc** and choose **Insert**.
2. Press: **F1** to display the list of macros.
3. Move: the **highlight** to the macro desired.
4. Press: **Enter** to run.
5. Respond to screen prompts.

Note: *If you load the file named README onto the screen and print it out, you will have a hard copy of the names of the supplied macros, which includes the names of the keys used to run the macro.*

To run a macro using the control code (the keys named following the "Ctrl" in the macro name):

1. Move: the **highlight** to the position where the macro is to be inserted.
2. Press: **Ctrl** and the control codes (the two assigned letters).

The macro will automatically begin running on the screen.

USING THE MACRO PROGRAM

You can create a macro by <u>recording</u> keystrokes as they are typed, or by <u>writing</u> a macro which means you type representations for various keystrokes.

To record (create) a macro and assign a control code for using it:

It is best to plan the keystrokes to be included in the macro before you begin. This helps you create a macro which is accurate when it is used. However, if you make mistakes while recording keystrokes, it is possible to correct them while the macro is being created, or you may edit the macro after it has been saved.

1. Press: **Shift F3** to begin recording keystrokes. (RM--record macro--will be displayed in the status line.)
2. Enter the keystrokes to be included in the macro. These may be keystrokes for entering <u>commands</u> as well as keystrokes for entering <u>text</u>.
3. Press: **Shift F3** to stop recording keystrokes, and to display the message: "COPY to: ()."
4. Type: **filename.mac^<Ctrl** alphabet key**>** alphabet key.

Example: **letterhead.mac^<Ctrl l>h** could be the macro name for a macro which runs the keystrokes for a letterhead.

Note: *The "less than sign--<," "Ctrl plus a letter," the "greater than sign-->," and the following letter, assign the control codes used to run the macro.*

5. Press: **Enter** to save.

To run the macro using the control codes:

1. Move: the **highlight** to the position where the macro is to be entered.
2. Press: **Ctrl** key plus the two assigned letters.

Using Microsoft Word Advanced Functions, Appendix II

To run the macro from a list displayed in "Glossary":

1. Move: the **highlight** to the position where the macro is to be entered.
2. Press: **Esc** and choose **Insert**--<u>do not</u> use the "Insert" key.
3. Press: **F1** to display the list of glossary entries and the macros.
4. Move: the **highlight** to the macro to be run.
5. Press: **Enter**.

To edit a macro

1. Clear the screen.
2. Press: **Esc** and choose **Insert**.
3. Press: **F1** to display the list of macros.
4. Move: the **highlight** to the macro to be edited.
5. Type: ^ (Shift 6). This instructs the system to display the macro commands and text rather than to run the keystrokes.
6. Press: **Enter**.

<u>To make revisions:</u>
7. Edit the text of the macro as you would edit any other text. If you have to enter new commands, type them as they appear in the macro, <Esc> to represent **Esc** or <Enter> to represent **Enter**.

To save the edited macro:

1. Press: **Shift F10** to "select" the entire macro.
2. Press: **Esc** and choose **Copy**.
3. Press: **F1** to display the list of macros, or type the macro name.
4. Move: the **highlight** to the macro name, if you used F1 to display the list.
5. Press: **Enter**. A message will be displayed "Press Y to overwrite the Glossary, etc. . ."
6. Press: **Y** to overwrite and save the edited macro.

To delete a macro:

1. Press: **Esc** and choose **Transfer, Glossary, Clear.**
2. Press: **F1** to display the list of macros, or type the name of the macro, if you know exactly how it is written.
3. Move: the **highlight** to the macro name.
4. Press: **Enter** to display the message to confirm the deletion.
5. Press: **Y** to delete.

If you want to delete several macros at once, type each name, separated by a comma, or highlight each name, and type a comma, then press **Enter**, and press **Y** to delete.

To write a macro:

Writing a macro takes a good deal of planning. You have to know the keystrokes involved in using the various features you want to include in the macro, plus the various macro instructions which may be included. You also must know how to write the representations for those features. The Word manual gives complete information on the format for these features and instructions.

The following is an example of a written macro. The macro, which is one of the supplied macros that is part of the Word program, can be used to copy and move a block of text.

```
«pause Select text to be copied, press Enter when done»

<esc>c<enter>«pause Select destination point, press Enter when done»

<ins>
```

The basic procedure for writing; however, is as follows:

1. Write the text, the macro instructions, and the representations of keystrokes.

2. "Select" the entire written macro as it is displayed on the screen.

3. Press: **Esc** and choose either **Copy** or **Delete.**
4. Type: the name for the macro which includes the filename, the extension, a caret and the control codes. See the following example.

filename.mac^<Ctrl F>M

5. Press: **Enter** to save. The macro will be stored in the current glossary.

6. When you Quit the current word processing session, you will be prompted to save the glossary. Respond by typing **Y** to save the macro permanently.

MATH

You may add, subtract, multiply, divide, and calculate percentages using Microsoft Word.

Operators must be entered to perform the calculations:

Functions:	Operator
Addition	+ or no operator
Subtract	−
Multiply	*
Divide	/
Percent	%

To add:

1. Type: all of the numbers to be added.

```
Example:   147      or   23 + 56 =
           2189
```

2. "Select" the numbers.
3. Press: **F2** to add.

The result will be displayed in "scrap."
4. Press: **F6** to turn off "Extend."
5. Move: the **highlight** to the position where the total is to be inserted.
6. Press: **Insert** key to insert the answer from "scrap."

Note: If no operator is entered, "selected" numbers will be added.

To subtract:

1. Type: the first number.
2. Type: −(minus sign).
3. Type: the number to be subtracted.

```
Example:  $79.50    or 15 - 5 =
         - 7.25
```

4. "Select" both numbers and the operator.
5. Press: **F2** to display the answer in "scrap" and press **F6** to turn off "Extend".
6. Move: the **highlight** to the position where the answer is to be inserted.
7. Press: **Insert** key to insert the answer.

To multiply:

1. Type: the first number.
2. Type: * (asterisk).
3. Type: the second number.

```
Example:  5 * 5=     or    95
                           *2
```

4. "Select" both numbers plus the operator.
5. Press: **F2** to display the answer in "scrap" and press **F6** to turn off "Extend."
6. Move: the **highlight** to the position where the answer is to be inserted.
7. Press: **Insert** key to insert the answer.

To divide:

1. Type: the first number to be divided.
2. Type: / (slash).
3. Type: the second number.

```
Example:  144/12=    or    2000
                           /100
```

4. "Select" both numbers and the operator.
5. Press: **F2** to display the answer in "scrap" and press **F6** to turn off "Extend."
6. Move: the **highlight** to the position where the answer is to be entered.
7. Press: **Insert** key to insert the answer in text.

To calculate a percent:

1. Type: a number followed by the % sign.
2. Type: an * and the number to be multiplied by the amount of the percent.

or

3. Type: the number, then an * and the percent.

```
Example:  7% of *75 =        or 85
                                *7%
```

4. "Select" both numbers.
5. Press: **F2** to display the number in "scrap" and press **F6** to turn off "Extend".
6. Move: the **highlight** to the position where the answer is to be inserted.
7. Press: **Insert** key to insert the answer.

MERGE: FILLING IN FORMS

To create the form document similar to the example below:

```
«DATA·STUDENTS.DOC»↵

Last·name·«lname»→                First·name·«fname»→              ↓

Address·«address»→        →                →                        ↓

City·«city»→                      State·«state»→ Zip·«zip»→         ↓

Classification·«class»→   →                →                        ↓
¶
```

1. Go to the Options menu and set "show non-printing symbols" field at "All" so you will be able to see your tab marks as you create the form.

2. Format a paragraph mark with a box. Then as you enter the text, use **Shift Enter** to begin each new line. Tab marks which will be formatted with the underline character are used to draw the horizontal lines within the box.

3. Type: the data instruction as displayed above.
4. Press: **Shift Enter** to begin a new line.

<u>To set tabs for appropriate positions:</u>
5. Press: **Alt F1**.
6. Type: the position number for each tab in the form.
7. Press: **Enter** to return to the document.

<u>To enter the labels and field names:</u>
8. Type: the first label followed by a field name and chevron as shown in the example.
9. Press: the **Tab** key.
10. Repeat for the remaining labels and field names.

Using Microsoft Word Advanced Functions, Appendix II 267

To format the field name, the chevron, and tab mark with the underline character:

11. Move: the **highlight** to the first field name.
12. "Select" the field name, the chevron, and the following tab mark.
13. Press: **Alt U** or **Alt XU** if you are using a style sheet to format with the underline character.

Note: *This will draw the lines as displayed in the box in the example. Any method of drawing lines may be used; however this is an easy way when creating a form that will be filled in using the merge program.*

14. Repeat for the remaining labels and fields names.

To create the data file:

1. Type: the data file similar to the example shown below.

```
lname,fname,address,city,state,zip,class¶
Sullivan,Roger,1501 Seneca,Seattle,WA,98103,Junior¶
Voges,Jan,1015 Grand Blvd.,Montebello,CA,90640,Senior¶
Miles,Ronda,879 Boyles Ave.,Phoenix,AZ,85028,Freshman¶
```

2. Check the data file for accuracy.
3. Save the document.

To use Print Merge to fill in the form:

1. Load the form document on the screen.
2. Press: **Esc**.
3. Choose: **Print, Merge** or **Print, Merge, Document**.
4. Type: a filename if you are merging to a document.
5. Press: **Enter** to merge.

MERGE: FORM LETTERS

Use the merge function to produce personalized form letters.

There are three basic steps in a merge procedure:

1. Create the main document which contains (a) the statement asking for the appropriate data document, (b) the field names in the data document which are to be used in the merge, and (c) the text of the letter.

2. Create the data document which contains the header record consisting of the field names and the data records which contain the information about each individual-- name, address, city, state, zip, etc.

3. Merge the main document with the information in the data document.

To create the main document:

Press **Ctrl [** and **Ctrl]** to type the chevrons which enclose the "data instruction" and the field names.
Field names may contain up to sixty-four characters.
Field names may not contain decimal point.
Field names may not contain spaces.
Field names do not have to appear in the same order in the main document as they do in the data document.

1. Type the DATA» instruction on the first line, enclosed in chevrons. See the example below. The filename must be the same as the filename of the data document. See "To create a data document" below.

```
«DATA FILENAME.DOC»

«title» «fname» «lname»
«address»
«city», «state»  «zip»

Dear «title» «lname»:

Thank you for your letter of «date».

Sincerely,


Your name
Your title
```

2. Save the file and clear the screen.

or

3. Split the window, and create the data document in window 2. This allows you to view the various field names used in the form document and reduces the chances of error in typing the heading line in the data document.

To create the data document:

The data document must contain the following information:

The **field names** are the names in the header record (first line) at the top of the document. The field names are separated by commas, and there are no spaces between the names.

A **record** for each individual, which consists of all the information (fields) pertaining to that one individual. A record is ended with a hard return (**Enter**). Do not have a paragraph mark on the line below the last record. This may cause the merge to be unsuccessful.

The **fields** consist of each item of information about one individual and must be separated by commas. If a field contains a comma, then you must set off the field in quotation marks.

Using Microsoft Word Advanced Functions, Appendix II

1. Type: the text for the data document according to the example below.

```
title,fname,lname,address,city,state,zip,date
Mr.,Allen,Baker,123 North
Ave.,Seattle,WA,98109,February 15
Ms.,Ruth,Simons,"Apt. 1, First Ave.
S.",Renton,WA,98245,March 21
```

Note: *The text may wrap in a record. This is acceptable, as long as you didn't press* **Enter** *to insert the line end at that point.*

2. Save the document and clear the screen. The filename must be the same as the filename in the "Data" message in the main document (see the example above).

To merge the main document with the data document and print the final output:

1. Load the main document on the screen.
2. Press: **Esc** and choose **Print, Merge, Printer**.
3. Press: **Enter**.

Note: *If the merge is not successful, check both documents for field names which are not spelled exactly the same way. Also look for extra paragraph marks in the data document, including an extra paragraph mark at the end of the document--this will stop the merge. An extra comma after the last field name in the header line will also cause the merge to be unsuccessful.*

To merge to a document:

1. Load the main document on the screen.
2. Press: **Esc** and choose **Print, Merge, Document**.
3. Type: a filename for the merge output.
4. Press: **Enter**.

The merged document may then be loaded, edited, and printed at a later date; however, this obviously does take up disk space.

MERGING RECORDS WITH DIFFERENT NUMBERS OF LINES

To create the main document as follows:

```
«DATA FILENAME.DOC»

April 15, 1989

«address»

Dear «name»:

Thank you for your recent inquiry.

Sincerely yours,


Your name
```

1. Type the data instruction similar to the example above.
2. Enter the field names in the appropriate positions.
3. Type the text for the main document.
4. Save the document.

To create the data document:

See the example below. A screen print is displayed to show the new line marks at the ends of the lines, and the paragraph marks at the ends of the records.

1. Press: **Shift Enter** rather than **Enter** at the ends of each line in the address. This formats the address as one field.

2. Enclose the address field in quotation marks when it contains a comma.

3. Press: **Enter** after the field which will be used in the salutation to indicate an end to a record.

```
address,name¶
"Mr. Alfred Brown↓
2041 S. W. 85th Blvd.↓
South Bronx, NY 10024",Mr. Brown¶
"Ms. Joan Bannister↓
ABC Corporation↓
16079 S. W. Olive Way↓
Seattle, WA  98073",Ms. Bannister¶
```

Save the document (be sure the name matches the name in the "DATA" message in the main document), and clear the screen.

Using Microsoft Word Advanced Functions, Appendix II

To merge:

1. Load the main document
2. Press: **Esc** and choose **Print, Merge, Document.**

or

3. Press: **Esc** and choose **Print, Merge, Printer** to merge with the data document.

To merge only specified records:

1. Load the main document.
2. Press: **Esc** and choose **Print, Merge, Options.**
3. Move: arrow key to "range" field.
4. Press: space bar to set "Records" as the response.
5. Move: arrow key to "record numbers" field.
6. Type: the numbers of the records to be merged with the main document.
7. Press: **Enter.**
8. Complete the merge procedure as outlined in instructions above.

To use IF/ENDIF statements

IF/ENDIF instructions are included in field names to eliminate blank lines when certain fields are empty. For example, if some addresses contain one line instead of two, the blank line in the final output will be avoided if an IF/ENDIF instruction is included.

The following is an example of how these statements are used:

```
«company»
«name»
«streeta»
«IF streetb»«streetb»
«ENDIF»«city», «state» «zip»
«IF country» «country» «ENDIF»
«IF streetb=""» «ENDIF»
```

The last line is entered to insert a blank line at the end of the address if there is no "streetb." This would be used only when setting up the form document for labels when the spacing needs to be controlled because of label size.

MERGE: LABELS

LABELS IN A SINGLE COLUMN

To create a main document:

The main document contains the field names and must be formatted to reflect the label size (for example, 1" X 3"). Each label will be printed on a "separate page" which is 1" long.

See example below:

```
«DATA FILENAME.DOC»«title» «fname» «lname»
«address»
«city», «state» «zip»
```

To set the margins to correspond to the label size being used:
1. Press: **Esc** and choose **Format, Division, Margins**.
2. Set the menu fields as follows:
   - top: = 0
   - bottom: = 0
   - left: = 0.5
   - right: = 0
   - page length = 1" (or whatever the label height is).

Name and save the main document.

To create a data document:

Create and save a data document similar to text in the box below.

```
title,fname,lname,address,city,state,zip,date
Mr.,Allen,Baker,123 North
Ave.,Seattle,WA,98109,February 15
Ms.,Ruth,Simons,"Apt. 1, First Ave.
S.",Renton,WA,98245,March 21
```

To merge to a document file:

1. Load the main document.
2. Press: **Esc** and choose **Print, Merge, Document**.
3. Type: a filename for the merged output.
4. Press: **Enter**.

To merge and print:

1. Load the main document.
2. Press: **Esc** and choose **Print, Merge, Printer**.

SHEET-FEED LABELS IN THREE COLUMNS

To create a main document:

1. Type: the text for the main document as displayed in the example below.

```
«DATA FILENAME.DOC»«title» «fname» «lname»
«address»
«city», «state» «zip»
```

Copy the text for as many labels as may be printed in the one column (probably nine) and add the message «NEXT» at the beginning of each label form. See example below.

```
«DATA FILENAME.DOC»«title» «fname» «lname»
«address»
«city», «state» «zip»

«NEXT»«title» «fname» «lname»
«address»
«city», «state» «zip»

«NEXT»«title» «fname» «lname»
«address»
«city», «state» «zip»
```

2. "Select" all of the text for the first label except the "DATA" message.
3. Press: **Alt F3** to copy into scrap.
4. Move: the **highlight** to the line below the first label form.
5. Press: **Insert** key to copy.
6. Move the **highlight** to the beginning of the second label form, and add the message «NEXT».
7. Copy the second label form into scrap and insert it below the second label form.
8. Repeat until you have about ten label forms in the first column. (You may have to adjust this number, and also adjust the spacing depending upon the size of the labels you are going to be using.)

To set Format Division Layout for three columns:
9. Press: **Esc** and choose **Format, Division, Layout**.
10. Move: the **highlight** to "number of columns" field.
11. Type: **3**.
12. Move: the **highlight** to "space between columns" field.
13. Type: **0**.
14. Move: the **highlight** to "division break."
15. Set: at "Column."
16. Press: **Enter**.

To copy the form for the labels from the first column to the second and third columns.
17. "Select" all of the forms in the first column, plus the division mark for the first column.
18. Press: **Alt F3** to copy to scrap.
19. Move: the **highlight** below the division mark.
20. Press: **Insert**.
21. Repeat for the third column.

To create the data document:

1. Create the data document like the example in the box below.

```
title,fname,lname,address,city,state,zip,date
Mr.,Allen,Baker,123 North
Ave.,Seattle,WA,98109,February 15
Ms.,Ruth,Simons,"Apt. 1, First Ave.
S.",Renton,WA,98245,March 21
```

2. Save it (be sure the filename matches the «DATA» message filename in the main document) and clear the screen.

Then either merge to a document (**Esc** and choose **Print, Merge, Document**, type file name and **Enter**) or merge and print (**Esc** and choose **Print, Merge, Printer**). It's a good idea to print the first page on regular paper to see if your spacing is correct.

MERGE: SET AND ASK VARIABLES

Information may be entered from the keyboard during a merge, by using SET and ASK variables in the main document. You do not use a data document with this procedure.

The **SET** variable will set information in every document during the merge.

The **ASK** variable will allow you to enter text from the keyboard in each document.

An example of a main document containing **SET** and **ASK** variables is on the following page.

* The words following SET and ASK are the field names.

* The text following the question marks are messages which will be displayed on screen during the merge to prompt you to type specific information at each "ASK" pause.

```
«SET date=?Type today's date»
«ASK name=?Type title, first and last names»
«ASK street=?Type street address»
«ASK city=?Type city»
«ASK state=?Type state»
«ASK zip=?Type zip»

«date»

«name»
«street»
«city», «state»   «zip»

(Type the text of the main document).
```

To create the main document:

1. Type: the text in the format displayed in the box above.
2. Name and save the document.

To merge with data entered from the keyboard:

1. Load the main document.
2. Press: **Esc** and choose **Print, Merge, Document** to merge to a new document.
   or
3. Press: **Esc** and choose **Print, Merge, Printer** to print the final output.

<u>At the date prompt:</u>
4. Type: today's date and press **Enter**.

Using Microsoft Word Advanced Functions, Appendix II   275

At the remaining prompts:
5.   Type: appropriate response depending upon the screen message.
6.   Press: **Enter** after each response.

Repeat steps 4 through 5 for additional documents. Once the date has been set, it will not have to be typed again, since it was entered as a SET variable.

7.   To end the merge, press **Esc**.

OUTLINE

The outline feature allows you to type an outline and add document text in the same file. The outline feature is a part of your text, not a separate file, as it is in most word processing systems. In order to view the text in outline form, press **Shift F2** to toggle between the outline view and document view. Also, if you wish to reorganize the various sections of your outline, press **Shift F5** to go to "Organize" view. In this mode, you may highlight large sections of text, which are displayed only by their headings, then move those sections by moving the heading.

To enter headings in outline form:

1.   Press: **Shift F2** to go to outline view. The word **Level 1**, will be displayed in the lower left corner of the screen.
2.   Type: the text for the first entry in level 1.
3.   Press: **Enter** to return--note the level number remains the same.

To type headings in level 2:
4.   Press: **Alt 0** to increase the outline level to 2.
5.   Type: the heading and press **Enter**.

To return to a previous level (to the left)
6.   Press: **Alt 9** to reduce the outline level (notice the display in the lower left corner of the screen).
7.   Type: the heading and press **Enter**.

To add text under a heading:

Note: You may be in either "Outline" view or "Document" view.

1.   Move: the **highlight** to the end of the heading level where the text is to be added.
2.   Press: **Enter**.
3.   Press: **Alt P** (or **Alt XP** if you are using a style sheet) to display the word "Text" in the lower left corner of the screen when you are in "Outline" view, or to display **SP** in the left column when you are in "Document" view.
4.   Type: text.

To collapse or expand heading levels and text:

You must be in "Outline" view to collapse or expand outline levels or text.

Press:	To:
Minus	Collapse subheadings and text
Plus	Expand subheadings
Shift minus	Collapse text only
Shift plus	Expand subheadings and text
Asterisk	Expand headings throughout document
Shift F10 and Asterisk	Expand all headings and text

To organize (or rearrange) headings and accompanying text:

From "Outline" view:
1. Press: **Shift F5** to display "Organize" in lower left corner of screen and go to the outline organize mode.
2. Move: the **highlight** to "select" the heading to be moved.
3. Press: **delete** to move text into scrap.
4. Move: the **highlight** to a new position.
5. Press: **insert** key to insert the heading and all text under that heading.

To add numbering to outline levels:

1. Press: **Shift F2** to go to outline view from document view.
2. Press: **Esc** and choose **Library, Number**.
3. Choose: "Update" and set "restart sequence" at "Yes."
4. Press: **Enter** to number.

To remove numbering from an outline:

1. Press: **Shift F2** to go to "Outline" view.
2. Press: **Esc** and choose **Library, Number**.
3. Choose: "Remove."
4. Press: **Enter**.

SIDE-BY-SIDE PARAGRAPHS

Side-by-side paragraphs are useful for typing schedules, scripts, results of studies where questions are displayed with corresponding responses, or any type of document where you wish to have information displayed in paragraphs which are next to each other.

The steps to create a document using side-by-side paragraphs are:

1. Type the text for each paragraph with no blank lines between paragraphs.

2. Format each paragraph, setting indents from the left and right margins to correspond to the left and right sides of each column, set each paragraph with "1" line in the "space before" field, and set each as a "side-by-side" paragraph in the Format Paragraph menu.

To type the text:

1. Type: each paragraph in normal paragraph format as shown in the example below.

```
9:00-10:00
General Session:   Washington State Business Education
Association.
Room 106
```

Determine the layout, (i.e, the size of the indents from the left and right margins) of your columns as you want them to appear in the final output. See the example below for the document as it will be printed.

* The right side of the first column is "indented" from the right margin.
* Both sides of the middle column are "indented" from both the left and right margins.
* The left side of the third column is "indented" from the left margin
* Be sure to allow for space between the columns.

```
9:00-10:00         General session:                Room 109
                   Washington State Business
                   Education Association
```

To format the paragraph in the first column:

1. Move: the **highlight** into the first paragraph.
2. Press: **Esc** and choose **Format, Paragraph**.
3. Set fields as follows:
   - "right indent" = 4.5 (the amount of space from the right margin to the right side of the first column)
   - "space before" = 1 (if you want a blank line between rows of columns)
   - "side-by-side" = "yes"
4. Press: **Enter** to format. (A "]" is displayed in the ruler line.)
5. Move: the **highlight** to the remaining paragraphs to be entered in the **first column**.
6. Press: **F4** to repeat the edit, i.e., apply the formatting for the first column.

To format the paragraph in the center column:

1. Repeat the steps outlined above except set both "left indent" and "right indent" fields to be indented to the point where the center column will be entered, i.e.:
   - "left indent" = 1.75 (to indent 1.75" from the left margin)
   - "right indent" = 1.75 (to indent 1.75" from the right margin)
   - "space before" = 1
   - "side-by-side" = "Yes"
2. Press: **Enter.**
3. Move: the **highlight** to the remaining paragraphs to be formatted for the center column.
4. Press: **F4** to repeat the edit.

To format the paragraph in the third column:

1. Move: the **highlight** to the paragraph to be entered in the third column.
2. Press: **Esc** and choose **Format, Paragraph**.
3. Set fields as follows:
   - "left indent" = 4.5
   - ""space before" = 1
   - "side-by-side" = "Yes"

4. Press: **Enter**.
5. Move: the **highlight** to remaining paragraphs to be entered in the third column.
6. Press: **F4** to repeat edits.

After formatting each paragraph go to "show layout" mode to see how the text will look when it is printed:

1. Press: **Alt F4** to go to "show layout."
2. Press: **Alt F4** again to leave "show layout" mode.

SORT

The sort function allows you to sort text in paragraphs, lists, tables, or in data documents used in merge. The sort may by either alphanumeric, or numeric, and in ascending or in descending order.

If the sort is alphanumeric, Word sorts in the following order:
1. Paragraphs or lines with punctuation marks at the beginning are displayed first.
2. If you set "case" field at "Yes," lines beginning with uppercase letters will come before lowercase letters.
3. Lines or paragraphs beginning with letters will come before numbers in an alphanumeric sort.

To sort a paragraph:

The paragraphs will be sorted on the basis of the <u>first word</u> in the paragraph.

1. Type the paragraphs to be sorted.
2. Save the document. Since the "sort" program requires a large amount of memory, always be sure to save the document before the sort program is run.

<u>To sort the paragraphs in alphabetical order:</u>
3. "Select" the paragraphs to be sorted.
4. Press: **Esc** and choose **Library, Autosort**--note that Alphanumeric is highlighted.
5. Press: **Enter** to sort the paragraphs.

To sort a list:

Sorting a list is actually the same as sorting a paragraph, for each line in the list is considered a paragraph by Word.

1. Type: each entry and press **Enter**.

Note: Do not press **Shift Enter** *(New Line)* at the ends of the lines. *The text will not be sorted. However, when you sort a* <u>column</u> *in a table, the sort will be successful when* **Shift Enter** *has been used at the ends of lines.*

2.		"Select" the entire list.
3.	Press:	**Esc** and choose **Library, Autosort**.
4.	Set:	"by" field at alphanumeric.
5.	Press:	**Enter** to sort the list alphabetically. (The sort will be on the basis of the first word in each line.)

To sort the list in descending alphabetical order:

6.		"Select" the list.
7.	Press:	**Esc** and choose **Library, Autosort**.
8.	Move:	the **highlight** to "sequence" field and choose "descending."
9.	Press:	**Enter** to sort.

To sort a column in a table:

1.	Move:	the **highlight** to the first character in the column.
2.	Press:	**Shift F6** (column selection).
3.	Press:	right arrow and the down arrow to "select" the entire column, including the paragraph codes.
4.	Press:	**Esc** and choose **Library, Autosort**.
5.		Change any of the fields in the Autosort menu.
6.	Press:	**Enter** to sort.

To sort records in a data file:

Sorting records in a data file is a paragraph sort.

1.	Move:	the field to be sorted to the <u>beginning</u> of each record.
2.	Move:	the **highlight** to the first record. (Do not include the header record at the top line.)
3.	Press:	**F6** to turn on Extend.
4.	Press:	the **down** arrow and **End** key to "select" the rest of the records.
5.	Press:	**Esc** and choose **Library, Autosort**.
6.		Set sequence for either ascending or descending.
7.	Press:	**Enter** to sort.

STYLE SHEETS

A <u>style</u> is a collection of formatting commands which may be applied as one command to a character, a paragraph, or a division.

After several styles have been created, they are saved in a file called a **style sheet.** This style sheet may then be attached to a document, and the formatting is applied to text in the document by pressing the **Alt** key with the key code (see the definition of a key code on the following page).

USING THE NORMAL.STY STYLE SHEET

If you don't create a style sheet, Word automatically attaches a style sheet to your document. The file name of that style sheet is NORMAL.STY. (The extension .STY is always used in naming style sheets.) If you wish to change a default value (i.e., change the margins for example), that change is made in the NORMAL.STY style sheet.

To change a default in the NORMAL.STY style sheet:

1. Press: **Esc** and choose **Gallery** to go to the area where a style sheet is displayed. If this is the first time the NORMAL.STY is to be changed, the screen will be blank. (The file name is displayed in the right corner of the window.)
2. Press: **I** for Insert--the menu is displayed at the bottom of the screen.
3. Move: the **highlight** to "usage" field and choose the option to be changed.

   a. If you wish to change <u>character formatting for the entire document</u> (for example, to change the default Font Name) choose "Paragraph" usage rather than "Character" usage.

   b. Choose "Character" usage to format single characters such as page numbers, footnotes numbers, etc.

   c. If you wish to change paragraph formatting, choose "Paragraph."

   d. If you wish to change margins (or any other division formatting characteristics), choose "Division."

4. Move: the **highlight** to "variant" field and press F1 to display a list of variants.

Note: *A* **variant** *is a preset* **style** *identified by a number or a name. The variants with names (i.e., "standard") are applied automatically to the document when the style sheet is attached to it. There are variants for each type of usage.*

The highlighted variant in the "Character" list is "Page." The highlighted variant in the "Paragraph" or "Division" list is "Standard."

5. Move: the **highlight** to the variant to be selected.
6. Press: **Enter** to display the formatting commands included in the variant selected.

<u>To change the default formatting commands:</u>
(The style must be highlighted.)
7. Press: **F** to choose **Format**.
8. Make the changes as you would in regular document text.
9. Press: **Enter** to return to the Gallery screen.
10. Press: **E** to choose **Exit** and return to the document screen.

When you clear the screen, close the window, or exit WORD, you will be prompted to save the style sheet. Respond with a Y to save.

Note: *If you have changed the NORMAL.STY style sheet, you will have to press Alt X and the letter representing the type of formatting to be applied, instead of Alt and the letter. For example, to apply "justify," press Alt XJ rather than Alt J.*

Using Microsoft Word Advanced Functions, Appendix II

CREATING A STYLE SHEET

You may create a new style sheet which may be attached to a document replacing the default style sheet NORMAL.STY.

1. Press: **Esc** and choose **Gallery**.

Note: *In the style sheet screen, NORMAL.STY will be displayed in the lower right corner of the screen. If you had made changes to the normal style sheet, those "styles" will be displayed on the screen. The styles should be deleted so that new styles may be created, unless you want those styles to be included in the new style sheet. To delete a style, highlight it and press D to choose Delete.*

To create a style:

1. Press: **I** for Insert to display the style menu.

The following are the fields in the style menu and the responses to them:

Field	Response
Key code:	Type one or two characters which will represent the style. (For example: **SP** for standard paragraph.) This key code is used with the **Alt** key to assign the style to a character, paragraph or division in your document.
Usage:	Choose the type of formatting to be used, i.e., character, paragraph, or division.
Variant:	Press F1 to display a list of names and numbers of styles which may automatically be included in the style sheet, or type a number or name to be selected. (Refer to the previous page for more information about variants.)
Remarks:	Type a short descriptive term which will help identify the style.

At "key code"
2. Type: the one or two keys to press with the **Alt** key to apply this style to text.
3. Move: the **highlight** to "usage" field and choose the usage to be used.
4. Move: the **highlight** to "remarks" field.
5. Type: the description of the style.
6. Move: the **highlight** to "variant" field.
7. Press: **F1** to display the variants
8. Move: the **highlight** to the variant to be used.
9. Press: **Enter**.

The preset formatting commands included in that variant will be displayed on the screen.

To format the style (change it to include formatting commands which you want):

The style must be highlighted.
1. Press: **F** to choose **Format**.

Note: *The format menu displayed will depend upon the "usage" which has been selected:*

    If "Character" was selected, the Format Character menu will be displayed.

    If "Paragraph" was selected, Character, Paragraph, Tab, and Border option will be displayed.

If "Division" was selected, Margins, Page numbers, Layout, and Line numbers options will be displayed.

2.	Choose:	the appropriate submenu, and set each field for the formatting characteristics to be selected.
3.	Press:	**Enter**.
4.	Repeat:	for each type of formatting (character, paragraph, division) to be applied to the style.

To name and save the style sheet:

1.	Press:	**Esc** and choose **Transfer, Save**.
2.	Type:	a filename.
3.	Press:	**Enter** to save.
4.	Press:	**E** to choose **Exit** to return to the document area.

USING A STYLE SHEET

To attach the style sheet to a document:

1.	Press:	**Esc** and choose **Format, Stylesheet, Attach**.
2.	Press:	**F1** to display the list of available stylesheets.
3.	Move:	the **highlight** to the style sheet to be selected.
4.	Press:	**Enter** to attach.

Note: *If you know the name of the style sheet, press Esc FSA, type the filename, and press Enter.*

To use the styles in a document

<u>To set "show non-printing symbols" field at "Partial" to display the paragraph marks.</u>
1.	Press:	**Esc** and choose **Options** to set "show non-printing symbols" at "partial" and press **Enter**.

<u>To set "show style bar" field at "Yes" to display the key codes in the left margin.</u>
2.	Press:	**Esc** and choose **Options** and set "show style bar" at "yes" and **Enter**.

<u>To apply a style:</u>
3.	Press:	**Alt** and the key code corresponding to the style to be applied. The key code characters will be displayed in the left margin.
4.	Type:	the text to be formatted with that style.
5.	Repeat for other styles.	

To revise the formatting of a style:

1.	Press:	**Esc** and choose **Gallery**.
2.	Move:	the **highlight** to style to be changed.
3.	Press:	**F** for Format and choose the type of formatting to be used to make the changes. (This procedure is the same as changing formatting in documents using the character, paragraph, and division formatting menus.)
4.	Press:	**Enter** to make the changes to the style.
5.	Press:	**E** for Exit to return to the document.

To delete a style:

1. Press: **Esc** and choose **Gallery**.
2. When the style sheet is displayed, move the **highlight** to the style to be deleted.
3. Press: **D** to Delete and **E** to Exit.

Note: *When you "Quit" Word at the end of the session you will be prompted to save the Style Sheet. Be sure to press "y" for "yes" to save the edited style sheet.*

To create a style by example:

<u>In the document screen:</u>
1. Type: the text and format it--for example, in Italic and double-spaced.
2. "Select" the text.
3. Press: **Esc** and choose **Format, Stylesheet, Record** or **Alt F10**.
4. Set the "usage," "key code," "remark," and "variant" fields as you did in the previous steps to correspond to the formatting.
5. Press: **Enter** to create the style.

Note: *This procedure will add the style to the style sheet which is attached to the current document; however, you will need to respond with y for yes to save the stylesheet when you clear the screen or quit.*

To see a list of supplied styles:

1. Press: **Esc** and choose **Gallery, Transfer, Load**.
2. Press: **F1** to display the list.

Note: *The supplied styles are in the same directory with the Word program files when the program is installed. Be sure you look in that directory for the list of supplied styles. The name of that directory is probably "Word5" if you followed the Microsoft Word manual directions for installing the program on a hard disk.*

TABLE OF CONTENTS

Text may be marked or designated to appear in a table of contents. Then Microsoft Word will automatically copy this designated text to a table of contents area and display the entries with their corresponding page numbers.

The steps for designating text for the table of contents are similar to those used in designating text for the index.

1. Choose **Options** and set "show hidden text" field at "Yes."

2. Press **Alt E** or **Alt XE** to begin hidden text format.

3. Type **.c.** to designate level one in the table of contents, or **.c.:** for level two. You may designate text for up to five levels in the table of contents. The number of colons following **.c.** designates the level of the subheading.

To show hidden text on the screen:

1. Press: **Esc** and choose **Options**.
2. Set: "show hidden text" field at "Yes."
3. Press: **Enter**.

To designate the entries for the headings which will appear in a table of contents:

Note: *The .c. must be formatted as hidden text so that it will not be printed out with the document.*

1. Move: the **highlight** to the first entry to be designated.
2. Press: **Alt E** or **Alt XE** to begin "hidden text" formatting.
3. Type: .c. to designate the text for the table of contents.

Note: *The text to be designated must be followed by a paragraph code or a division mark. If it doesn't have a paragraph code or a division mark at the end, insert a semicolon formatted as hidden text at the end of the text.*

4. Repeat for each of the remaining entries. Use the **F4** key to repeat entering .c.

To designate entries for subheadings:

1. Move: the **highlight** to the entry to be designated.
2. Press: **Alt E** or **Alt XE** to format as hidden text.
3. Type: .c.: for the first subheading
   or: .c.:: for the second subheading.

Reminder: *The number of colons following .c. designates the level of the subheading.*

4. Repeat the formatting the same way you formatted for the main heading.

To compile the table of contents:

Note: *Set "show hidden text" at "No." If hidden text is displayed on screen it may change the repagination of the document.*

1. Press: **Esc** and choose **Options**.
2. Set: "show hidden text" field at "no" and press **Enter**.

<u>To compile:</u>
3. Press: **Esc** and choose **Library, Table**.
4. Set: "from" field at "Codes."

Note: *If you used the "outline" feature when you created your document, you may choose "outline" in the "from" field to compile the table of contents; however if you intend to use this option, you must first display your text in Outline view, and show the headings and subheadings which you want to appear in the table of contents. The text typed at the various outline levels will then be copied to the table of contents in corresponding levels.*

5. Make changes to other fields in the Library Table menu if it is appropriate.
6. Press: **Enter** to compile.

Note: *When the process is complete, the table of contents will be displayed at the end of the document, and will be in a separate division. This allows you to make formatting changes that affect only the table of contents. For example, you may wish to set the margins at a measurement which is different from the rest of the document or change the page number format to "i" for example.*

To use the supplied macro "Toc_entry.mac" to designate text for the table of contents.

1. "Select" the text to be designate for the table of contents. The entire block of text must be "selected" so the beginning and ending codes may be added.
2. Press: **Ctrl TE** to run the macro.
3. Use the Library Table menu to compile the table of contents.

VERTICAL TABS

Refer to LINE DRAW for instructions for setting a tab with an underscore as a leader character to draw horizontal lines.

Vertical tabs are used to draw vertical lines in tables.

To set a vertical tab:

1. Press: **Alt F1** to go to the Tab Set menu.
2. Type: the position number for the tab.
3. Type: **V** to specify Vertical.
4. Repeat: for as many vertical tabs as you need.
5. Press: **Enter** to return to the document.

To use a vertical tab:

When **Enter** is pressed from the Tab set menu, the vertical lines will be displayed on one line of text. Each time **Enter** is pressed, the vertical lines will be repeated on the next line. When other tabs are used, the **highlight** skips over the vertical tabs, since they are already entered.

APPENDIX III

PROMPT SHEET FOR USING MICROSOFT WORD

USING THE FUNCTION KEYS

Calculate	F2	Print	Ctrl F8
Collapse body text	Shift F11	Print preview	Ctrl F9
Collapse heading	F11	Record macro on/off	Shift F3
Column select on/off	Shift F6	Record style	Alt F10
Copy to scrap	Alt F3	Repeat last edit	F4
Expand all	Ctrl F12	Repeat search	Shift F4
Expand body text	Shift F12	Save	Ctrl F10
Expand glossary name	F3	Select current line	Shift F9
Expand heading	F12	Select next paragraph	F10
Extend selection on/off	F6	Select next sentence	Shift F8
Font name	Alt F8	Select next word	F8
Footer	Alt F2	Select previous para.	F9
Go to page	Alt F5	Select previous sentence	Shift F7
Header	Ctrl F2	Select previous word	F7
Line draw	Ctrl F5	Select whole document	Shift F10
List field choices	F1 in menu	Set tab	Alt F1
Load	Ctrl F7	Show layout on/off	Alt F4
Next char. in menu	F10 in menu	Show line breaks	Alt F7
Next window	F1	Spell	Alt F6
Next word in menu	F8 in menu	Step macro	Ctrl F3
Outline organize	Shift F5	Text/graphics	Alt F9
Outline view on/off	Shift F2	Thesaurus	Ctrl F6
Overtype on/off	F5	Undo	Shift F1
Previous char. in menu	F9 in menu	Upper/lower case	Ctrl F4
Previous word in menu	F7 in menu	Zoom window on/off	Ctrl F1

SPEED KEYS FOR CHARACTER FORMATTING

Use Alt X with the alphabet key when a style sheet is attached.

Bold	Alt B
Double underline	Alt D
Hidden text	Alt E
Italic	Alt I
Normal character	Alt space bar
Small caps	Alt K
Strikethrough	Alt S
Subscript	Alt -
Superscript	Alt + or Alt =
Underline	Alt U

SPEED KEYS FOR PARAGRAPH FORMATTING

Use Alt X with the alphabet key when a style sheet is attached.

Centered	Alt C
Double spacing	Alt 2
Hanging indent	Alt T
Increase left indent	Alt N
Indent first line to next tab	Alt F
Indent from left and right	Alt Q
Justified	Alt J
Left flush	Alt L
Normal paragraph	Alt P
Open space above paragraph	Alt O
Reduce left indent to next tab	Alt M
Right flush	Alt R

DIRECTION KEYS/INSERT AND DELETE

1st char. next para.	Ctrl down arrow	First command/field	Home in menu
1st char. next word	Ctrl right arrow	Insert scrap	Insert
		Insert scrap, replace selection	Shift Insert
1st char. prev. para.	Ctrl up arrow		
1st char. prev. word	Ctrl left arrow	Last command/field	End in menu
Bottom of window	Ctrl End	Left 1/3 window	Scroll Lock left arrow
Delete to scrap	Delete		
Delete, not to scrap	Shift Delete	Left one character	Left arrow
Down one line	Down arrow	Left one command/field	Left arrow in menu
Down one line in menu	Down arrow in menu	Right 1/3 window	Scroll Lock right arrow
Down one windowful	Page Down		
End of document	Ctrl Page Down	Right one character	Right arrow
		Right one command/field	Right arrow in menu
End of line	End		
Extend down one line	Shift down arrow	Scroll down one line	Scroll Lock down arrow
Extend down one window	Shift Page Down	Scroll up one line	Scroll Lock up arrow
Extend left one char.	Shift left arrow	Start of document	Ctrl Page Up
		Start of line	Home
Extend right one char.	Shift right arrow	Top of window	Ctrl Home
		Up one line	Up arrow
Extend to end of line	Shift End	Up one line in menu	Up arrow in menu
Extend to start of line	Shift Home		
Extend up one line	Shift up arrow	Up one windowful	Page Up
Extend up one window	Shift Page Up		

OTHER KEYBOARD FUNCTIONS

Help	Alt H	New paragraph	Enter
Mark all document-retrieval files	Ctrl space bar	Next form field	Ctrl >
		Next show layout object	Ctrl Keypad 5 right arrow
Mark/unmark document-retrieval files	Space bar	Nonbreaking hyphen	Ctrl Shift -
Move between document/menu	Esc	Nonbreaking space	Ctrl space bar
New column	Ctrl Alt Enter	Optional hyphen	Ctrl -
		Previous form field	Ctrl <
New division	Ctrl Enter	Previous show layout object	Ctrl Keypad 5 left arrow
New line	Shift Enter		
New page	Ctrl Shift Enter		

APPENDIX IV
GLOSSARY OF TERMS

Block	A group of characters (words, digits, commands) held together and worked with as one unit.
Byte	A unit of measurement which is about the size of one character.
Cursor	The highlighted symbol on the screen which indicates the position where text or commands may be entered or edited.
Default value	An assigned response or quantity for a program that is set by the manufacturer. For example, margin settings, page size, and line spacing are default values which the manufacturer includes with a word processing program.
Directory	A division (or file) which contains the names and locations of a group of files. Directories are useful for locating programs and data files on disks.
DOS	An acronym for Disk Operating System. A software program which enables the user to send commands from the keyboard to the computer.
Drive	The component (device) which is necessary for writing data to a disk, or for reading data from a disk.
Field	One item of information in a database file. For example, an individual's telephone number could be a field.
Filename	The characters used to identify a file.
Filename extension	Additional characters added to a filename and separated from the filename by a period. It is used to identify the type of data in the file.
Format a disk	The DOS process which divides a disk into tracks and sectors so files may be stored and retrieved.
Format text	The process of setting margins, tabs, line spacing, centering, changing font name or size, using bold, underlining, or italics, for example, to change the way the text in a document will look when it is printed.
Gallery	The Gallery displays the screen where styles (a collection of formatting commands) may be created, and where the style sheet (a file containing a group of styles) is displayed.
Glossary	The glossary is the place where keystrokes--either text or commands--which are frequently used in documents may be stored. The glossary includes macros as well as glossary entries.
Hanging indent	Formatting a paragraph so the first line is aligned at the left margin and remaining lines are automatically indented. The position of the indent is

	determined by the position of the tab stops and the number of times the indent command is entered.
Hard copy	The printed copy of a document such as a letter, table, spreadsheet, or a graphic.
Hard return	The line return which is entered by the user when the Enter key is pressed. It is sometimes called a required return.
Hard space	Sometimes called a "required space." The space is entered in such a way that a line break will not occur at that space. It is used to keep text, such as a title with a name or a month with the day, together on one line.
Highlight	Highlight is the term Microsoft Word uses to identify the cursor.
Indent from both margins	Formatting a paragraph so all lines of the paragraph are indented from both margins. The position of the indents is determined by the position of the tabs and the number of times the indent command is entered.
Input	Entering data or commands into the computer by typing from the keyboard.
Insert mode	The mode which allows new text to be entered in a document without replacing or typing over existing text. The text which is already in the document automatically moves ahead of the new text as it is being typed.
Left Indent	Formatting a paragraph so all lines are indented automatically from the left margins. The position of the indent is determined by the position of the tab stops and the number times the indent command was entered.
Load a document	Load is the term Microsoft Word uses to refer to retrieving a document.
Macro	In a word processing program, a macro is a recorded series of keystrokes that may be played back whenever you want those keystrokes to be entered. The keystrokes may consist of text or commands or a combination of both.
Menu	A list of choices displayed on the screen when various functions keys are pressed. The user may then make a selection from the various options displayed in the menu.
Merge	Combining information from two or more files into one sequenced file.
Merge program	A program that allows the user to combine a file which contains a form document with a database file to produce personalized documents such as form letters.
Mode	The method or condition of operation. For example, "insert mode" or "overtype mode."
Operating system	A software program used to run the computer. For example DOS, CPM, and UNIX are the names of operating systems.
Overtype mode	The mode which allows new text to be entered in place of old text (typed over old text). Text which has been typed over is deleted.

RAM	Random access memory. The area of internal memory, called the "working memory," where your data is temporarily stored. Part of your application programs are also loaded into RAM to enable them to be used in working with the data input.
Record	All related items pertaining to one unit. In a database file used in a merge program, a record contains all the information (fields) pertaining to one individual.
Retrieve a document	The procedure used to display on the screen the contents of a file which has been saved on a disk.
ROM	Read only memory. This is permanent memory and cannot be erased or changed by the user. ROM is generally a storage chip which is programmed at the time of manufacture.
Save a document	Writing the text, which is displayed on the screen and which is residing in RAM, on the disk.
Soft returns	The line returns which have been inserted in text by the computer program.
Startup	The method of turning on the power in the computer and loading the application program to be used. It is sometimes called a "boot."
Style sheet	A style sheet is a file which contains a group of styles used to apply formatting to text. A style is a collection of formatting commands.
Summary sheet	A summary sheet contains information about a document--author, operator, title, keywords, creation date, revision date--and is attached to the document. It may or may not be printed, depending upon the user's choice, when the document is printed. It is used to sort or select files, or to display information about the document.
Syntax	The order in which computer commands must be given. The syntax varies with the program which is being used.
Wordwrap	The feature in a word processing system which allows paragraph text to be typed without pressing the Enter (return) key at the ends of lines. The program enters soft returns automatically so the lines fit within the existing margins.

INDEX

Add, 22, 114-15, 264-65
Addresses, and merge, 94-96
Advanced functions, quick reference guide, 249-85
Annotations, 156-57, 249
Arrow keys, and line drawing, 41-43
ASK, 274-75
    and form letter, 87-89
    and macros, 135-38, 139-44

Banner, create and position, 46-48
Basic functions, quick reference guide, 213-48
Block, 217, 289
Block functions, 213-14
Boilerplate paragraphs. *See* Standard (boilerplate) paragraphs
Bold, 214
Bookmarks, 158-60, 249-50
Borders, 250-51
Bottom margin, 229
Box
    create and position, 49-50, 64-65
    and format border, 36-37
    and line, 42
    and text, 43
Breaks, column, 9, 50-51
Byte, 289

Calculations, multiple, 119-22
Caps, small, 240
Capture.COM, 44, 59-64, 258-59
Centering, 214
Character, normal, 229
Character formatting, 214-17, 287
Choose a command, 217
Clearing, tabs, 22
Clear the screen, 217
Codes, control. *See* Control codes
Collapsing, outline subheadings and text, 191-92

Columns
    breaks, 9, 50-51
    copying, 24
    deleting, 22
    and headings, 48
    and merge, 90-93
    moving, 21-22
    multiple, 6-8, 38-39, 46, 251-52
    newspaper style, 6-10, 38-39, 251-52
    sorting in table, 105-6
    and tab set position, 20-21
    three, 15-18
    totalling, 116-17
    two, 11-15, 46, 52-53
Command menu, 217
COMMENTS, and macros, 135-38, 139-44
Compiling
    index, 197
    table of contents, 203-4
Contents, table of. *See* Table of contents
Control codes, and macros, 133
Copy
    block of text, 217
    columns, 24
    hard. *See* Hard copy
Create a document, 217
Cross-reference, 159-60, 252
Cursor, 289

Data document
    and merge, 84-87, 93
    and sorting, 106
Data records, 86-87
Default value, 289
Delete, 218-19, 288
    columns, 22
    footnote, 154
    and macros, 135
Dictionary, supplemental, 219-20
Direction keys, 288

Directory, 289
Disk, format, 289
Disk Operating System (DOS), 289
Display, screen, 237-38
Divide, 116, 265
Division formatting, 220-21
Document
    create, 217
    data. *See* Data document
    load (retrieve), 228
    and page numbering, 204
    print, 233-34
    retrieval menu, 227
    retrieve, 236, 291
    save, 237, 291
Document view, 186, 187
DOS. *See* Disk Operating System (DOS)
Double spacing, 221
Double-underline, 246
Drive, 289

Editing
    index, 197-98
    macros, 134
    repeat, 235
    and style, 171-72
    table, 19-24
END IF. *See* IF/END IF
Erase, and line, 42
Expanding, outline subheadings and text, 191-92

Field, 289
File, naming, 229
Filename, 289
Filename extension, 289
First line indent, 221
Flush left, 226
Flush right, 236-37
Fonts, names and sizes, 215-16

Footnote, 252-53
    deleting, 154
    entering, 152-53
    formatting numbers, 155
    menu, 152-55
    moving, 154
    print, 155
    revising, 153-54
Format border menu, 34-39
Format position menu, 44-52, 254, 256
Formatting
    character, 214-17, 287
    disk, 289
    division, 220-21
    footnote numbers, 155
    italic, 225
    multiple columns, 6-8, 251-52
    normal character, 229
    normal paragraph, 230
    paragraph, 232-33, 287
    side-by-side paragraph, 11-18, 276-78
    and style sheets, 178
    text, 289
    uppercase, 216-17
Form letter
    and merge, 84-87, 93, 267-71
    and SET and ASK, 87-89
Forms, 66-75, 254
    creating, 66, 68-71
    filling in, 66, 71-72
    filling in using merge, 99-101
    guide for preprinted, 66-67, 72-75
    and merge, 266-67
    preprinted, 254-55
Function keys, 287
Functions
    advanced. *See* Advanced functions
    basic. *See* Basic functions

Gallery, 289
Glossary, 221-22, 263, 289
Glossary of terms, 289-91
Graphics, 65, 255-59
Graphics layout, 44-65

Guide
    for preprinted forms, 66-67, 72-75
    reference. *See* Quick reference guide

Hanging indent, 222-23, 289-90
Hard copy, 290
Hard return, 290
Hard space, 290
Header record, 86
Headings, and columns, 48
Heads, running, 237
Help menu, 223
Highlight, 290
Horizontal lines, drawing, 39-40
Hyphenation, 223-24

IF/END IF, 96-97, 135-44, 271
INCLUDE, 97-99
Indent
    from both margins, 290
    first line, 221
    hanging, 222-23, 289-90
    left, 224, 226, 290
Index, 194-99, 259-60
    compiling, 197
    editing, 197-98
    and macros, 198-99
    and text, 194-96
Insert, 288, 290
Insert menu, 130, 131
Italic formatting, 225

Justified right margin, 225

Keyboard functions, 287-88

Labels, merge, 90-93, 271-74
Landscape mode, 225
Layout, graphics, 8, 44-65
Left flush paragraph, 226
Left indent, 226, 290
Left margin, 228
Letter, form. *See* Form letter
Library, Link, Graphics menu, 44, 63-65, 257-58
Library document-retrieval menu, 227

Library run, 227-28
Library table menu, 203-4
Line
    and arrow keys, 41-43
    and box, 42
    horizontal, 39-40
    sorting in table, 105
Line draw, 34-43, 260-61
Link. *See* Library, Link, Graphics menu
Load, document, 228

Macros, 130-44, 261-64, 290
    and control codes, 133
    creating, 131-33
    deleting, 135
    editing, 134
    and index, 198-99
    and SET instructions, 135-44
    supplied, 130-31, 261-62
Manual hyphenation, 224
Margins
    indent from both, 290
    indent from left and right, 224
    justification, 225
    left/right, 228
    paragraphs outside, 54-59
    top/bottom, 229
Math, 114-22, 264-66
Memory
    RAM. *See* Random access memory (RAM)
    ROM. *See* Read only memory (ROM)
Menus, 290
    command, 217
    footnote, 152-55
    format border, 34-39
    format position, 44-52, 254, 256
    help, 223
    insert, 130, 131
    Library, Link, Graphics, 44, 63-65, 257-58
    library document-retrieval, 227
    library table, 203-4

Merge, 84-101, 266-67, 290
    and addresses, 94-96
    and filling in forms, 99-101
    form letter and data document, 84-87
    and form letters, 267-71
    and labels, 90-93, 271-74
    program, 290
    and SET and ASK, 89, 274-75
Microsoft Word
    advanced functions quick reference guide, 249-85
    basic functions quick reference guide, 213-48
    introduction, 2-4
    prompt sheet, 287-88
    quit, 234-35
    startup, 242
Mode, 290
Move
    columns, 21-22
    footnote, 154
    and line, 42
Multiple calculations, 119-22
Multiple columns, 6-8, 38-39, 251-52
Multiply, 115-16, 265

Naming, file, 229
Newsletter, and format position menu, 44-52
Newspaper style columns, 6-10, 38-39, 251-52
Nonbreaking spaces, 240
Normal character formatting, 229
Normal paragraph formatting, 230
NORMAL.STY style sheet, changing, 167-68, 279-80
Numbering
    footnote, 155
    outlines, 189
    page, 204, 230-31

Operating system, 290
ORGANIZE, and outline view, 192
Outline, 186-93, 275-76
    collapsing and expanding, 191-92
    numbering, 189
    and printing, 193
    and style sheet, 174-76, 193

Outline view, 186, 187-88, 192
Overtype, 230

Page numbering, 204, 230-31
Pagination, 235
Paper, size, 231-32
Paragraph
    flush right, 236-37
    formatting, 232-33, 287
    left flush, 226
    normal, 230
    positioning outside margins, 54-59
    side-by-side, 11-18, 276-78
    sorting, 102-4
    standard (boilerplate), 98
PAUSE, and macros, 135-38, 139-44
Percentages, 118-19, 266
Portrait mode, 233
Preprinted forms, 66-67, 72-75, 254-55
PreView, print, 9-10, 14-15, 234
Print
    annotations, 157
    document, 233-34
    footnotes, 155
    and graphics, 65
    merge, 101
    and outlines, 193
    and preprinted forms, 75
    preView, 9-10, 14-15, 234
    and style sheet, 176-78
Prompt sheet, for Microsoft Word, 287-88

Quick reference guide
    advanced functions, 249-85
    basic functions, 213-48
Quit, Microsoft Word, 234-35

RAM. *See* Random access memory (RAM)
Random access memory (RAM), 290-91
Read only memory (ROM), 291
Record, 291
    data. *See* Data records
    header. *See* Header record
    sorting in data document, 106

Reference, cross-. *See* Cross-reference
Reference guide. *See* Quick reference guide
Referencing, and bookmarks, 159-60
Repaginate, 235
Repeat edits, 235
Repeat last edit, 16
Replace, 235-36
Retrieve, document, 228, 236, 291
Return
    hard. *See* Hard return
    soft. *See* Soft return
Revise, text, 236
Right flush paragraph, 236-37
Right margin, 228
ROM. *See* Read only memory (ROM)
Ruler line, display and view, 53
Running heads, 237

Save, document, 237, 291
Screen
    clear, 217
    display, 237-38
Scrolling, 238-39
Search, 239
Selecting text, 239-40
SET, 274-75
    and form letter, 87-89
    and macros, 135-38, 139-44
Setting, tabs, 23
Show layout on/off, 8, 52-53
Side-by-side paragraph formatting, 11-18, 276-78
Size, paper, 231-32
Small caps, 240
Soft return, 291
Sort, 278-79
    columns in table, 105-6
    and data document, 106
    lines of table, 105
    paragraphs, 102-4
    text, 102-6
Spaces
    double, 221
    hard. *See* Hard space
    nonbreaking, 240
Speed keys, for character and paragraph formatting, 287

Spelling, 240-41
Standard (boilerplate) paragraphs, 98
Startup, Microsoft Word, 242, 291
Strikethrough, 242
Style sheets, 166-79, 279-83, 291
    changing NORMAL.STY, 167-68, 279-80
    creating, 168-72, 281-82
    and outlines, 174-76, 193
    printing, 176-78
    revising formatting, 178
    using, 172-74
Subscript, 244
Subtract, 115, 265
Summary sheets, 243-44, 291
Superscript, 171, 244
Supplemental dictionary, 219-20
Syntax, 291

Table of contents, 200-204, 283-85
    compiling, 203-4
    and text designation, 200-202

Tables
    creating, 19-20
    editing, 19-24
    lines in, 40-41
    and multiple calculations, 119-22
    sorting columns in, 105-6
    sorting lines of, 105
    totalling column in, 116-17
Tabs, 244-45
    adding, 22
    clearing, 22
    and columns, 20-21
    and horizontal lines, 39-40
    setting, 23
    vertical, 40-41, 285
Terms, glossary of, 289-91
Text
    and bookmarks, 158-59
    and box, 43
    collapsing and expanding, 191-92
    format, 289
    and index, 194-96
    and outline, 189-90
    and outline view, 187-88
    revise, 236
    selecting, 239-40
    sorting, 102-6
    and table of contents, 200-202
    use of, 2-4

Thesaurus, 246
Top margin, 229
Totalling, columns in table, 116-17

Underline, 117, 246
Undo, 246-47
Uppercase, formatting, 216-17

Vertical tabs, 40-41, 285
View
    document, 186, 187
    outline, 186, 187-88, 192

Windows, 247-48
Word. *See* Microsoft Word
Wordwrap, 248, 291